The American Crisis Playlist:

From Political Pestilence to Pandemic

by

Terry Barr

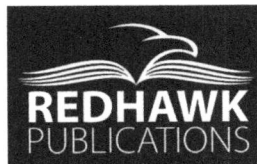

REDHAWK
PUBLICATIONS

Redhawk Publications
The Catawba Valley Community College Press
2550 US Hwy 70 SE
Hickory NC 28602

ISBN: 978-1-952485-89-3

Library of Congress Number: 2022946789

Printed in the United States of America

redhawkpublications.com

Copy editing by: Ashlyn Blake

Advance Praise for Terry Barr's *American Crisis Playlist:*

Terry Barr takes us on a rollicking ride with The American Crisis Playlist, a weekly deep dive into old favorites and new releases throughout the era of Covid. Packed with musical memories and surprises, it's a booster shot to put that turbulent time in our rear-view mirror.

— Frank Mastropolo, author, *Fillmore East: The Venue That Changed Rock Music Forever*

2021 is perhaps a year best forgotten. From a pandemic to political strife, we were a nation at war—with an unseen virus and with ourselves. We were, in short, a nation in crisis. Terry Barr chronicled it all with his weekly American Crisis dispatches. Weaving together playlists with his heartfelt writing, this was more than simple reporting. Each of these posts served as a light guiding the way, helping us remember that even in the darkest hour, there is always hope.

Terry Barr's heartfelt writing beautifully meshes current events with the healing power of music. In an era many of us spent in isolation, Barr's American Crisis series reminded us that our story is one written collectively.

In an era where music consumption is fueled by soulless algorithms, and bots pour fuel on the fire of social discourse, Terry Barr offers a refreshing antidote; writing that is straight from the heart. Weaving remarkable music playlists with his weekly take on the day's issues, he's not afraid to share his fears, rage, and joy. He cuts through the white noise, reminding us that in the end, all we have is each other.

—Kevin Alexander, author, Managing Editor of the online music publication, *The Riff*

As both a music lover and a human being who was deeply affected by the various American crises in 2020 and 2021, I found a lot to enjoy and relate to in this excellent book by Terry Barr. Not only does Terry share his own experiences and feelings from those challenging times, but he also shares music that helped him, and I'm sure many others, through those very dark days. It's often been said that the music each person listens to is the personal soundtrack for their own life. If this is true, and I believe it is, Terry Barr's music playlists in this book have provided each of us with hundreds of wonderful additions to our own personal soundtracks. Music to help make our dark days brighter and our light days even lighter.

—Pierce McIntyre, Founder and Chief Editor of *Plethora of Pop* on Medium.com

Terry Barr's *American Crisis Playlist* masterfully weaves memoir with the collective cultural narrative of music to mitigate terrifying, polarizing shifts in the political landscape that obliquely whisper all the way back to his young years in the South. You can pick thread's of Terry Barr's life in recurring characters and forgotten faces that come back to haunt like a song. *American Crisis Playlist* holds vigil through music to cope with the Orange Plague, the ultimate guise of emerging violence, hate, intolerance and fear. Barr offers refuge and a place to relate where music becomes a lens for literature, culture, politics and personal growth. The 520+ song playlist contains decades of eclectic tunes with deep cuts, concert trips, music history and narratives of growing up through music. His playlist sustains, gives us pause and feels as warmly relatable as his voice. Reading Dr. Barr will feel like sharing records in his living room. I can't think of memoir or diary writing that has the same fidelity.

—Jessica Lee McMillan, author, *What You Exceed*

Other books by Terry Barr:

Don't Date Baptists and Other Warnings from My Alabama Mother

We Might As Well Eat: How to Survive Tornadoes, Alabama Football, and Your Southern Family

Secrets I'm Dying to Tell You

States' Rights Really Means White Supremacy: An Essay (Kindle Single)

The American Crisis Playlist (2020-2021)
Table of Contents

The American Crisis Playlist

Click the QR code above to access the American Crisis Playlist on Spotify and listen as you read.

Please enjoy other playlists from other Redhawk Publications books.

Foreword

In recent years, it's become increasingly challenging to make sense of this American life.

Hollywood itself would fail spectacularly if tasked with developing an eccentric plot so off-the-rails preposterous as the one we're living.

With a population befallen by a global pandemic from a continually mutating virus responsible for millions of deaths, combined with our American political landscape devolving into a nightmarish hellscape of absurdity and dysfunction, this has culminated in a tragic tale almost too surreal and harrowing to believe.

Yet, somehow, in this chaotic era we consistently manage to eclipse the insanity of each passing year, one-upping on a near daily basis the previous traumatic news cycle with an alarming escalation of shock and awe. Invariably, in this current climate things quickly go from bad to worse in the blink of an eye.

Mark Twain wrote that truth is stranger than fiction because fiction needs to make sense; truth does not.

These days very little makes sense, and so in such troubled times we turn to that which brings us comfort, leaning heavily on those things which calm our anxious minds and soothe our troubled hearts.

In The American Crisis Playlist (2020-2021), Terry Barr expertly guides us through our seemingly never-ending dark night of the soul with qualified commentary and a sublime selection of music aimed at reinforcing belief in ourselves and bolstering faith in the existence of our better angels.

When it seems all hope is lost, music is always there to save us either from outside forces or from ourselves.

Fittingly, this playlist series begins and ends with classics. "Once in a Lifetime" by Talking Heads and "Jungleland" by Bruce Springsteen bookend the collection, but between there are hundreds of time-appropriate songs from such disparate artists as David Bowie, Marvin Gaye, Bob Dylan, Taylor Swift, Solomon Burke, Leonard Cohen, The Black Keys, Aretha Franklin, Tame Impala, The Clash, Lou Reed, Howlin' Wolf, Local Natives, Spoon, Neil Young, Otis Redding, Sonic Youth, and The Raconteurs, to name but a few.

And speaking of raconteurs, Terry is among the finest storytellers to ever put pen to paper or digital ink to screen. His writing is an amazing tapestry of personal stories, nostalgia, astute observations on current affairs, and popular music all woven together in a unique style all his own.

Terry's singular voice comes through in this magnificent collection of essays with clarity and commiseration, reassuring us that we're not living through these unprecedented times alone and that we are not lost despite having no roadmap for navigating the great unknown which lies before us all, growing more uncertain by the day.

This book is a gift, both timely and timeless, recounting tales of ages past and present, with a narrative both sentimental and futuristic emerging. Terry provides a gripping exploration of one of the most anarchic and turbulent eras ever witnessed by the American people.

Historical times, indeed.

Any road trip is only as great as the endless supply of accompanying tunes one brings along. As a true connoisseur and lover of music, Terry guides us on an extremely emotional musical journey here, with a year's worth of songs both classic and new.

These fifty-two playlists—consisting of ten songs each—serve to remind us where we've been, show us how far we've come, and reassure us over the great distance we've yet to go.

As Terry would say, here's coping...

—Chris Zappa August 2022

Acknowledgments

The needle has found its groove, so before the music starts **let me thank my growing family**, as always, and particularly this year for buying me a new turntable and powered speakers. I know: I keep exceeding my record budget, but you understand, right?

Next, thank you to Robert Canipe and Patty Thompson at **Redhawk Publications** for hosting my fourth book and all the others. Ten years ago, even one book seemed like a dream of 78 rpm records.

The third track, the centerpiece of this side, is a hearty thank you to *The Riff*, **Medium's Premiere Music Publication,** and to its editors, past and present, for publishing this series originally: Rob Janicke, Noah Levy, and workhorse **Kevin Alexander**. Your support is the bass-line to everything.

To my Medium music family—Keith, Stan, David A., C. Robin, Pierce, Paul C., Jeffrey, Nicole, Alex M and B, JP, Frank, Charlie, Sarah, Robert, Anthony, and especially **Chris Z and Jessica**—"I can't live, if living is Without You."

To my Bessemer friends whose music sensibilities helped to form and accompany mine: Joe, Jack, Jim, Steve, Fred, Jimbo, Sallie. Quick, name all the tracks from *Aja* in order, fast.

To John, Beatle lover extraordinaire.

To Phillip: let's go crate-diving in Landrum again.

To Les, whose idea that I compile these playlists got the whole thing started.

To **my brother Mike** whose love of Elvis, The Monkees, and the Beatles makes me remember all those trips to K-Mart in search of the lost chord or picture-sleeved 45's.

To **Max**, my best friend—sorry when I play the music too loud, pal.

To those I've lost.

And to those I've gained, especially, **Pippa Adele**.

Introduction

In 1967, two major cultural icons poked me into understanding that more existed in my world than Alabama football, or Mary Jane, my fifth grade girlfriend, who decided in sixth grade that we were done. The first cultural icon came via my teacher, Beth Thames, who told our entire sixth grade class about a novel that influenced her: George Orwell's *1984*. She described Big Brother and told us that he stood as a figurehead for something called a Totalitarian society, something modeled after Soviet Russia. I didn't exactly have nightmares for the next seventeen years, but part of me did get uneasy as the fateful year grew closer.

Do you remember 1984? Ronald Reagan got himself re-elected and no one of any importance seemed to understand what Iran-Contra meant, or whether Oliver North was a patriot or scoundrel, or both. I got married in that year, to an Iranian immigrant (which made my parents nervous and caused some of my friends to re-enter their bigoted closets), so life, if not a Big Brother nightmare, had its jagged edges for me.

1967 also saw the release of, almost inarguably, The Beatles most famous album, *Sgt. Pepper's Lonely Hearts Club Band*. Beth Thames also told us about this event, too, but she left out the part about "Lucy in the Sky with Diamonds" maybe being a loose symbol for LSD. She let us bring music to class one week and talk about why we loved what we loved. One kid brought The Lemon Pipers' "Green Tambourine," while my friend Robert brought "Judy in Disguise (with Glasses)," by John Fred and His Playboy Band. Sadly, no one brought The Beatles, because this was Bessemer, Alabama, a suburb of Birmingham where two disc jockeys had advocated and staged a Beatles' bonfire after

John Lennon questioned who was more popular, them or Jesus. I might have brought The Turtles' "Happy Together," my one 45, but maybe not.

Memory plays tricks after so many years.

On Sgt. Pepper, my favorite song now is "A Day in the Life," a song which also reminds me of James Joyce who once had a character in *Ulysses* say,

"Life is many days, day after day."

Which makes me think of one year that seemed to last a decade, from the almost summer of 2020, till the following summer of '21. One year, a series of plague days; a crisis in America unlike any I've ever lived through, though my mother—had she not passed in 2018—might have reminded me that she lived through the Great Depression, World War Two, the smallpox and polio epidemics, and McCarthyism.

Whew.

Still living through the presidency of Donald Trump (forever after labeled here as the Orange Plague or OP) and the onset of the CoronaVirus motivated me to compile a weekly series of ten songs— an **American Crisis Playlist**—that for me captured the bleakness, the fear, the paranoia, and the wonder of what each new day might bring and how long this series of days, this life under Covid, might go on. My **Medium** home, *The Riff*, published this weekly series, trusting me to be honest, to get my feelings down, to motivate others to write back, listen, and maybe even be inspired to keep going even though no one was even much trying to predict, much less guarantee, a happy ending, or ending at all.

Really, the only plan I had when I began this series is to listen and write about music, to try to stay sane and let the songs I love do what they've always done for me: make me happy, make me reflect, make me feel less alone, and maybe most importantly, make me want to share and talk about them with my friends and family. Sometimes, a week's events would insist that I make mini-themes for the list, as I did for the just-passed Juneteenth. For other weeks, I might decide to include a few old songs that helped others get through crises of past eras (for such weeks, I could have always included Marvin Gaye's "What's Going On?"). At other times, I'd hear a new song, or something from a band I'd forgotten, and I'd get so happy that I'd almost forget that I couldn't wisely go to a record store or any live venue that night.

As each weekend approached, I'd compile a list of songs to include, and then select ten for that week's playlist. I would always be willing to adapt that week's list, though, because this is the way music functions: when you're writing about one song, another song that you'd forgotten might assert itself, insinuate itself, into the mix. So best to be flexible and go with the more natural segues.

It would usually take me two hours to write each week's playlist and then link all the songs. My shoulders would ache; my dog would wonder why I refused to walk him; my wife would disappear and, upon her return, wonder if I had become one with my computer. And maybe I had.

Please understand: I am not a music critic. I am not a trained musician (the only instrument I ever played was the Flutophone in 6th grade), though I did sing in school and church choirs throughout my childhood and adolescence. I am a writer, however, and have been writing about the music I love for decades in various forums. And like most of you, I cannot claim any objectivity about what I love and don't love. And yet, before I started this playlist, I didn't care for Taylor Swift, Kacey Musgraves, Sampho, or even know about bands like The Black Pumas, Dizzy, London Grammar, or Wild Pink. Now, all are on my steady rotation, as are old faves like Neil Young, Johnny Cash, Jackson Browne, Bruce, Otis, The Clash, Stevie Wonder, Santana, The Kinks, Aretha, Sonic Youth, and, of course, The Beatles.

Their music sustains me, and got me through the worst of this year (of course my wife, daughters, son-in-law, friends, and Max did the most for my sanity). So that's what I want to say most here: these playlists, this book, were my attempt to restore my soul.

I think it worked, too.

And speaking again of The Beatles, *Sgt. Pepper* also contains that Paul ditty: that cliched and almost throw away tune, "When I'm Sixty-Four." How many people, upon hearing that song as I did when we were young and foolish and in love with a girl/boy who just rejected us, ever thought we'd make it to sixty-four, "...older and losing [our] hair?" Did that seem possible when I was eleven, some fifty-three years in the future?

I bring that song up because in the American Crisis year of 2020, I turned sixty-four, and for my birthday, my wife gave me a surprise zoom party—not so much of a surprise, since it's my zoom account and she had to get my password and other info to set it up, and so...But really, how could I, at age eleven, ever guess that when I turned sixty-four, I would have been married to an Iranian immigrant for thirty-six years, that we would have to have a virtual party because human contact had become that precarious and fragile, and all the while, young black men were being murdered in the streets (sadly, a reality I've been second-hand witnessing all my life), and our president was a cretin of the highest order, not so much Big Brother as the bully down the street who would rather puncture your basketball with a blunt knife than play H.O.R.S.E. with you. And I'm being kind in my analogy.

The "many years from now" are NOW. I can't say that we have averted the crisis, even though the country is still here along with its constitution. Over half a million have perished due to the virus. The former president is still commanding crazy legions of supporters, some of whom are currently likening being asked/forced to wear masks to being victims of the Holocaust, a horror that, back in 1967, I wasn't really aware of, despite being half-Jewish.

By the time you read this, maybe the covid corner will have been turned so completely that the future will amount to getting one more vaccine a year. Trying to predict the political landscape, however, is akin to predicting which leaf will fall on a tree two streets over that you might pass by every other day. And with the Jan. 6th House Select Committee hearing increasingly damning testimony about a failed fascist coup, I feel almost drowned in those political leaves.

One thing that hasn't stopped, that will be regular though never "the same,' is music. Live shows are back, and each Friday, new music drops in record stores and on whichever streaming service you want. Thank God.

So, as I put "Happy Together" on my new turntable, put something on to please yourself as you "enjoy" the past year from this perspective—an American Crisis Playlist year that I promise, I don't have on repeat.

One more note: doing your math will tell you that there are 520 songs on these compiled playlists. I tried to add new, unwritten about songs each week. I didn't want to or plan to hit repeat, and I promise, I left so many songs out, too. Yet, there are some repeats. I won't name them here, but have some more fun and see if you can figure out what they are. I promise: they aren't what I would have expected them to be, either.

§

The first set of playlists take us through the broiling summer months of 2020, when murders of young Black men amped up, and the OP tried to convince us that he knew the Bible frontwards and backwards, upside down and right side up. It was clear that Biden would be the Democrat's candidate, but unclear as to who his running mate would be, and if anyone would matter or give Joe a better chance of winning. I dreaded Independence Day, because I feared someone might do something idiotic like storming the Capitol or blowing some Bastille-like structure up. In those coming weeks, I'd commemorate both my birthday and the second anniversary of my mother's death. I was hopeful about defeating the virus and the OP, but as to the latter, I also was getting squeamish about November, and wondering if I'd look back to the summer and reflect on how any glimmer of hope would be better than an even more grim reality of four years more of the OP.

Like most Americans, I'm stunned at where we are today. People in my town move about as if there's no pandemic, as if there never has been. Friends, including my wife, ask, "What if we're the crazy ones"—we who are social distancing and trying not to go into the public sphere?

Even more stunning is our Orange Plague, our Great Divider/ Denier. He thinks he's Churchill as he purses his lips and attempts to look stony-faced while parading a prop Bible for all to see and disbelieve. I'm not sure what petty tyrant is his analogous double—I used to think it was Mussolini, what with the pout, the folded arms, the sheer pomposity. Maybe Papa Doc? Jim Jones?

Four years ago, I had never heard of General James Mattis, and now I want to kiss him. I'll never forget George Floyd, and wish I could have kissed him, too.

But since I can do none of those things, I will present ten tunes for your playlist pleasure. I'll leave to your various tune methods of adding, downloading, and listening to your heart's content, especially when you need just a little break from the news and all the unfolding tragedy.

So let our American Crisis Playlist (No. 1) begin.

AMERICAN CRISIS PLAYLIST #1

1. "**Once in a Lifetime**," Talking Heads, from 1980's *Remain In Light*. What's the more appropriate title message, the song or the album? Yes, sadly, in every lifetime we face a monumental crisis, and it's not very uplifting to ask, "What's the deadliest crisis you've ever

experienced?" I used to think mine/ours was 9/11. Before that, the twin assassinations of MLK and RFK. Before that, the four little girls. How do/can we remain in light? Show me yours and I'll show you mine. Isn't that the way we play, and live?

2. "**Venus,**" Television, from 1977's *Marquee Moon*. I first heard of Television back in 1981, on the day I first heard The Clash's *Sandinista* album, featuring "The Magnificent 7." Do you remember when we were supposed to fear the Sandinistas? Ah, the good old Reagan era, which does seem golden these days. Television, though, was another beast entirely, ripped from the NYC art scene. Planet, goddess of love, oh Tom Verlaine, you knew too much, but what would you say now?

3. "**Amerigo,**" Patti Smith, from *Banga* (2012). "Where are you going, and are you going anywhere?" Patti traces the circles for us, imagining what it must have been like to see this new land 500 years ago, and to have it named for you. What do we see in those western skies, and what if we never see them, or stop seeing them? How do we keep breathing with all that we've done and sanctioned in the name of a mad Italian? This song entrances me, and if I don't get to see Patti perform live before I die, I will add it to my losses.

4. "**This Maudlin Career,**" Camera Obscura. From the 2009 album of the same name, "This maudlin career has come to an end, I don't want to be sad again." I don't either, and so...music. I had flirted with listening to this band but couldn't commit. And then, in one of our burned playlist exchanges, my friend Les sent me this song. I have never been the same. It's strange, though, that I've played it for so many people, and no one has reacted even remotely as I do. What's the matter with you? Listen to that piano, that voice. What more could there be?

5. "**America Is Waiting**," David Byrne and Brian Eno from 1981's *My Life in the Bush of Ghosts*, which should get somebody's award for best album title of the 1980s. Back in those Knoxville days when cool people had to own this record, I kept expecting to hear "America Is Waiting" in one of my local dance clubs. I figured the gay club would be the one, but alas, never. So pardon me while I try to get my hips aligned, and yes, still waiting, America, for the Constitution to mean what it's supposed to.

6. "**Running Up That Hill**," Kate Bush, from *Hounds of Love* (1985). Clearly I have an 80's vibe running up whichever hill I'm climbing. I regret that I couldn't find the 12-inch single to run here, as its beats once led me to a hill house on top of Ft. Sanders, Knoxville. Can't tell you what happened there; wish I could, but it involved a haircut and, of course, a girl named Noelle. I audited a History of Rock and Roll course at UT, and this was the first song our instructor played on an incredible sound system. There were 75 people in the class; half of them reading *The Daily Beacon*, and 80% of the others asleep. Fuck 'em.

7. "**Never look back**," Run The Jewels. Oh, now you're awake? From *RTJ4*, just out this week. Killer Mike: I'd kiss you, too. Still, I have to look back because history demands it. I keep seeing poseurs who want to believe that Confederate monuments are about history. Put them in a museum then. Birmingham knocked down one that had been there since 1915. *Yes.* Oh, and yesterday, in Mountain Brook, AL—a Birmingham enclave that is 97% white—500 protestors gathered to honor George Floyd. Wish I had been there, and Killer Mike, too.

8. "**I Feel Love**," Donna Summer. You can find this on her double record *On the Radio*, as well as other obscure discs. The first time I heard it was at Belle's, a gay bar in Birmingham. I'll repeat, a gay bar in Birmingham. The Magic City. Anyway, I did feel love for you, Donna, and my hips moved better back then (1978) too. Say it over and over, and maybe we'll all believe.

9. "**Morningside**," Moby, from his new *All Visible Objects* record. Each morning I wake up wondering if we're still here. And so far, we are. Listening to Moby makes me want to call my old pal Jimbo and thank him even if he has moved past Moby now, or long ago. Pure emotion here, and that's why I've kept up with his music. He's a softer Laurie Anderson, with beats in the Bush of Ghosts. Everything is too visible now, but what exactly are you seeing, dear?

10. "**Everyone Else**," London Grammar, from 2017's *Truth is a Beautiful Thing*. "Everyone else knows why, everyone else knows why, look what you've done." Apply that to your favorite violent actor or head of state. You'll get it even if he doesn't. But he might one day, when he is in jail or out of office, or both. Keep Hope Alive. And most of all, keep breathing. You've shown us the way, George.

There's an episode of PBS's *Eyes on the Prize* series called "Mississippi: Is This America?" in which we see the grisly aftermath of the murder of Emmett Till, a fourteen year-old boy brutally killed by two adult white males because the boy allegedly "got fresh" with the wife of one of these men. The two men were found "not guilty" by a true jury of their peers: 12 other racist white men. The jury was out about 30 minutes, and one juror was quoted as saying it wouldn't have taken that long, but they sent out for Coca-Colas.

All this took place in 1954, in Money, Mississippi. Look it up. Look it all up. So, without getting too incendiary, let me say that when I say "Black Lives Matter," and you want to amend it to "all" or otherwise argue the point, I say that you need some anti-racist training.

So do I, for that matter.

Now, while we go to our respective training corners, let's inspire ourselves with some tunes. They aren't all American tunes, because America isn't the whole world, as we all know.

Sometimes, I'm not sure what we all know, or if all of us know and agree on any one thing. So, I'm not saying all of these songs are "great," but if you think they are—or most of them anyway—we're on to something good. I hope we can build from there.

AMERICAN CRISIS PLAYLIST #2

1. "**Let's Go Away for a While**," The Beach Boys, from 1966's *Pet Sounds*. The album was Brian Wilson and the boys' answer to "Sgt. Pepper." Neil Young also used this tune in his film *Journey Through the Past*, which is where I first heard it. Isn't it strange how we come by

certain information? Such a wistful tune...if we only could, and in my state of South Carolina—a hot spot now—I wish people would go back inside...for a while.

2. "**Laughing**," David Crosby, from 1971's *If I Could Only Remember My Name*. Check out the steel guitar, and yes, that's Neil Young singing in the background. Crosby's voice was, and to an extent, still is so lovely. "I was mistaken...only reflections of a shadow that I saw..." Oh shit. No laughing matter, our shadow selves. They're popping out all around now. Dark stuff, emanating from somewhere on Pennsylvania Avenue. "I was mistaken, only a child laughing in the sun...."

3. "**Inside Out**," Spoon, from *They Want My Soul* (2014). There was that night in Asheville, after "Tennis," when Spoon got my soul. We were three: Owen, my wife, and I. Owen kept wading into the crowd, jostling around, while the two of us hung back, holding each other. What a fucking image to hold onto, given what would happen just a few months later, his life ending like that. I have played this song over and over as if I understand something; as if it can help me. "I know that time's gone inside out/ And now it's only like we told you/
Hm, oh then they wash my feet/They do not make me complete." No, not those holy rollers like Franklin Graham, for sure. My soul is mine, and the only one I gave it to is with me.

4. "**Born Like**," Hazel English, from 2020's *Wake Up!* Here's one that the more I listen to, the more I feel my eyes, inside self, soul. I love songs that sound like both now and then. Somehow, it reminds me of Brenda and the Tabulations' "Right on the Tip of My Tongue." It doesn't really sound like that, though — it's rather the mood, someone asking and longing for what just passed. "We're breathing in time now/ Your lips are near mine now/We're dancing in time now/ This moment's divine." And I forgot to say, I love you.

5. "**Mercury in Retrograde**," Sturgill Simpson, from 2019's SOUND & FURY. Love the line about people asking him what his songs mean. Go on, use some imagination, right? This is one of my older daughter Pari's favorite songs, and Sturge was the last live show we saw. I hope I can amend that last clause some time in the next year or two, wherever Mercury is or winds up. Still remembering that guy vomiting in the seats below me, the operative word being "below."

6. "**Summer Girl**," Haim, from their forthcoming (2020) record, *Women in Music, Part III*. Some of us have been in love with summer girls; others of us were those girls. Think of all the summer songs you know: "Theme from a Summer Place," "Hot Fun in the Summertime," "Summertime," "Hot Town, Summer in the City," and they're all pretty great, but Haim puts something extra into this one, kind of jazzy and free. I see pools and lakes, and a frisbee lying forgotten in a field as we ride off in someone's old truck or Vega.

7. "**Transformer Man**," Neil Young. From 1982's *Trans*, a record that might sound to you and me a little bit, or a lot, like Kraftwerk. I soooo preferred this record to *Everybody's Rockin*, one of its Neil-contemporaries. If you know much about him, you likely know that he has some severely disabled kids. This record and the later Re-Ac-Tor tried to get inside a traumatized mind, a shifting perspective. Worth many other listens these days.

8. "**Angie**," The Rolling Stones, from *Goat's Head Soup*. Not my favorite Stones' song, but I heard it so often back in 1973, when I was in my senior year of high school. Nixon was still president then, and look at me, I'm no longer wincing. I was never not sorry to hear a Stones song play on my AM radio, but I also fear that in my own mind, I've still never given them their due. Among so many things these days—including a November Tuesday coming—that has to change.

9. "**I Hear You Knocking**," Dave Edmunds, from *Rockpile* (1972), in the days where we'd barely heard of Elton John, Cat Stevens, or the horizon-edge of Glam. I couldn't figure out this song, its style, and what it was making me think of and feel. Yet, every time it ventured out of WSGN-AM 610, I cranked the radio in my mother's old Pontiac and...grooved? Coming down the road soon would be Elvis Costello—soon as in another six years—and this next band, who really mattered.

10. "**Somebody Got Murdered**," The Clash, from 1980's *Sandinista!* Sorry, I have to go now, leaving you with an upbeat tune about a downbeat reality. I'm sure this one is for keeps. "But where they were last night? No-one can remember/Somebody got murdered Goodbye, for keeps, forever."

Take care in the streets, at home, and with your soul.

You might be forgiven for forgetting what year we're living in (not to mention the commemorative day—JUNETEENTH—or even the day of the week). I am looking forward to yoga with Jessica at noon, so it must be a Friday. My older daughter is in town and will be practicing too. We won't be in the same room—too little space, too much feedback—but we'll be together in Namaste.

I'm unsettled this morning, though. I had forgotten that the state of Mississippi still harbors the Confederate battle flag within its state flag. That's quite a message. I thought life was easing some in the Old South. The Southeastern Conference is asking Mississippi to remove that emblem of defiance and slavery. What place does it have, what purpose does it serve, today? When I was a kid growing up in Alabama, we studied the Civil War in at least three grades.

History, despite what some believe, doesn't evaporate just because we no longer fly or worship certain symbols of oppression.

And speaking of Alabama and the SEC, former Ole Miss and Auburn head coach Tommy Tuberville is running for the US Senate, hoping to displace Democrat Doug Jones. Jones successfully defeated accused pedophile Roy Moore for that seat back in 2017. Jones also successfully prosecuted Klansmen who bombed the 16th Street Baptist Church in Birmingham back in 1963, a story I feel sure you've heard about.

Tuberville's claim to fame is leading Auburn to an undefeated season in 2004, but still **finishing third** in the final poll that year, and defeating Alabama six times in a row—a remarkable achievement, which absolutely qualifies him in Alabama to enter politics, with the endorsement of Orange Plague. Tuberville's primary opponent is Jeff Sessions, and far be it from me to say **who goes with Satan** more closely in this matchup.

But I don't live in Alabama any longer, and I don't vote Republican—not even as a crossover renegade.

As Joseph Goodman at **AL.com** writes this morning, once Tuberville wanted Ole Miss students to quit bringing the Rebel flag to football games. Now...well, let's say that he doesn't end his twitter feed with #BLM.

I wonder what music Tuberville, Sessions, and Orange Plague listen to? Actually, I don't really care.

So here are more tunes to disquiet you or rouse your inner anti-Confederate spirit.

AMERICAN CRISIS PLAYLIST #3

1. "**People Make the World Go Round**," The Stylistics, from 1972's *The Best of the Stylistics,* which absolutely should be in your Apple Tunes library. Old 1970's Soul rushes through me like nothing else I hear. I see my mother driving us to Birmingham on a rainy day, our radio helping us negotiate traffic and my anxious moods. Man, the brass section in this one and the steady, soothing rhythm. Plus the voice. It's hard to love people these days, yet it's what we have. Ourselves, that is.

2. "**1979**," Smashing Pumpkins. From *Mellon Collie and the Infinite Sadness* (1995). When the bass kicks in, I drink more coffee by reflex and want badly to dance. The song looks back to a year we can all claim. I graduated from the University of Montevallo in '79. Twenty-three years old, I thought I knew so much. What does infinite sadness mean to me or you? "Justine never knew the rules, hung down with the freaks and ghouls." I knew girls like her. Like Jada, who for a time definitely made the world go round.

3. "**I'm Afraid of Americans**," David Bowie, from 1997's *Earthling*. I stole this one from a story my **Medium friend Jessica Lee McMillan** wrote a while back, found on The Riff. I miss David and had somehow missed this song. There's an alternate version, enhanced by Trent Reznor, so have fun and take a moment or two to wonder what non-Americans think about that stupid flag still flying over Mississippi. Despite what you might think, Bowie was British, and Finland is not a part of Russia.

4. "**Straight to Hell**," The Clash from 1982's *Combat Rock*. I've written before how watching The Clash on SNL back in '82 felt so strange then and so impossible now. My friend Les told me about a friend of his who more or less freaked out at watching a mohawked Strummer do this song. But responding freakishly to Strummer only means he didn't listen closely or think about the residual by-products from our incursion into VietNam. It's where we consigned those poor Amer-Asian children; it's where our Leader, The Orange Plague, is pushing us today.

5. "**An Cat Dubh**," U2, from their first album, *Boy* (1980). I remember when Jimbo bought this record at Charlemagne in the 5 Points South section of Birmingham. This was 1980, and I wondered what else Jimbo knew that I didn't. Think about the first New Wave record you ever heard and what doors it would open for you. This was my first, not counting David Bowie who, as we all know, transgenred/ transgendered white rock earlier and more often. In some ways, I think U2 was never better than on this record. In most ways, I'll amend. Boy.

6. "**A Day in the Life**," The Beatles. If you don't know this album (1967), what is so wrong with your world? Do you live in Mississippi or Alabama? In Alabama, we used to burn Beatles' records. How many Beatles songs can Jeff Sessions name? I think today is Paul's birthday. "Woke up, fell out of bed..." Sorry, that was me. My favorite Beatles'

song, next to "**Cry Baby Cry**." And while I'm not putting it on this list, follow this one sideways with ELO's "**Mr. Blue Sky**," but only if you're happy or stoned. Or both.

7. "**At Your Door**," Chromatics, from 2012's *Cherry*. In case you want to know, while I write I drink medium roast coffee from Red Rooster roasters out of Floyd, VA. I also listen to heavy doses of Chromatics. I used to listen more to Beach House or The XX. "Give me your hand..." I think I want this playing in the minutes that I fade on out of here—a good while from now, so please note and remember. And don't open if you see the whites of their sheets.

8. "**Double Oh-Oh**," George Clinton, from the 1985 record, *Some of My Best Jokes Are Friends*. So much I could say here. Actually, I just wrote about jokes and friends a few days ago: **https://medium.com/get-inside/can-we-still-be-friends**. But back to George: now, when he says "This is My Country...My Country Tis of Thee," it somehow means more. Still out there from the Mothership? You can dance and protest at the same time on this one.

9. "**yankee and the brave**," Run the Jewels, from *RTJ4*. I think they know "charlatans" when they see 'em. RTJ gets better with every release, I think, but what do I know? More doors to enter and discover what I didn't consider before. More people are turning on to Killer Mike these days, and we know why. I'm not gonna bait The Great Divider/ Denier, aka, The Orange Plague, by asking what he thinks, because I know he doesn't. He can't. Nor can he dance, though I can't get the image of him and Jeffrey boogying that one night at one of his clubs.

10. "**Missed the Boat**," Modest Mouse from 2007's *We Were Dead Before the Ship Even Sank*. Danceable, too, but I'm afraid that everyone isn't ashamed and though I'm feeling positive right now about "change," as they say, I might be "laughing all the way to hell."

But let this one carry you and me on the newer wave of anti-racism and prove that all of us were and are created equal. Which means we have to face our inner Tommy Tuberville some day. Why not start with this moment?

People get bothered by the strangest things:

—Those who wear masks in public (see this story: **https://medium.com/warm-hearts/i-am-that-masked-man-**).

—The Banning of Confederate flags from NASCAR (I know, that's like separating the RC Cola from the Moon Pie).

—Pro football players like Brett Favre and Drew Brees finally having Colin Kaepernick's back (How dare they betray all that's racially white?).

—David Brooks interviewing Bruce Springsteen (more Socialist propaganda, you see).

Such is the world of Facebook and all those who like to poke bears, donkeys, elephants, and old friends. One day I swear I'm ending my relationship with that crazy social media platform. Maybe I should set a goal: if I can lose the extra five pounds in my midsection, Facebook is history.

So much for the other homemade almond cookies sitting in our glass canister.

Is the Confederate flag one of the banners included in Six Flags over Georgia, or was Stone Mountain enough?

Many points to ponder, but while we do, let's play and discuss a few tunes to lighten, embolden, and make us dance.

AMERICAN CRISIS PLAYLIST #4

1. "**One More Time (in the Ghetto)**," The Clash, from 1980's *Sandinista!* I've been reflecting on The Clash more regularly since Jessica Lee McMillan brought them up a few weeks back. This Reggae-influenced track stood out to me forty years ago when *Sandinista!* was released. I

knew I had been missing a lot, musically, though I had been keeping up with the atrocities committed by US-backed rebels in Nicaragua, and the democratic attempts in repressive El Salvador. Somehow, I forgot about American ghettos and all the dying men in them. And women. Isn't it cool that the U.S. government has always been so adamant about ridding us of inner-city poverty?

2. "**Living in the Past**," Jethro Tull, from the album of the same name (1973), if you can find it anywhere. Speaking of Confederate flags, now that was a past all right. The Past, which for too many translates into The Lost Cause. Why live there, especially in the South? Especially when things didn't go so well for the people in gray, not to mention the people in Black. Reconstruction brought freedom and self-autonomy. And that lasted an entire fifteen years. And then retrogression, leading to legalized segregation. Yep, that past.

3. "**It Tears Me Up**," Percy Sledge, from *Warm and Tender Soul*, a 1966 gem. Mr. Sledge was an Alabama guy, like me. I'm betting he didn't vote for Mrs. Wallace in '66. Still, maybe he understood how George used his wife for his own gain, and then moved on so very quickly after Lurleen died of cancer two years into her term. She had cancer before she ran, and George knew it. Talk about being torn up. Sledge's voice is almost too much, and I always wished I could sing like him, except I'm white, and a baritone.

4. "**No Surrender**," Bruce Springsteen, from 1984's *Born in the USA*. "We learned more from a three-minute record than we ever did in school." So those Libertarians who were disparaging Bruce on Facebook? Go ahead man, I'm sure Bruce can hear your puny laments about his so-called subversion of whatever you pretend to hold dear. Not my fault that Ronald Reagan tried to use Bruce for his own gain. Politicians: what do they know about soul music, the power of Rock and Roll, or a spirit that soars like this? At least Reagan tried. Not sure

the guy who claims to be in charge today ever had a radio, much less an eight-track. And this is a pretty great three-minute record, released in the year of our lord, George Orwell.

5. "**Sprawl II (Mountains Beyond Mountains)**," Arcade Fire, from *The Suburbs* (2010). Why is it that whenever I hear Arcade Fire I feel like anything good is possible? I picked this one because when The Suburbs was released ten years ago, it stood out. I had been listening to the record on my drive home, and this song came on just when I crested a certain plateau on the outskirts of my city, and I saw beyond: the mountains and beyond them, more mountains. I'd drive any distance to see them live.

6. "**Neighborhood #3 (Power Out)**," (double-play!) Arcade Fire, from 2004's *Funeral*. So today, I had to go to my wife's office to clean the grounds. So much ivy and thorny vinery, and of course today the humidity decided that it really was time to feel like South Carolina in the summer. But as I was about to exit my car, Sirius-XMU thought it a fine idea to play this one. I let the air conditioner waft over me for a few minutes longer, and then a dog and his owner walked by, and I swear I almost asked them to dance. So now, I'm asking you.

7. "**Just Like Honey**," The Jesus and Mary Chain, from *Psychocandy*. In 1985, I had been married for a year. I used to hang out at Raven Records in Knoxville looking for the next great band. One day, this one came in. Jay Nations, who ran Raven, put it on the turntable, and I kept thinking that The Strawberry Alarm Clock had been reinvigorated or something like that. I bought the record, played it for my wife, who always surprises me (she hates PJ Harvey and loves Tom Waits). But she loved this, and so it made our heavy rotation back in the days when we lived in a small apartment in an old Victorian mansion on Clinch Avenue. Turn out the lights, play it loud, and see what happens.

8. "**I Summon You**," Spoon, from 2005's *Gimme Fiction*. A little old band from Texas (post-ZZ Top), and isn't Texas in trouble right now? Not that I wish the virus on anyone, but come on Texas (and Florida and Arizona and South Carolina). You very red states. Remember when being Red meant being Communist? Way to go Republicans. How many Republicans like Spoon? Just asking, or summoning.

9. "**Lean On Me**," Bill Withers, from *Still Bill* (1972). It seemed like such a pleasant, almost innocuous song when it debuted back when I was a high school sophomore. Turns out, people from all over the world have adopted the song as a refrain of hope, togetherness, and beacon of strength during the travails of life. Like right now. My wife started crying when she heard "Lean On Me" last week, as used in one of the great mass marches and vigils for George Floyd. Now that's another reason why I love her. [And sidebar, you can follow this with The Hollies' "**He Ain't Heavy, He's My Brother**," if you wish]

10. "**It's Too Late**," Carole King, from *Tapestry*. 1971, and I was too enthralled with Neil Young to give Carole's mega-hit its due. It was played constantly on the old AM, and I didn't quite get it. Yet the piano refrain and King's voice kept getting closer, inside of me. I really don't feel pessimistic or bleak right now, because I know we're going to beat the virus one day, and I feel and am trying so hard to believe that the other, more orange, plague will be vanquished in November. "Still, I'm glad for what we had and how I once loved you," which I hope isn't a lament for the country.

Enjoy, and coming next week, a not-so-Patriotic list for our Independence..

I can't believe it's July already, my birthday month, and the month in which both my mother and grandmother passed. This will be my second birthday without my mother, though on the last one I had while she was alive, she was really sick. She wanted me to go out and buy a nice shirt, and she'd pay me back, she said. I know I bought a shirt at some point afterward, but not until after she passed, and I doubt that I considered it as coming from her, though I should have. Not that I remember any shirt right now.

My mother loved to barbecue on the 4th—ribs, Boston Butt, you name it—and she'd make the entire summer BBQ feast: potato salad, deviled eggs, slaw, homemade peach ice cream, baked beans. It's funny what I remember: when my dad was still living, he insisted that the beans had to be Van Camps. But after he passed, my mother switched to Bush's. Who knows why, and when I asked, she said,

"They taste better."

Aren't canned pork and beans all the same?

What beans do they serve for breakfast throughout Great Britain? I wonder whether anyone knows, and is that where we got them? Another British import?

An old joke: do the British observe the 4th of July?

Of course they do, and the 5th, 6th, and 7th, too.

Our commemoration of Independence is upon us, however, and my brother and I, living eight hours apart, aren't sure whether we're barbecuing or not this year.

It's just so hot and everything.

Not to mention, it's just my wife and me at home, and going through the grill motions seems like overkill at this getting stranger all the time moment.

Our great divider/denier knew nothing about Putin paying for American soldiers to be killed, or at least that's the party line at this moment. "Knew nothing" is right, but let's not confine that to only one aspect of American policy, politics, or life in general.

I hope this is the year that America will become independent of this orange plague. I'll definitely be barbecuing on that great day. Until then, here's a list of Independence Day tunes to keep you humming:

AMERICAN CRISIS PLAYLIST #5

1. **"You Got Me Hummin',"** Lydia Pense and Cold Blood, from 1969's *Cold Blood*. "I don't know what you got..." At age thirteen, I wondered what I didn't have. Many of my guy friends had girlfriends, and I didn't want to be independent. I wanted to be joined at some girl's hip. Lydia looked pretty exotic, and when she sang the title line, I had no idea what she meant. I know now, and I didn't get a girlfriend until I was sixteen.

2. **"Walk in the Park,"** Beach House, from 2010's *Teen Dream*. Why is this the perfect title for an album? Maybe Jessica Lee McMillan knows. Anyway, parks seem emblematic of Independence Day, though maybe they're not as safe as they used to be. Were they ever safe for all of us, though? I remember that Cowsills' song, "The Rain, the Park, and Other Things." I always wanted to go walking in the park with my lover. When I was growing up, our main park, Roosevelt, had a World War I cannon in it. As a boy, I climbed all over that thing, not really understanding what it meant. Now, that's quite a monument, but I wonder where it is now?

3. "**No One to Depend On**," Santana, from *Santana III*. "I ain't GOT nobody that I can depend on." Somehow the way Carlos sang that pierced me back then, and it still does. I spent $3.69 for the album at K-Mart, all my grass-mowing money, and I felt so cool and out-of-this-country when I played it on my old portable turntable. Whom to depend on these days? My family. My dog. My Medium readers. Ssshh, don't tell anyone, I'm depending on you, but I have a new book coming out soon about secrets. American secrets. "No tengo nadie."

4. "**Smiling Faces Sometimes**," The Undisputed Truth, from 1971's eponymous album. Speaking of no one to depend on: "beware the handshake, it hides a snake" indeed. You know something? The Orange Plague has no idea how to smile. Have you ever watched him try? It's like when I was five and my dad was trying to make my picture, and he'd say "Smile sonny," and I would tight-lipped try, not knowing how to force something so unnatural. We laugh at those old pictures. The OP doesn't know how to laugh, either. So we don't have to worry about his smiling face—an undisputed truth, for sure.

5. "**Police on My Back**," The Clash from 1980's *Sandinista!* An obvious choice, right? An old reggae gem that the punk boys made their own, with sirens and plaintive cries, and that relentless, driving rhythm. All the time, burning. "What have I done?" has too many meanings. Always has, if you're on the wrong side of the status quo. I used to dance to this back in grad school at English Department parties when its meaning hadn't quite filtered in. I knew so much but clearly not enough.

6. "**Something in the Air**," Thunderclap Newman. In 1969, *Hollywood Dream* was produced, containing this song. I first heard it, though, on the soundtrack for a film called *The Strawberry Statement*, inspired by the SDS and campus protests that seem all-too-familiar now. I

bought the record because it was permeated with Neil Young songs like "**Down By the River**." But I couldn't quit playing this one. If no one told you that it wasn't released back then, you'd figure its lyrics were about today. Whatever is in the air—and it has to be so many things—is even more complex than ever. I would love us to get together sooner, rather than later. And I do know that it's right.

7. "**The Message**," Grandmaster Flash and the Furious Five. Find it on a 12-inch single, like I did back in 1990. How do you keep from going under? I love the lines, "All My Children in the daytime, Dallas at night. Can't even see the game or the Sugar Ray fight, so don't push me cos I'm close to the edge. I'm tryin' not to lose my head." Speaking of timeless. Messages come and go, like their messengers. We can read, we can hear, we can see. Yet, we don't. He's telling us, clearly, but how many of "us" bought this record back then, or knew it existed?

8. "**We the People**," A Tribe Called Quest. Guess the year. From *We Got It From Here, Thank You 4 Your Service*. I heard this on SNL the week after the election. And then the following spring at the Grammys. I've written about it many times, played it for others, and it retains the same power it shot out that night on SNL, the same night when Kate McKinnon sang Leonard Cohen's "**Hallelujah**," dressed as Hillary, with all attending somber irony. I think we watched SNL because we were still in shock. Imagine all we didn't know then, though many of us, we, the people, could foretell.

9. "**Imagine**," John Lennon, from *Imagine*, 1971. My mother had this song played during her memorial service at the church. Now that took guts on everyone's part. People can change. She didn't care whether it was Marxist, atheistic, Buddhist, or whatever. She didn't believe it was unpatriotic, either, though I'm sure that she didn't worry about imagining "no country." She just imagined "all the people living life in peace." Such a dreamer, my mother.

10. **"Turn, Turn, Turn!"** The Byrds, from 1965's eponymous album. Pete Seeger wrote the song, or rather Solomon did, and Seeger added six words. What I remember most about this is my mother wanted these words said at my grandmother's service in July 1971. My family wasn't the most progressive group out there, and they did love this country. Though loving a country's people isn't so easy, especially when they demand their right to hate, to not wear a mask, and to oppress others. Seeger was right, prophetic, hopeful, and stubborn: "A time for peace, I swear it's not too late."

Oh well, that's me: still idealistic, still refusing to give up hope. Still remembering all the songs I loved and need to this day. Especially this day.

Now, keep those celebrations safe, and please remember those who aren't.

As the second half of the summer unfolded, I faced birthday zoom parties, my yearly physical, and constant reminders, it seemed, that America's discussion of Race had really gone nowhere, mainly because we had an oaf in the White House who somehow thought that skin color was tied to hereditary rights. Or maybe that thought was even too articulate for him. Many in the country, taking a cue from the OP, denounced China for inventing the virus, and so we were back to the world of Freedom Fries.

Maybe because I was still hoping for impeachment, I thought back to the president who opened the China door, and his impeachment trial and then resignation, back in my high school years—1971-4. I thought of the music back then, too, which dominates the playlists of this next section.

The ChiLites, Neil Young, Issac Hayes, 3 Dog Night, Alice Cooper, John Ono Lennon, Alive N Kickin'.

Crabby Appleton.

I was also landing some new bands like Springtime Carnivore, Neon Trees, STRFKR, Dizzy, and Poolside, because in our leisure activities, we often rode around town with Max, listening to Sirius-XMU.

Life tried to go on. An estate sale in my neighborhood, unmasked people pouring over the remains of an old man who passed, truly made my head spin (right round like a record), and I wondered in those late summer days how in the world, despite the Covid plague, anyone could muster up the courage, nerve, or idiocy to want to wander through close quarters with other unknown strangers, though I know that "unknown strangers," while a redundancy, is the least troubling part of what I just wrote.

My family also took a trip to the beach, to Edisto Island, holding our breath at every rest stop, and properly sanitizing the Air B&B place we rented. We bought all our food from masked Costco, and played music every night while we drank and worked puzzles or dominoes, and ate ate ate.

Baseball started, and football was coming, because if you can go to an estate sale...it must be MAGIC.

I gave blood today for my yearly physical. As a famous band once proclaimed, "I feel fine," and both my temperature and urinalysis were normal (aren't you pleased to know?). I was smart enough to make and bring a Yeti of coffee with me so that after the tests were done, I could combat the caffeine headache that was surely coming.

My dog thought it odd and then disconcerting that I was leaving the house without him, dressed, as it seemed to him, for a walk. When I returned after 30 seconds—forgot a note for my doctor—he was extremely happy to see me. He was happier still when I returned an hour later, not only because I was home and he loves me, but I was now toasting a bagel with lox and cream cheese, and he LOVES all three, especially the lox.

My dog also loves yogurt because he's just that zen.

What isn't so zen is the sign I saw at our local locksmiths. It should be comforting to know that a locksmith lives so close to us, but the signs they post mar any comfortable or fuzzy feelings. The one today proclaimed:

"No Wuhan Virus here."

So, I don't need my locksmiths to smack me with their political opinion, their ethnic slurs. Maybe I'll just stand out front with my urinalysis results, proclaiming:

"Urine clear, pH correct, no American virus near."

I used Grandmaster Flash last week, but I need an echo:

"Don't push me cause I'm close to the edge...

I'm trying not to lose my head."

Trying so hard, or maybe not hard enough, depending on how you want to read those lines.

Anyway, now that I've mentioned some music, let's get on with a new playlist in these hot times, and yes, I will refrain from posting Nick Gilder's "**Hot Child in the City**."

The subtitle reference will appear momentarily.

AMERICAN CRISIS PLAYLIST #6

1. "**B-A-B-Y**," Booker T. Jones (featuring Ayanna Irish), from his 2019 release *Note By Note*. Booker T is still making good music after all these years, and this tune makes me think I'm still living in 1964, and that would be nice for some folk, though maybe not in the Deep South. Soul music tried so hard to unite us back then, and if we let it, it still could. This record is a great place to start, and your significant other might hug you for playing it. And more.

2. "**Jesus, Etc**," Wilco, from 2005's *Kicking Television, Live in Chicago*. I heard this on the way back from my doctor's office this morning, and kept thinking about it after, and how much I truly LOVE Wilco. I mean, I LOVE WILCO. "Our love is all we have. Our love, our love is all of God's money/ Each one is a burning sun." Figure that one out, or not, but the one thing I know is that when we get things under control, and our locksmith allows us to, I'm driving somewhere to see Wilco, with My Love. So there.

3. "**Lost in the Dream**," from The War on Drugs' 2014 album of the same name. One of my favorites of the latest wave of indie artists, I listen as often as I can, though sometimes I drift off into one of those darker clouds if I listen too long. Lost in the emotions of loss and uncertainty. There's a lot of that going around, but don't let it get you down, I say to myself more often than I like to admit, though I just did, let it, that is. Maybe a stronger dose of L'Theanine?

4. "**One of My Submarines**," Thomas Dolby, from 1982's *The Best of*....
Speaking of dreamy and lost, I've always found this song strangely
comforting, its echo effect during "Bye-bye empire, empire bye-bye/
Shallow water—channel and tide," making me want to sing and shout
at a locksmith. I also think of the clubs I haunted when this song was
popular, back in Knoxville on those fall Friday nights when no one
knew me.

5. "**Always Something There to Remind Me**," Naked Eyes from their
Best of, 1983, the perfect follow-up in my ears to "Submarine." I loved
the original by R.B. Greaves, and I remember going to a bar called
Badlands and dancing with someone I barely knew to this one. The
music video, back when those were "things," was strong, too, or so
my memory tells me. We've all been there, so when you listen, think
of a place, club, bar, or townhouse apartment in West Knoxville, that
reminds you of something so past it can never come back.

6. "**Heal Yourself**," Ruthie Foster, from 2007's *The Phenomenal
Ruthie Foster*. Thanks to Miyah Byrd, I learned of Ruthie Foster's
voice, person, power. Every song on the album speaks to the heart
of hope, pain, and inspiration, and I'm not one to use the word
"inspiration" lightly especially when it comes to art. At least I didn't
use the word "uplifting." I hear that in the piped-in music at my
dentist's office, or at least that's what the station they play says
about itself. Why can't they play Ruthie Foster, though? That would
ease the pain of all that drilling.

7. "**Harvest Moon**," Poolside, from 2012's *Pacific Standard Time*.
Normally I don't like Neil Young covers, and if you told me that the
cover would be from an indie electronic band...well, I'd probably say
"All Right," for Neil did turn to electronica, too. My dog and I, after the
lox, danced to this one, because he's a "loxsmith," and about the only

one I'll let see me dance these days. Poolside has got me going now, and their new release, *Low Season*, is pretty good, too. I feel calmer. What a great name for an electronica band.

8. "**That's How Rumors Get Started**," Margo Price from her new record of the same name. Speaking of phenomenal, Price speaks to me in many voices; her writing is true and ready for both the country, the city, and all roads in between. If it weren't for rumors, where would we be? I wonder that a lot right now, as we whisper and scream about each other and the destiny in front of us. In any case, while we're on that destiny, why not take Margo Price along for company? Or...

9. "**This Town**," Kacey Musgraves, from 2015's *Pageant Material*. "This town's too small to be mean." This song kills me, in part because it reminds me a bit of my home town, as well as the town my older daughter lives in now, as well as the town I teach in. I thank my younger daughter for helping me find Kacey, and my colleague Justin who, when he heard me playing this one, came bounding into my office yelling, "I love her. Living here, she's got us down." I miss those office days, but Kacey helps.

10. "**Running Dry (Requiem for the Rockets)**," Neil Young and Crazy Horse. I didn't find this 1969 song, from *Everybody Knows This Is Nowhere*, until 1971. I was barely fifteen, and while I knew my life was good and nothing was really "running dry" for me, I still responded to this song more than any other on the album. Neil's ballads have always moved me (though I love his rockers and, like him, I am PISSED that the Orange Plague has appropriated "**Rockin in the Free World**" for his virus rallies. Asshole). Anyway, the Rockets were an old band that Neil said goodbye to, and this song would be one I'd be honored to call my own, requiem or not. "I'm sorry for the things I've done." Simple acknowledgment, and a gesture to end on.

Birthdays come faster these days, maybe because I'm slowing down. I hope my slow down is pretty imperceptible to most others who don't have the pleasure of watching how long it takes me to get into the kitchen each morning to get the coffee going.

Coffee works wonders, as does a wife who plans a zoom surprise party for her husband's birthday but then uses his zoom account and his email address to issue the invitations.

She has the best heart, though, and pulled off a minor miracle, allowing me the gift of seeing on my screen so many legends from my life. I am a lucky man.

I got my yearly physical yesterday, too, and as I was checking out and scheduling next year's annual, the receptionist asked those words I've so longed to hear:

"Will you be using your Medicare next year?"

So time moves forward, with a few hiccups, but in these rolling years I have been thinking more of how things keep coming back—how rounded life is—or maybe how rounded I have always been, as evidenced by the baby photo of me that my friend Fred posted during the party. I was maybe one year old, and the little rounds of fat on my arms made me look very Buddha-ish, according to Fred. Or Budd-ist, and that's another rounded, inside joke.

So as I think of the recurrence of yearly festivals, how all things begin and come back again, I have a few songs to tide us over as we try to figure out our schools, our end-of-summer dreams, and the most burning question:

Do we boycott Goya beans?

1. "**You Spin Me Round (Like a Record)**," Dead or Alive, from 1985's *Youthquake*. Pete Burns appears like a vision in a lost dream, and since he's no longer with us, I'm wondering about how we keep on spinning. I remember dancing to this one in a D.C. club back in the days when my wife wore heavy boots, had Yoko-hair, and looked pretty mean. Being spun by such a woman was fine, fine, fine. Watch out...

2. "**More, More, More,**" The Andrea True Connection, from 1976's *More, More, More*, which I was reminded today had something to do with Ms. True's work as an adult film star. I so love euphemisms. Maybe only white disco artists could sound so banal, so casually disaffected from what they were singing or dancing to. And the other thing: in our Bicentennial year, what said "Happy Birthday America" more or better than this song? Wasn't there a movie back then about Linda Lovelace for President? Hhhhm.

3. "**Tighter, Tighter**," Alive 'N Kickin', from 1970. "Nobody else before you gave me such a beautiful feeling." I didn't know what that meant in 1970, but I hoped to know it one day after I passed a certain birthday. This was a big hit that year, the year I entered high school. I always loved the way Soul wedded horns to beautiful harmonies, and added a killer electric guitar riff somewhere in between or near the end, in this case. "I love you so much and I can't let you go, no, no, no."

4. "**Go Back**," Crabby Appleton, from 1970's self-titled album, perhaps their only one, though I haven't made a careful study. And speaking of electric guitar—pretty psychedelic, almost like The Strawberry Alarm Clock (name three songs of theirs, fast). Bonus points if you know who the original "Crabby Appleton" was. Or is. I'm sure he's still out there in Google-land. Nothing really dies. Now, name me one person, thing, or Great Divider/Denier you'd like to sing this one to.

5. "**The World Spins**," Julee Cruise, from 1989's *Floating Into the Night*. Apple Music categorizes this record as "Pop." Well, maybe. Would David Lynch think so? Did he, when he found this amazing artist and used her sound for *Twin Peaks*, that epic escape into Laura Palmer's dream diary, the red curtain, the Black Lodge? Go back and watch the series (s2e7) and wait for this song to "appear" at the Road House. Never has a tone like this been less perfectly aligned with what you see on the screen. I remember James and Donna, the looks on their faces. All they didn't know, but soon enough would. Floating, spinning, reeling, again and again.

6. "**Round and Round (It Won't be Long)**," Neil Young from 1969's *Everybody Knows This Is Nowhere*. "...to mend the tear that always shows." Who's going to mend our hearts and minds, and when? Biden? November? Maybe that the tear is showing so glaringly is our hope. Nowhere to run, no place to hide. "States' rights" has morphed into "All Lives Matter," codes for people to hide behind and do all the wrong things because of. According to Mary Trump (and I believe her), her uncle has used the "N"-word often and has also said some nasty things about Jewish people. Round and round it goes.

7. "**Name on a Matchbook**," Springtime Carnivore, from 2014's self-titled record. Her real name is Greta Morgan, and she apparently grew up on 60's and 70's singles that her father had stacked in his basement jukebox. So there. Where will we be come next springtime? Will I still be making playlists? Will you still be reading and listening? Is the jukebox still alive, Greta? Can we go there, and dance?

8. "**Tomorrow**," The Strawberry Alarm Clock, from 1967. I'm only trying to be helpful. Now you have two more to name. I still think this is psychedelic. Is it on that jukebox, Greta? Listen to the organ solo, followed by a guitar that always made me think of the animated series "Birdman." But that's me. "Right now, I'm with you, and together we can make it through." There you go.

9. "**Die Young**," Sylvan Esso, from 2017's *What Now*. No question mark: I love that. When I heard this one again the other day, I was power-walking in the heat of the South Carolina 2:00 pm sun. Not very bright of me. So I slowed down, did a pulse check, and thought of my wife who loves this song and asked one day if I had heard it. She didn't know that I'd had it in my heavy rotation, but then, we all have our secrets that sometimes we don't mind sharing. I'm not planning to, either, by the way.

10. "**I Like America & America Likes Me**," The 1975, from 2018's *A Brief Inquiry Into Online Relationships*. I've always liked America, and always thought she reciprocated. But what do I know? Maybe I've been wrong these past 64 years. What can I do now? I'm ready to listen, to change, though my online relationships—except through **Medium**—are starting to drag me down. And if I did let Facebook go, would anybody know? Just asking.

The fear of goon squads launched more widely in American cities. The fear of voter suppression. The fear of showing up to the polls when people aren't wearing masks or socially distancing. The fear of schools reopening too soon.

Okay, after a large dose of hemp oil, I'm ready for some tunes to keep me on the upbeat, even if some of them speak more to lo-fi instincts.

Last night as we were on our nightly drive for sanity, my wife reminded me that this current state of viral affairs won't last forever. That was good to hear.

"I don't know when it will end, but it WILL end," she said.

And knowing her so well, I understand that she means not a death-ending, but one where we'll go on living, maybe not quite as before, but with new meaning, and newer/older tunes to keep us company and bolster our fearful hearts.

So, on and on, right?

AMERICAN CRISIS PLAYLIST #8

1. **"For God's Sake (Give More Power to the People),"** The Chi-Lites, found on 1971's *20 Greatest Hits*. Now, in 1971, no one had heard of the Watergate complex in Washington, D.C., VietNam still seemed an endless war, a ravaged country, and George Wallace was yet again running for president. What a screwed up time, and I'm guessing that few among American white people would have embraced a Black Lives Matter movement then. Too afraid of Black Power. So Nixon was about to be re-elected. Who remembers that he ran in 1968 as the "Law and Order" guy? At least he didn't pose with a Bible, for God's sake.

2. "**For the Good Times**," Isaac Hayes, from 1971's *Black Moses*. I confess: in 1971 when I heard the Black students at my high school proclaiming "Black Moses," I got worried. I wondered not "if," but "when" there'd be trouble. I mean, a sacred biblical figure declared as "Black." It didn't occur to me then that skin color was not only relative, but that in the middle eastern part of our world, people were generally darker than those I was mainly surrounded by in my social sphere. Of course, Isaac wasn't talking about the Hebrew "Moishe" as much as calling attention to a new promised land. Now, was that land America? Maybe so, since he sang some old tunes on this record, including this one written by Kris Kristofferson and popularized by Ray Price, one of my mother's favorites.

3. "**People Have the Power**," Patti Smith, from 1988's *Dream of Life*. "People have the power to redeem the work of fools." Now, how prescient. Maybe Patti had read *The Art of the Deal* and knew what was coming. It hurt me to italicize that title, by the way. I remember when *Easter* was released in the late 1970's and some of my friends objected to Patti's display of underarm hair. Sometimes I have no hope for people, but that's the best time to crank this one up. "The power to dream" and to do, "to wrestle the earth from fools." I love that Patti is such a badass, still.

4. "**Norman F******G Rockwell**," Lana Del Rey, from the 2019 album of the same name. I can't figure out why people have such problems with Lana, as if somehow she paid less dues than others. Anyway, this one kills me, because of her voice, of course, but also because how often does someone say "You're just a man, you do what you do," which puts us in a place that is so f*******g true. A place men don't seem to understand given how important we think we are. I remember in 1984 when Geraldine Ferraro was Mondale's running mate, and a friend told me that she "didn't look vice-presidential." I wondered what he

meant. I wish I had been around him in 1988. Remember that VP? Or the one now in 2020, whom YouTube comedian Randy Rainbow just satirically outed as a "Queen?" And check out some Rockwell art from the 60's and 70's, too.

5. "**Ballad of Dwight Fry**," Alice Cooper, from 1971's *Love It To Death*. "Sleeping don't come very easy in a straight white vest." I think rock music should be unsettling and when I heard this song back in those heady high school times, I didn't quite know what to do. Weren't we all just a little bit insane? It was fun talking to people about Alice Cooper, that now tame precursor to the next artist on this list. Alice runs through his vocal range in this one and I remember playing it so loud and hoping that my parents weren't listening too close to the words. Remember, they called this "hard rock" back then.

6. "**The Beautiful People**," Marilyn Manson, from *Antichrist Superstar*, way back in 1996. I'm sure my parents never got around to Marilyn, since I had long since moved out of their house. My daughters and I listened to this one sometimes, and I was kind of proud that they knew it and liked it. I once told them to tell any boy who got too close that they liked Led Zeppelin—my keen parenting skills at work. Remember the Bill Maher show that had both Marilyn and Pamela Anderson on it. Look it up; Pam was not the most beautiful one in the room, btw. Rage.

7. "**Power to the People**," John Ono Lennon, again from 1971, and found on *Power to the People, The Hits*. I swear that I didn't single out 1971 before starting this list, nor can I believe that I was fifteen when this song hit AM radio—or that it did hit AM radio. You could probably have predicted given the songs above that this one was coming. In fact, if you didn't predict it, then I'm disappointed. A former colleague in the Business Dept at my college once told me that I reminded him of Lennon. Was I ever prouder? Right on.

8. "**Liar**," Three Dog Night. 1970, from *Naturally*. Also, if you don't know why this song makes this week's list, then you really haven't been paying much attention. But I know you have. This was the same year that I saw them live. I think I wore white shoes on my feet. Not "bucks," but they did have buckles. When Nixon said he wasn't a "crook," few believed him. I keep picking on old Tricky Dick, but he did do so much of it to himself. Does anyone want to blame him now for opening the door to China?

9. "**Divorce Song**," Liz Phair, from 1993's *Exile in Guyville*. "Your license said you had to stick around until I was dead." I'm guessing this is the song Melania starts and ends her day with. Or maybe it's "Polyester Bride." I hope it's only days away, rather than the horrible alternative. Did you hear that Barron's school won't be reopening on time? I'm so sorry.

10. "**On and On and On**," Wilco, 2007, *Sky Blue Sky*. I wrote a piece about this song and all my losses that Tre L. Loadholt published on *A Cornered Gurl* and in *Quintessence*. Thanks so much Tre. I really love you, like I really loved Owen. And Wilco. "Please don't cry; we're designed to die." Despite that, this song fills me with joy, which is usually what happens when I hear Wilco. Also, it proves that my wise wife is right, and it's best to end here, now.

Here it is, August, and Major League Baseball has started and college football still thinks it's possible to have a season. Like many, I hope it works out, health-wise, for all. I will watch, because I love these sports, and I'm not going anywhere, as I've been cleared to teach online this fall.

Anyone for a course in Southern Jewish Literature?

As I walked my dog this morning, I saw tons of people headed into a house in my neighborhood where an estate sale is going strong. That most of these people were not wearing a mask distresses me. No way can they be social distancing either. Am I the one who's crazy? I don't watch the news every day, but haven't we passed 150,000 deaths? Didn't Godfather chain CEO Herman Cain just pass from Covid-19? Hasn't former Alabama football player and AD Bill Battle just tested positive? Aren't the Miami Marlins in deep shit?

Max and I kept walking, far apart and very far away from everyone dying to pick up goods from a dead man's house.

We are truly a strange species. Especially here. Especially now.

No wonder so many of us rely on music to see us through, to help us hear the many wonders and possibilities of what we can do with our voices, our hands, our minds when we seek creativity, use our imaginations, and think of all that might be.

Some of the artists here have escaped me in the past, but I love how they're evolving, or maybe it's I who am finally ready to hear more than ever now.

So thanks to all who read and listen to these words and sounds. I hope you continue to do so, and are here with me week after week.

1."**Flamingo**," Herb Alpert & the Tijuana Brass, from *S-R-O* (1966). Fifty-plus years ago, my parents bought every Herb Alpert record that came out. Here was one of those intersections and unions of sets that allowed us to all listen and whistle and be one in music. Like most of his numbers, "Flamingo" was an old cover, written by Ted Grouya, and first recorded in 1940 by The Duke Ellington Orchestra. I don't know, it just makes me feel happy, and it makes me see us by our old stereo in the den, wondering how it could ever get any better.

2. "**Baby I'm For Real**," The Originals, from *The Originals* (1969). I think it was the winter of 1970 when this song couldn't be played enough on hit radio. I wasn't even fourteen yet, so how did I know to like a song where a man is crying, begging a woman to see him as authentic? I know that whenever the song came on, I turned the volume up and understood that I would never have "soul" like this, but I sure wanted some. Badly.

3. "**Cowgirl in the Sand**," The Byrds, from their 1973 reunion album. I barely tolerate anyone covering Neil, but covering this song—my absolute favorite Neil song? Well this one passes, because The Byrds are gorgeous and they don't try to mess with anything or play an extended electric guitar solo. Acoustically appropriate, and their voices, still harmonizing, still strong and quiet. "Purple words on a gray background, to be a woman and to be turned down."

4. "**Lefty**," Dizzy, from this year's *The Sun and Her Scorch*. I've been listening to Dizzy for a few months now, ever since I heard them on NPR's The World Cafe. There was no particular reason for my picking this song, other than "the stars being written on tonight," and once, almost forty years ago, I house sat for friends who had a dog named Lefty. Man, I loved that dog, a harbinger of my best friend today, Max.

Good old dogs. I can still hear her slamming into the back screen door when I wouldn't let her inside the house. Lefty, I love you dog, and I'm so sorry that I wouldn't let you in. I think Max is you, reincarnated, though, so I'm making amends.

5. "**Good Side,**" Liz Phair, from a 2019 single. "There's so many ways to fuckup a life...done plenty more wrong than I've ever done right...At least I'm not a criminal." It's funny to think about the many things I've done wrong, and still do wrong, so I know what you mean, Liz. I'm glad you're still out there, recording good ones like this. Any more coming? Please.

6. "**Have You Seen the Stars Tonite,**" Paul Kantner and the Jefferson Starship from 1970's *Blows Against the Empire*. I loved the Airplane/ Starship's ballads, a far cry from their more raucous tunes like "Plastic Fantastic Lover" or "Volunteers." Well, I loved those, too, but sure hated when the Airplane split in two. Actually, even that wasn't so bad, as we got the early J. Starship and Hot Tuna for our listening pleasure. Another great ballad is "**Today,**" so give that a listen, too. Such great guitar. Bless Its Pointed Little Head!

7. "**Cardigan,**" Taylor Swift, from her new release, *folklore*. It feels like she's been with us forever, and finally, here I am, ready to listen and love. My daughters have been fans since the beginning, but I guess I don't always trust their tastes, since way back in their Shania days. I shouldn't mention Hillary Duff, but....I like the darker Taylor, and that she's in tabloid feuds with Kanye and Katy makes me love her more. "When you're young they assume you know nothing." Guilty, Taylor, and my own girls.

8. "**Black and White,**" Three Dog Night, from 1972's *Seven Separate Fools*. Okay, it might sound trite now, given all the crap being promulgated by the White House. It's not even close to my favorite

3 Dog song, but I was thinking of it the other day, and how 1972 didn't guarantee anyone anything, and yet, here we are. Better? Worse? Still the same old people doing the same old shit? Anyway, they weren't fools, this band, but have you read Mary Trump's *Too Much and Never Enough* yet. Wow.

9. "**my future**," Billie Eilish, from her brand new single. "Check your reflection to find your complexion...I've changed my plans because I'm in love with my future." Go on, tell me why I shouldn't love this record, and when you make that stab, go on and explain why I haven't listened to her other stuff either. Or give me a break and let me keep listening now that I've found her.

10. "**Strangers,**" The Kinks, from *Lola vs. Powerman & the Moneygoround Pt 1* (1970). For Jessica Lee McMillan, because she tries so hard, writes so well, and this is her favorite tune from "Lola...." And for Sarah, wherever you are.

Bye Lefty. I still love you.

.

Justin Willman has a compelling show on Netflix, *Magic for Humans*, now in its third season. It's such an incredible antidote to watching the news and accepting the reality that we have at least several more months of the Orange Plague (at least) and who knows how many more months to deal with our other pandemic.

I've always understood that magic is about misdirection, sleight of hand, getting the audience to see and believe what the magician wants us to.

Oh God. Look what I just wrote. What's the percentage of the country that truly believes that Justin can pull a full-grown woman out of his backpack? 40%? And if this is the number, is that just Justin's base? Can he get more converts, or has he plateaued?

I swear, if he ran for president I'd vote for him, and maybe not just IF the Great Denier/Divider were the only other candidate.

Last night, from the only show in my memory, Justin got way serious, somber even, as he interacted with his mother, who is suffering from Alzheimer's. It was almost unbearable. She still knows her son, but just barely. As he said, they still have these moments; in fact, all we really have, ever, is the current moment.

Nothing magic about that, but it does or should cause us to pause in this moment and think of ways we can manage to do better, and then do so in the next moment. We'll fail, maybe even often, but we'll have successes, too.

So here's to Justin, his mom, and all the successes to come. May they all be rich in spirit, with a bit of music thrown in for accompaniment.

1. "**Magic**," Olivia Newton John, from *Xanadu* (The Original Soundtrack Album) 1980. ELO had a hand in this, not that I need to justify loving a pop song because an eccentric rock band backs it. I knew guys back in the 70's who would have dropped everything to marry Olivia, not that she was interested or even looking. For me, her brand of pop felt soothingly good. My mother loved this song, and I see nothing wrong with that. We'll take our magic whenever/wherever it comes.

2. "**Dear Stranger**," STRFKR, from this summer's *Future Past Life*. This is one of those songs that, if you told me it was produced back in the 70's or 80's, I might believe you. But you wouldn't do that, would you? Dreamy synth pop living in the alternative world these days, it makes me really yearn for The Dream Academy, or for taking a trip to a northern town in England. Everyone there would be a stranger, or just stranger, like I'm feeling now. Listen to the way this one builds at the end. Wow.

3. "**Breathe Deeper**," Tame Impala, another new one from his/their latest record, *The Slow Rush*. I keep thinking I'm going to grow tired of this act, headed by Kevin Parker, who must be some kind of magic man. I keep wondering how he weds dance grooves to another form of Beatle-sound. I'm too musically dumb to understand, so if he's fooling me and getting me to look somewhere over my shoulder, over a rainbow, or above it in a more Lucy-like sky, good for him. I'll pay, I'll bite. I'll pick his card. "Breathe deep(er) the gathering gloom. Watch lights fade from every room."

4. "**On the Floor**," Perfume Genius, another brand new one from *Set My Heart on Fire Immediately*. Mike Hadreas has a way of bringing us visions of dance floors in space. Can't believe this is already his fifth record. How time does fade/slip away. Oh yeah, just this moment. I'll stop here and listen.

5. "**Magic Man**," Heart, from *Dreamboat Annie* (1976). I saw them on the *Dog and Butterfly* tour, with some friends. But I should have taken my other friend, Cheryl, who understood all about dogs and butterflies, and thought too well of me before I could think better of myself. She was my true college friend, in those moments when if you looked too fast, people were transformed beyond what you hoped for or even needed. Just couldn't slow down enough to see what any moment meant. So, Heart, for Cheryl.

6. "**Midnight Room**," Springtime Carnivore, from 2016's *Midnight Room*. "In my midnight room, I never stop dreaming of you." What might that room look like? What moments, what time? I'm attracted to their lush, Camera Obscura vocals, and looking forward to more. And I think we all get the midnight room in our house, in our mind.

7. "**Nights**," Neon Trees, from *I Can Feel You Forgetting Me* (2020). This one definitely sounds like the 80's, on a FM corporate rock station near you. I didn't care for the "Hair Bands" so much, but every now and then, a Mister Mister or Bon Jovi might find me driving late at night, and I'd have to turn my poor car radio up and wonder at myself and my penchant for being suckered by the power of pop.

8. "**Up from a Dream**," Haim, from *Women in Music Pt III* (2020). So I've been driving a lot recently, with Max by my side, and lately, too, I've tuned in more to XMU to see what's new in this particular moment. Haim keeps calling, so I answer. "Are we already up from the

dream, or do we need to wake up again?" I think it's the latter, but I'm just one guy typing. They're on my must-see concert list when I wake up the next time, though.

9. "**Dreaming**," Blondie. Hell yeah, from 1979's *Eat to the Beat*. Was Blondie overrated or under-rated? Or both? Man, when I hear this song I think about how punk and new wave and rock and pop are split hairs in someone's wastebasket. I once scared a friend by playing this record. She preferred Jonathan Edwards' "**Sunshine**," a nice tune, but still. She was also an Auburn fan, but she was my friend anyway and a good one.

10. "**Magic Bus**," The Who, which you may find on *Meaty Beaty Big and Bouncy* (1971). Who doesn't love a good Who song? Look at their photo from 1965 on the cover of *My Generation*. Could anything have been that simple and easy, that innocent and alarming? I saw them in Lexington, KY, after Keith was gone. It felt tainted, like something happened to the magic, but it was the moment we had. Not so psychedelic, but pretty hard. Every day, you'll see it. Keep searching.

I bet you're glad I refrained from mentioning Barry Manilow. I know I am. Donna Summer once covered "**Could This be Magic**," but you didn't hear that from me.

That vacation trip was a solid and soiled experience. Solid, because my wife, daughters, and our three dogs refreshed ourselves with ourselves, and I started really believing that we would get through all of the crises at our feet. Soiled, because at our sandy feet was a compound of T***p trainers and Q people, frolicking and waving more banners than I'd ever seen in one beach place—such a prelude of what was to come.

The love fest known as The RNC also played out, but I didn't watch. For there was paint drying in our house and you know how exciting that is.

And then, we all lost RBG, and our loss set the battle for the next court seat to be only a notch worse than the one in our minds and hearts.

In these weeks, I also began teaching again, found a new therapist because I felt I was falling, falling, and not in love again.

Taylor Swift records started grabbing me, too. It's never too late, baby, especially when your young daughters get to groovin.

Florida was making news for all the wrong reasons, too, and not because their football teams sucked (actually, they didn't so much). DeSantis opened up bars, etc., and I still wonder how many people died, and Alabama students stood in line maskless to go to bars and get football tickets. Life goes on in stranger ways.

Musically, I was all over the place, dreaming of Blondie, Tame Impala, New Order, Shelby Lynne, Public Enemy, Broken Social Scene, Lykke Li, Slowdive, The Buffalo Springfield, the Stones, Badfinger,

Sergio Mendes, Malo, Human League, the Thompson Twins, and...

Jerry Falwell, Jr, who, it seemed, wasn't exactly as honest and pure as he let on. I was never so glad to see a T***p supporter revealed as such in my life.

.

Playlist #11: August 18, 2020.
Rising Tides

After a trip to Edisto Island, where my family and I were decidedly socially distanced and conscious, it's back to the ongoing new reality of life. The semester at our college started yesterday, and so far, so good. At least for my Creative Nonfiction class and me. Like most people, I wake up every morning hoping that our lives have remained as regular as possible. I saw some people on the beach who likely don't worry, except in that crazy QAnon sort of way.

I would ask, "Who believes that weird shit?" but do I really want an answer?

Likely not.

I miss my daughters terribly, and I know we just had nine days together. It's never enough and the house is too quiet again. Don't worry, music is coming to fill our fevered void.

I do have to say that I watched the DNC last night, and among all the wonderful speeches—especially by Amy Klobuchar, Bernie Sanders, and of course Michelle Obama—I was heartened by the Republicans who spoke out against the Orange Plague and for Biden/ Harris. Love you John Kasich.

I probably haven't been going as high as Michelle would like, and so I hope my better angels emerge here and now. No promises, but here's to trying, and to ousting orange plagues come November, and other viruses as soon as humanly possible.

Wear your mask (we got a "Roll Tide" version) and figure out how to vote and:

#BLM.

1. "**Dead of Night**," Orville Peck, from 2019's *Pony*. C'mon, you know you love him. Listen to this dirge-country ballad and tell me why he isn't in your steady and heavy rotation? Those guitar notes at the beginning perfectly complement his voice. "We laugh until we cry." That pretty much sums up life, unless you want to do it backwards, which sometimes happens. How many other past traditional country stars do you think were gay? Not to out anyone, but it's something to ponder in the ...

2. "**Dreams**" (for Layla), Fleetwood Mac, from 1977's *Rumors*. Something else that happens in the dead of night to many of us. I keep dreaming about my lost cats—the ones who passed naturally and the ones who left in other ways that I'll never understand. Why do I keep dreaming about them? My therapist said it was because I loved them so and they're assuring me that they are still with me and know that I loved them. So. Do I believe that? Why shouldn't I? If only those crystal visions, which I don't, apparently, keep strictly to myself, were real. I guess you'd say, who's to say they're not?

3. "**Hey Baby (They're Playing Our Song)**," The Buckinghams, 1968, from *Portraits*. This one came to me at the beach. Originally, it came to me by mistake. I was 12 in '68, and went downtown to Pizitz to buy the latest Paul Revere and the Raiders 45, a picture sleeve of "Don't Take It So Hard." When I got home, I did take it hard when I discovered that the record I wanted was not there and in its place, this great Buckinghams tune. I could have whined until my mother drove me back and exchanged it, but instead, I put it on our stereo. Still have it, too: "It's the one with the pretty melody."

4. "**Get Ready**," Rare Earth, 1970, covering The Temptations' hit on their debut record of the same name. Now, if you have that album, you alone know that the title song clocks in at 21+minutes. What on this

rare earth? I saw them in the summer of 1970 at the WVOK Shower of Stars, with Mary Jane, Jimbo, and Mary Jane's cousin, "Wheatie." Not sure how she spells it, nor do I remember what it's a nickname for. No matter. Neil Diamond was the headliner that night, but no matter, too, for listen to the moment the bass and tambourine kick in. You'll remember summer romance, if you ever forgot it, that is.

5. "**Bizarre Love Triangle**," New Order (1984), which you may find on their *Singles* LP. We used to dance to them at The Factory in Knoxville, though on our first date, my future wife also invited her boyfriend. He was a nice guy, and maybe neither of us knew what on this rare earth was happening. She was only 21, so all wrinkles should have been expected. I almost gave up after that night, but a month later, there she was again. Without him. With me, dancing still.

6. "**Beds Are Burning**," Midnight Oil (1987) *Diesel and Dust*. We definitely danced to this one in our first Greenville apartment. Then we actually got to see the band in Atlanta, though I don't remember the name of the venue. Maybe because we got so stoned before going in, after we had consumed Ethiopian food at The Blue Nile in Virginia Highlands. Anyway, this song won't go away because the issues it addresses won't either. "The time has come, a fact's a fact..." Dump the Orange Plague. How can we dance when our earth is turning?

7. "**Fool on the Hill**," Sergio Mendes and Brasil '66, which you may find on their 1970 *Greatest Hits* record. I had this 45, too, inherited from an older guy named Jim Snyder, though I could have garbled that last name. He and his wife let us have our high school graduation party at their house. I don't know when or why he gave me his 45's. I remember him talking to me that night, like he needed to let me know that life would go on, though we both knew that more than we could say was ending. I appreciate it, Jim, and thanks, wherever you are. Bet you thought this song was for the Orange Plague?

8. "**Los Angeles**," Haim, from *Women in Music Pt III*. I guess you have figured out that I love this record and keep finding new standout songs from it? "These days, these days." I love how jazzy they've gotten, these sisters. I'm thinking a lot about sisters these days and am reading a great novel about sisters, too: Silas House's *The Coal Tattoo*. I've only been to LA once, but hope my daughters make it there some day—not to live, but to see what others know and write about. A peaceful, easy feeling, this one.

9. "**The Rising**," Bruce Springsteen, from 2002's album of the same name. Maybe you heard this a time or two if you were watching the coverage last night from the convention. A good choice, I think, and for once, Bruce was taken by the right party. Man, I'd see him for the sixth time if he'd come back to Greenville like he did a few years back. We could celebrate, and he'd play this song, and this time I'd beg my wife to be with me for the show. Why'd you decline last time, honey? "Because I am an idiot sometimes."

10. "**Believe in Humanity**," Carole King, from 1973's *Fantasy*. It's an odd choice to name your album one thing and to include this song, which was a minor hit. But I think it's a fitting ending for this week, because I do. Believe. Another jazzy number to help me along as I try to not get too anxious over things like my dog's ear infection. My buddy. While I believe, I also think dogs and cats are more humane than we are, by far. Did you know that the Orange Plague doesn't care for dogs? Says it all right there.

Playlist #12: August 24, 2020.
Convention(al) Madness

Guess what? Mary Trump's Aunt Maryanne, the Orange Plague's older sister, told Mary that our current president "has no principles." I just read that in *Politico's* weekend roundup. Not that I needed to read it or hear it from TOP's older sister. But it's good to get family affirmation, right? If my brother ever said that about me...but then he wouldn't, because I do have principles, and so does he.

And the latest of these is that I am not watching one nano second of the RNC this week, which will feature TOP every night, at his request, demand, and brutal dictate. Because that's what he is or wants to be:

A Brutal Dictator.

I'm not sure why anyone thinks otherwise these days, though I know we're also still worried about street scenes in big cities, the virus up-ticking through colleges (c'mon Alabama students. Did you really need to stand in line for bar openings and without your masks? I guess you don't want to be healthy or to have football).

Am I angry? Yes.

Am I worried? Yes.

So what will I do this week instead of watching the republi-circus?

Maybe watch the Yankees play ball.

Maybe start watching **HBO's** "Lovecraft Country" now that "Perry Mason" has ended.

Teach my classes, and, oh yes.

Listen to my homemade playlists.

Hope you'll join me.

1."**Him or Me (What's It Gonna Be?),**" Paul Revere and the Raiders, 1967 (*Revolution!*). "If it's so, I got to know...what's it gonna be, him or...." Right down to it at the start. If you love me, you can't love him, vote for him, think he has normal human qualities, much less the ability to lead or unite a country. Who knew the Raiders could be so prescient? So kick-ass! I bet the OP can't even name a Raiders' song, the jerk. Get the record, and also listen to "**Tighter.**" wow.

2."**The Devil's Right Hand**," Steve Earle (1988) from *Copperhead Road*. So is the Orange Plague the devil or his right hand? Please don't spend too much time trying to decide—your brain cells can't take it—kind of like staring at the RNC on any night. I mean, what can they even say at this point? They started the darkness: "Caught a man cheatin', shot the dog down, shot the dog down, watched the man fall, never touched his holster, never had a chance at all." Not that I advocate violence, you understand. I DO NOT ADVOCATE VIOLENCE, not even against the devil.

3. "**Sympathy for the Devil.**" Now in 1968, The Rolling Stones recorded this one on *Beggars Banquet*. Maybe an obvious choice to follow another devil song, but potency is potency, even though what we've seen from this current administration is a lot of limp responses to our many crises. That 500 feet of wall that Bannon helped "finance" through a GoFundMe. Do you feel safer, freer, more enlightened and democratic? He should rot in jail; got no sympathy for his kind, and extrapolate that out to the orange guy he "worked" for.

4. "**Savior Complex,**" Phoebe Bridgers, from 2020's *Punisher*. Both the song title and the album title fit the bill. I'm not sure that the Orange Plague thinks he's anyone's savior, but apparently that base out there

imagines that he's gonna save their souls, or at least keep white males from ever feeling like they're not in power. Sorry to associate you, Phoebe, with this sea of madness, because you're so much better than the sycophants who surround this agent of our undoing. I know you'll rise above it—Phoebe, that is—and I hope all voters will, too.

5. "**Ambulance Blues**," Neil Young, way back on *On the Beach* (1974). "I never knew a man could tell so many lies; he had a different story for every set of eyes. How can he remember who he's talking to? Cause I know it ain't me, and I hope it isn't you." That was about Nixon, who seems like a poor forgotten Shakespearean tragic hero/villain now—worthy of MacBeth, I think, or even Richard III. What we have now is a guy trying to appropriate Neil's tunes for his own purposes. The least of his crimes, of course, but not to be forgotten. Almost picked Neil's "**Sea of Madness**," a worthy second placer.

6. "**Drive Me, Crazy**," Orville Peck, from this summer's *Pony*. I know this song is not about our current politics, but when I ran across the title this morning, I thought, "Yep, that's what I feel." I had just read the news today, oh boy, and I imagined going batshit crazy with worry and anxiety over all that I cannot control. All that's emanating from a man who absolutely did not get more votes than his rival back in 2016. Still. We got another chance, and so, what we have to, MUST do, is...

7. "**Fight the Power**," Public Enemy, from 1989's *Fear of a Black Planet*. What else is there to say? Except that it's too sad that what Chuck D and the guys were shouting back in '89 sounds just like what many of us are shoutin' today—about the planet, about racial discrimination, about the power against us coming from the seat of it. The back end of it. The butt of it. "Most of my heroes don't appear on no stamps." Think there will ever be a stamp with the Orange Plague on it? Let's cancel that before it's ever plate-blocked.

8. "**Your Lies**," Shelby Lynne, from *I Am Shelby Lynne* (2000). I guess I've already mentioned all the lying coming from Pennsylvania Avenue's 1600 block. So I'll venture into happier terrain. My wife and I got to see Shelby in Greenville at the old Handlebar. I think we might have taken our girls who probably couldn't appreciate this modern country sound back then. Bet they'd love her now. She was incredible, and back then, I had no idea she was Allison Moorer's older sister, or what they went through as sisters together when they were too young to know how to cope with lying and abuse.

9. "**Bad Weather**," Allison Moorer, from *Blood* (2019). As in so many pieces of art, the title of the record has a double meaning. We'll stick to the positive, though. Moorer also wrote a memoir of the same title that I'm reading right now. Her blood, her sister Shelby, is at the book's heart, as she attempts to reclaim all that she lost, or if reclaim is not the best word, to rise above it and declare her love for her soul, her sister. Bad weather, stormy weather, and please look out New Orleans...and Charlotte.

10. "**All I Have to Do is Dream**," The Everly Brothers, back in 1958, on any Best of compilation you want. I am dreaming of a day when I can see someone else in the White House. For the next four years, it's definitely Joe Biden, and then after, we can talk, keep dreaming, and find out more about America's better side, better angels, and more empathic best self.

Playlist #13: August 31, 2020. Who's Feeling Lucky?

Maybe I do. Tomorrow I have a consultation with a person whom I hope will be my new therapist. I've probably waited longer than I should have to re-start the process, and God knows, my wife needs the break.

Sometimes sighing is only sighing, and sometimes it's much more.

However, as down as I might feel—not in every moment of course—I also think to myself:

"Well you could be Jerry Falwell, Jr."

Sorry to keep kicking a guy when he's down (and way out at least by normal societal conventions and by the college he used to head), but when you assume a certain moral mantle and then become this degree of hypocrite, I think we're entitled to add a few more kicks to your rear end while you stand back and oh-so-helplessly have to watch.

Yep, way too easy.

And while Jr did not cause our current crisis, he definitely joined in and added to the mix. With leadership like his and the orange plague's, who needs robotic drones?

Or pool boys?

But even moral failures, religious hypocrites, and those who cry, "I was really just a businessman" need playlists in their honor, and so with that said:

66

1. "**Don't Touch Me There**," The Tubes, from 1996's *Goin' Down*. "The smell of burning leather as we hold each other tight... our jeans rubbing against each other. Darling, I want you so, your sweet lips and salty taste." Well, he had to be hearing something as the wife and the pool boy enticed, pleased, and tempted each other in the hotel room for eight years or so.

2. "**Don't You Want Me (Baby**)," Human League back in 1981 on the album, *Dare*. I feel like quoting the entire song: "It's much too late to find you think you've changed your mind...." Please, for God's sake listen to the song, learn the lyrics. This will one day be the soundtrack for the Lifetime or Hallmark movies based on the sordid affair. A religious icon of a man; his accommodating lady; and the pool boy who came between them (or made them more whole). This, again, is why I write strictly nonfiction.

3. "**Lies**," The Thompson Twins, somewhere in 1982 on a *Greatest Hits* album in middle America. So, really, what was the soundtrack of their affair, this three-way extravaganza playing out while poor unsuspecting Liberty U. students thought they were being governed by someone who was looking out for their academic and moral interests? Or, where was Jr in 1982? Which clubs or discos was he haunting, staring at the pretty boys and girls on public display? Is this sounding creepy yet?

4. "**The Policy of Truth**," Depeche Mode from...no, I can't, I just can't. It's too good, almost too unbelievable. 1980. *VIOLATOR*. "It used to be so civilized; you will always wonder how it could have been if you only lied." God knows what they'll wonder, be wondering in the future,

or where they'll turn up, offering more "truth." Are presidents of universities bound by their institution's honor code? "Never again is what you swore, the time before" indeed. Bonus: "**Personal Jesus.**"

5. "**Nausea**," X. 1980, *Los Angeles*. I suppose I don't have to explain much here. The good news is that X has a new album out and after forty years, punk still sounds good, even refreshing. Thanks John and Billy and Exene. This song is less punk and more "Yeah." Whatever that means. But I swear, the minute I read about that threesome, I thought of this song and its attendant sentiment. Though it was tinged with a tiny bit of glee.

6. "**It's A Sin**," The Pet Shop Boys from 1987's *Actually*. In my first year of teaching at my own college, I'd drive the dark days of a fall when I didn't think many people cared, listening to an FM station from Asheville that played this song almost every morning. "At school they taught me how to be so pure in thought, and word, and deed. They didn't quite succeed." Seriously. Aren't you as fucking tired as I am of religious hypocrites—those who yell at you to believe in Jesus and then, sure as shit—as sure of a thing as it takes five cards to play five-card stud—that they will commit the kind of sin that they most vehemently rail against? Of course, with the blessings of their real orange ally.

7. "**My Country**," tUnE-yA-rDs, on their album *Whokill*, 2011. Ever since our Puritan days, we've been obsessed by sex. And then I think of that funny Woody Allen movie—is it *Annie Hall*?—when Woody's persona Alvy wonders where all his school-age friends are now, and I'm pretty sure one of them says "I like to watch," which would be funnier if this weren't after what we know about Woody, and now maybe is again given what we know about Jerry Jr. Funny in that "My country tis of thee" kind of way. I used to think it was "My country tears of thee," and now I think I was right after all.

8. "**Blue Monday**," New Order, 1983, found in old clubs and other sundried legends. "How does it feel, to treat me like you do?" I haven't looked, but I guess the Falwells have kids (I just looked—they have 3 including Jerry III). Poor things. We know that Jerry Jr was once a kid, too. What did he learn from his Pop? How did it feel to be raised by the founder of The Moral Majority? Was the pressure too great? Did he need and find an outlet? "I thought I was mistaken, I thought I'd heard your words...those who came before me, lived through their vocations...." And I am quite sure that someone will tell them all how they should feel today.

9. "**It's No Secret**," Jefferson Airplane, from *Jefferson Airplane Takes Off*, in the very cool year of 1966, when I was ten and Jr was four. We've heard so often how rock and roll corrupts, how it's the devil's music, and how it's the road to illicit sex. But...surely no rock and roll found its way into the Falwell household. So how do we explain this behavior? Why do we think we can keep secrets of the heart (and eyes)? The Airplane had its issues, too, but then, they never claimed to be anyone's moral majority. Right?

10. "**We Have No Secrets**," Carly Simon, from her seminal record, *No Secrets* (1972). I refuse to quote these lyrics, because I love Carly so much and because this album is a precious memory from my high school years. We really don't want nor need to know our loved one's secrets, or at least all of them. I've thought a lot about this, especially given my recent essay collection's title, "Secrets I'm Dying to Tell You." Anyway, Carly's voice still gets me, and her words are so true, if only others would listen and heed them.

I've been feeling a bit off lately, like I'm trying to stay balanced on the curb, but I keep stepping off into something busier. Or maybe it's like the tree pose in yoga, and my limbs keep falling, try as I might to keep my focus steady.

I suppose I watched too much Woody Allen in my youth, and so whenever I feel a new pain, I think of doctors and CT scans and all that can go so dreadfully wrong. My wife reminds me,

"Well you know you do have that ever-so-slight hypochondriac streak in you."

"Hhhhm. What are you saying?"

She smiles and reassures, and then heads out for a kayaking lake crawl—she'll float along and restore herself, and I'll sit at home and read my students' creative nonfiction, where I'll discover just how petty my puny problems are. For I was never molested by someone I looked up to.

And then I'll put on some music and prepare the snapper creole for us that I've been craving ever since my brother and I talked about those foods we most need in these alien times. Thanks to reading Jessica Lee McMillan, I remembered some of the bands I'll list below and picked up a few new ones. The humidity has dropped and in this moment I sense fall, my favorite season, and something like hope feels possible again. Should be getting our Biden/Harris signs soon, speaking of hope.

And now, with hope for all, here's this week's

1. "**Skyline**," Broken Social Scene, from 2017's *Hug of Thunder*. We were watching some of the U.S. Open last night, and while I've lost my taste for tennis, I still long for New York. I missed who was playing whom, but I managed to glance up every time the blimp showed the skyline of Manhattan, daytime, nighttime, and from such a distance life seemed so normal. So I got up, put on this gorgeous, dreamy song, and measured the upcoming days with a soup spoon.

2. "**Myriad Harbor**," The New Pornographers, from *Challengers* (2007). We always end up in the city, seeing the sunsets in the sky. And from the sky. I've loved this band for almost 20 years, and I, too, would love to walk into my favorite music store and ask for an American anthology. I guess, though, such a work would mean different things to different people. The myriad reflections of who we are, and whom we pretend to be. My record store is open, though my turntable has long been closed.

3. "**It's My Life**," Talk Talk, found on their *Very Best* from a place in the 80's when all we had to worry about was Reagan, AIDS, and our human rights violations in Central America and elsewhere. More than anything, though, this song puts me in mind of my old lost friend David Bloomer. If anyone has seen him or knows about him, please tell him that our life together meant so much to me, and I wonder why we're lost now. He loved this song. And he loved to play tennis with me, too.

4. "**Long Live Rock**," The Who, 1979, *The Kids Are Alright*. "We were the first band to vomit in the bar." Well now, if that doesn't say long live rock, I don't know what does. Every now and then, I ask The Who to fix me up, and they usually oblige, and for my money, *Who's Next* is one of the five greatest rock albums ever produced. Rock isn't dead,

of course, because it never will be, and I might be old, but I'll dance to this one any day. And that, amongst so many other things, separates me from the Orange Plague.

5. "**A Rock 'n' Roll Fantasy**," The Kinks, 1978, *Misfits*. That summer before my last year in college, I worked days in my Dad's jewelry store, listening to K-99, and this song played almost every day, sometimes twice or thrice, as I, and the song's subject, spent our lives away. Maybe not quite on the edge of reality, but down enough to where I had to turn the volume up and never loud enough to satisfy. Is it weird that I miss everyone at that store, especially those I never said a proper goodbye to, or my Dad, whom I did, but he couldn't see me anymore? Maybe it has been a fantasy life after all. Love The Kinks for this.

6. "**The Last Great American Dynasty**," Taylor Swift from this summer's *folklore*. Despite our democratic pretensions, Americans love dynasties, it seems. Our neighborhoods are all about continuity, but look more closely, and watch the changes. When we moved into ours, we were young and foreign, and now we're so established that my wife brings flowers to the newbies as well as to the 90-year old able bodies. Things change all the time, and any dynasty is another way of fantasizing that you'll live forever. Volume low or loud, but one day, they'll turn you off no matter who you are or what your family pretends to be. This whole album is worth a new turntable, by the way.

7. "**I Don't Know**," Malo, from their out of print third record but available on 2001's *Celebracion*. I wrote a good bit about Malo in The Riff's summer song challenge. Maybe because the low humidity reminds me of the west coast, where right now, I'd love to be. Such smooth sounds. That horn section: to die for.

8. "**Blue Turk**," Alice Cooper from *School's Out*, back in 1972. Up through this record, Alice was making music that while some called it hard rock and left it at that, others understood that something more

complicated was happening behind the scenes—some jazz, some homage to show tunes. Alice would have been right in time with Berlin Cabarets, and likely would have lost his life trying to explain what he was all about and that the heavy mascara was just for show. Of course, I'm not sure where he fits in now. But I have felt resurrected listening to songs like this one; "You're so very picturesque, you're so very cold. It tastes like roses on your breath, but graveyards on your soul."

9. "**Whitey on the Moon**," Gil Scot-Heron, from *The Revolution Begins*, way back in time. Have you been watching "**Lovecraft Country**" on HBO? No? Do you know what a "Sundown Town" is? Have you ever heard of The Cthulhu Mythos? Or of "redlining?" You'll see a dynasty or two if you watch. This song/poem ended episode two, and I won't say anymore because watching is believing, or at least seeing some of your worst fears, or recent history, come true.

10. "**Mississippi Goddam**," Nina Simone, from 1965. Well, Mississippi did just free Curtis Flowers after six attempts to execute him for a murder he didn't commit. Thanks to the intrepid reporters from the podcast **In the Dark**, another black man wasn't lynched by the Magnolia State. But rumor has it, or rather Sue Eisenfeld in her book, *Wandering Dixie*, relates that between the 1890's and 1978, over 4000 lynchings in the South were documented. Of black people, and these were just the documented cases. Goddam. Why shouldn't we feel off and unbalanced? And go look at what happened to Ms. Simone.

I might have this wrong, but Florida Governor Rick DeSantis is ready to open bars in his state again, and nothing says "I'm ready for the pandemic" like sitting in a crowded barroom while the music is playing songs from Ted Nugent and that strange band of American sisters with Nazi leanings, Prussian Blue.

Sorry for the stereotyping, but Florida, really?

Well, the Seminoles are playing football today, and I guess the Canes are, too. The Gators are coming in two weeks, and as much as I love the idea of watching college football again, I don't need to go to no stinkin' bar to do it.

Sorry, had to throw in an allusion to *The Good, the Bad, and the Ugly* there. Because that's the way it feels all the time as I try and fail not to read too much of the news and, at times, forget that I'm not in Florida, and we're safe and wearing our masks and getting take-out food from the Thai place up the street.

So get behind me, Florida, and play some tunes worth the price of admission, or the price of a more distanced entry, or your own private house party.

And if nothing else, fall is almost here; the temps are moderating slightly, and live music is streaming somewhere near. Now, listen while I play...

AMERICAN CRISIS PLAYLIST #15

1. **"Dead Leaves and the Dirty Ground,"** White Stripes, from *White Blood Cells* (2001). I don't know what to do with myself: I love images of dead leaves wherever they are, because they remind me of my

childhood backyard where Dad never insisted I be so punctual about raking. So even in January, the leaves kept laying there, trodden under and definitely decaying. Ah, the Stripes fill me with joy, even at this great distance. Did they ever get the recognition they deserved? I first heard them in an old bar in Greenville— the glory days—and one of my writing students reminded me of them just last week. I have hope for our nation's "youth."

2. "**Never Been Wrong**," (for Gov. DeSantis) from Waxahatchee's 2017 record, *Out in the Storm*, the first of two Wax songs I'm listing this week. If you were in a bar and this song came on, what would you do? Ask the barkeep to crank up the volume? Order another pint of lager (or a cider drink)? Keep on shooting pool or darts? Grab someone you love, or would like to, and dance in the center of the room, or in some corner alone, where no one else can see or get to you? I'll hang up and listen now.

3. "**Can't Do Much**," from Waxahatchee's latest, *Saint Cloud* (2020). I love the way the opening guitar refrain reminds me of Junior Walker's "**Gotta Hold On to Your Love**." It feels like a summer holdout, but as she sings about her "uneasiness," I feel it—the general malaise of something's being wrong even in the dining room of my own house. Can't do much about it now, she says, but that's disingenuous of her since she's killing me with her voice and words. Doing quite a lot, actually.

4. "**Ohm**," Yo La Tengo, from *Fade* (2013). What does it mean when you wake up thinking about a song like this: "Sometimes the bad guys come out on top, sometimes the good guys lose?" I've had enough of losing, thank you. I got back into steady yoga practice this week and felt so much better. I have lost too much time "resisting the flow." Remember when we saw them at The Orange Peel in Asheville, and

they played this song acoustically right at the beginning? We were lost for a while then, because "nothing ever stays the same...and this is all we know." God, I love them.

5. "**Shelter**," The xx, back in 2009 on their debut LP, *xx*. I remember sitting in a coffee shop in Iowa City, writing in my journal while listening to this record, recommended to me by my best friend Owen's niece, Larkin, who is a NPR announcer in Pittsburgh. She is so much younger than us, and I do take comfort and shelter from people my daughter's age recommending sounds that I MUST hear, and their being so right about it. Between this band and Beach House, I wrote tons that summer at my summer workshop, led by James McKean, who has fallen off my email radar. Hope you're well Jim. So much has changed.

6. "**I Follow Rivers**," Lykke Li on her 2010 record, *Wounded Rhymes*. I've followed her since 2014's *I Never Learn*, so I decided to look even further back to this gorgeous song. I don't mind following the right people, and no, our governor isn't much better than Florida's, but then, I don't take my lead from politicians anyway. The creek behind our house is rising again after all the rain overnight, and if I followed it, I'd get to a waterfall downtown. I'd rather, though, listen and follow Lykke, because her sounds make me want to write more and not worry about "participating."

7. "**All I Know**," Washed Out, from 2013's *Paracosm*. I suppose I could have selected any song from this record, one of my top ten favorites of the decade. I have to be careful, though, and not listen too often, because something about it makes me feel heavy with the dream nostalgia of being fifteen and listening to sounds that made me want to cry, though I had no idea why. I knew too early, felt too early, all that I knew I'd be missing someday. That's what Washed Out is like for me: I miss what I've lost, what I understood I had only for those connected moments. It felt like this:

8. "**Expecting to Fly**," Buffalo Springfield, *Buffalo Springfield Again* (1967). Not to give myself too much credit, but when I was fifteen, this was my favorite song. I listened and sang to it every night, though my voice was baritone, and Neil's...? I hadn't found love by that point and so had nothing to lose, nothing that I had really lost. But what does that matter? Songs "sing" to you without any prelude, preamble, or past, really. You hear them, you love them, and they become part of you. And for me, this song, and the quick years following, will make Neil Young my rock muse forever.

9. "**Day After Day**," Badfinger, 1971, from *Straight Up*. Fred texted me this morning, at first to remind me that his alma mater, Tulane, was playing football tonight against South Alabama. Must see TV. But then he sent me a photo of his grandson Jesse and his son and daughter-in-law's dog. Oh, and Fred and I saw Badfinger in Birmingham back in 1972, way before Pete Ham decided that his days were done. Love this song, and so does Fred, and so did my mother, who always let me go, out of my "lonely gloom," whenever Fred called. Go Green Wave.

10. "**Creature Comfort**," Arcade Fire, from *Everything Now* (2017). This is likely my favorite AF record. And when you listen, yes, I am playing something more rhythmically upbeat, but when you consider the lyrics, sorry, nothing so comfortable, nothing so "painless." Still want to see them live, but I can wait till bars and arenas and anything in between are saner. "I don't know what I want, and I don't know if I want it." Yep, that's how it feels. That's today. ...a friend of mine, and one not nameless.

Of course, I wasn't feeling complacent or even steady. My wife and I chose to view Otto Preminger's *Anatomy of a Murder* Friday night, the perfect way to greet the Jewish New Year. Love James Stewart and Lee Remick—my mother looked like Lee Remick, which in this film kind of creeped me out.

We had made plans to order a kosher takeout pizza and share with friends, but my wife started feeling too bad for that.

And we both felt sick later when we got the news of Ruth Bader Ginsberg's death.

The madness and sorrow of this year just won't quit, and there are still three plus months left to go. It certainly feels "impossible to take" today, tomorrow and tomorrow and tomorrow, but what choice do we have? So I grieved again and then found some music yesterday to see me through, which I now want to share because you and I—those of you who follow this weekly list—we're in it together.

In this strangeness, we have each other.

▣ AMERICAN CRISIS PLAYLIST #16 ▣

1. "**You and I**," Local Natives, from 2013's *Hummingbird*. I tell myself that I must be strong, that we have to be strong, you and I, because whatever we're feeling or facing now, we might be looking back on soon and wishing that we were here again. The darkness can get darker, though I hope we wake up soon and keep the greater, truer light on. I so regret not seeing Local Natives back in Louisville when this record was hot. Looking back isn't always the best thing to do.

2. "**Alison**," Slowdive, all the way back in 1993 on a record called *Souvlaki*. I don't know what I was doing in 1993 not to know about this band. And where would I have heard it? FM radio played mainstream rock, and our alternative public station focused mainly on Americana. Bands like this found homes on college stations, I suppose, but I could have used the dreaminess then, in those days before our second child was born. Yep, looking back again, but those moments right before and right after her birth do seem all of a dream.

3. "**Hallucinogenics**," Matt Maeson, from his EP, *The Hearse*. I see the theme emerging: is all of this real, or am I on a drug that I forgot taking? Thanks to an old friend, who used to provide me the alternatives to my reality, I found this song and artist. I know what reality is: exiting Facebook, which I have informally done. Who needs the angst and the heartache and the vitriol? The news provides a daily dose, though I sometimes think we're all tripping.

4. "**Send in the Clowns**," Tyler Childers, from his just released record, *Long Violent History*. You should know this song from Stephen Sondheim's *A Little Night Music*, or from Judy Collins' version, found on her LP, *Judith*. Oh, you weren't so alive and well back in 1975? My sophomore roommate used to play this song over and over, almost crying, or maybe doing so for real when I wasn't around. His name was Mark, and maybe still is, though I haven't laid eyes on him since 1976. Anyway, the song's last line, "Don't bother, they're here," makes me want to cry, too. They wear orange hair, have orange skin and turkey necks. They don't call themselves clowns, though, so send in the drugs.

5. "**Bluebird**," Buffalo Springfield, from *Buffalo Springfield Again* (1967). I think it's the sky outside today, the bright sun, cool wind, and low humidity that put this song back in my head. Stephen Stills at his most brilliant, both in the writing and the singing. The banjo at the end

really takes me home, and if I had to have one record to take with me wherever I go, and this one was it, I wouldn't suffer a bit, even though sadness is my home. Good points to raise with my therapist tomorrow.

6. "**You're All I Want**," Cigarettes After Sex, a brand new single. I hear David Lynch really likes this band, and why not? Play this song to get settled and add the Alpha Stim to your earlobes. Pet your dog; have a cup of Red Rooster coffee and sit back, ease into it all. What's out there matters less than what's in there. It's easy to want more, and how do you know when you're content with what you have?

7. "**Breathe Deeper**," Tame Impala, from this year's *The Slow Rush*. When I first began teaching at my little college in the wildwood, I had such angst; people there still disparaged The Beatles, and the KKK was present in and out of all town shadows. So my wife—so present too—made a sign for me to hang on my office wall. The sign said "Breath," though she meant it to say "Breathe." Everyone gets confused and it's the same thing really, though she added a sideways "e" later. I kept it for years until I learned its lesson and heeded its message.

8. "**Get Gone**," Seratones on 2016's *Get Gone*. I want to say so much here; but instead I'll say that I discovered this band while watching an episode of John T. Edge's "True South" on the SEC Network. Maybe it was the Nashville episode, but who cares? What an edge they have, and I need edges, serotonin, and maybe some Alabama football this coming Saturday night. Won't cure my blues away but might keep the orange-haired devil from the door.

9. "**Help Me Stranger**," The Raconteurs, from 2019's *Help Us Stranger*. "If you call me, I'll come runnin'. You can call me anytime." Strangers and angels and devils and backwater musicians, but please, find me a better guitarist right now than Jack White. I do need my friends

and I am mistrusting strangers, though as Max and I walk through our neighborhood, I'm seeing all the potential friends—they have the right yard signs—and if it weren't for Covid, I'd have a house party and invite them all, to help.

10. "**Bridge Over Troubled Water**," Simon and Garfunkel from 1970's album of the same name. Play it and think of RBG and all we've lost and all that we need to have to ease our minds. Our weary and troubled minds.

It's a strange thing to be married to an optimist who boldly turned into a pessimist over the next few weeks in our country's life. I kept saying again and again, "We have a good shot," and she kept saying, "But we're so divided...." Hard to argue that.

Through these same weeks, we viewed (or at least some did) the presidential debates; we watched in...horror/dismay/glee/then it was announced that T***p had Covid. We endured another supreme court nomination process, and some of us voted early and others on election day.

Then, we waited.

We also heard that "we" had defeated Covid, though none of us had received a vaccine yet, and most of us were still refusing to go out in public without masks—except for those at certain White House affairs to celebrate another conservative, religious justice taking her seat.

And then we voted...and waited...

Part of me was losing my mind, so I decided to go back into therapy. Soon, I discovered that my therapist knew Lou Reed back when they attended Syracuse together, and I was filled with...hope? Definitely joy. Still, I wasn't sleeping well, and why should I have been?

The constant, again, was music, whether it came via older bands like The Pixies, Linkin' Park, even older sounds from Steve Earle, Waylon Jennings, The Beatles and Lou himself, Kris Kristofferson, Michael Jackson, Laurie Anderson, or from new-to-me artists like Miranda Lambert, Khruangbin, the Yeah, Yeah, Yeah's, Small Black, Arcade Fire, and Taylor Swift.

How can I tell you just how nervous I was? But I suppose you remember, and I'm sorry for reminding you. My therapist warned me that even if Biden won, our country was facing something dark and dire because, you know, some people don't take losing gracefully. My therapist is a wise man.

I've been dreaming about people I lost: my mother, my friend Owen, my cat Morgan. My recurring dreams of what I used to have. At least my mother wanted to hug me in this last dream and she held on, something she hardly ever did in "real life."

What are my dreams saying? Why don't I get the lessons they're teaching the first or the twelfth time (I picked "twelfth" because it's so damned hard to spell)?

My wife tells me that if I learn nothing else from her, then get this: when my mind starts—at the very start—to wander, I should start counting my breaths instead. This is supposed to help me sleep, and it is a practice also found in yoga where, like reality, my mind also tends to wander.

I keep thinking of Faulkner's character "Drusilla Hawke," from *The Unvanquished,* who tells her cousin Bayard that there's no point in sleeping anymore because too many things are flowing by her window, past her land and beyond. She's talking about freed slaves and returning, defeated Confederate soldiers. No point in sleeping, no joy or calm in it either.

I don't exactly share her views. I'm not nostalgic for, scarred by, the Confederate collapse and defeat, and **I'd like to sleep**, but when I have too many of those dreams, even when I'm hugged by a ghost, I wake startled and disturbed. It's like a paradox: I want the hug but I'm disquieted by getting it only in a dream.

I thought about including many Moody Blues songs this week, but then, I need a mood turnaround, not a more entrenched version of the bluer me.

Fortunately, I'm re-reading and teaching John Jeremiah Sullivan's *Pulphead* in my Creative Nonfiction class tomorrow night. In that collection, he writes of Michael Jackson, lovingly, critically, and with the deepest questioning sensitivity. He reflects on performances, recording sessions, and of course, the songs, always the songs.

So then I started thinking happier things, about dancing and shaking my poor, tired body, and so, in the midst of more crises (Yes, I will personally join the army to pull the Orange Plague out of the White House once he's defeated) I turn here to livelier sounds—anthems of spirit and joy, coming from within and beyond America.

I hope you enjoy, and I'll see you soon, on the other side.

AMERICAN CRISIS PLAYLIST #17

1. **"Shake Your Body (down to the ground**)," The Jacksons, from 1978, though you may find it on *The Essential Michael Jackson*. Might as well be startin' something with this badass dance tune from back when I used to club at least three times a week (oh those Wednesdays). I feel like I could hold my own on the floor, and I'm not ashamed to say to you that from time to time, more random people would ask me to dance with them. One or two of them tried to take me home, too, but I was never one to run off with perfect strangers.

2. **"Sheena is a Punk Rocker**," The Ramones, back in 1977, on *Rocket to Russia*. Speaking of perfect strangers, The Ramones figured out a way to marry punk and surf and sound fresh and happy, as disturbed as they certainly were. I knew some Sheena's, and "girl punk rockers" always turned my head. I was in a semi-mosh pit once with one named Noelle, and she knocked the shit out of a guy who got in our way. Later she cut my hair, too. I so loved her blond hair and combat boots. By day, she was an architect.

3. "**Carnival of Sorts (Boxcars)**," R.E.M., from their initial EP, *Chronic Town* (1982). I fell in love with them immediately upon hearing this song, and at grad student parties in old Knoxville, we played the shit out of this little record. R.E.M. played a tiny club on the strip back then, Hobo's, and fifty or so of us ventured in. Some of us left, too, but we were never the same in that way that rock music makes you want to keep dreaming of what you meant when you said I Love You to someone you barely knew.

4. "**Career Opportunities**," The Clash, from *The Clash* in 1977. How loud you'll play this one will tell me everything I need to know about you. Jessica is maxing her system out right now. And Les and Mary, wherever you are, I'm counting on equal doses of bursted speakers. That's busted to the rest of you.

5. "**Blown Away**," The Pixies, from *Bossanova*, in the ripe old Bill Clinton year of 1992. It was two of my students back then—Steph and Brad—who made me listen to The Pixies. Whenever they'd play something new, I'd ask, "Who's that now?" and the answer, not the song, always remained the same: "That would be The Pixies." Well, of course it would. I'm still blown away by moments like that when it seemed like I was teaching peers and they, me. Hey Steph, I do appreciate it all, and would love to see you again.

6. "**Buried Alive (feat. Dr. Octagon)**," Yeah Yeah Yeahs from the Deluxe version of 2013's *Mosquito*. You know what I think about the yeahs, so...Yeah. In my mind, and maybe dreams, I'm in a club and the DJ plays forgotten songs like this one and the dancers look around and think they've been dancing to all the wrong songs because how could any of those be better than this one? We're buried in plastic pop all too often, and we need a newer energy. Something more electric and even blue.

7. "**Electric Blue**," Arcade Fire, still a fave from 2017's *Everything Now*. Hit that perfect beat, boy. I keep wanting to know how they managed to find a way to make a great song keep sounding perfect after, what? 1000 listens? If my computer had a place to show a worn out and scratched place on the disc, this is it. I found out that I didn't know shit when I thought I knew what a classic dance track was back in 1978. But why compare? I never did in those moments when I was so...

8. "**Out of Control**," U2 from 1980's *Boy*. It's dark out there, or inside. So don't worry, just shake your head down to the ground and wonder why no one in 1980 could admit that U2 was the coming thing. I know, they seem old and faded now, but thinking is overrated, because, you know, nothing is neither good nor bad, after all. Is being out of control so bad? At least regarding music? Catch the drums as the song seems to fade and return.

9. "**Free at Dawn**," Small Black in 2013, on a record called *Limits of Desire*. Heirs of U2? What are our limits, and how **are** we free? What is happening to us? Where are we heading? Who will hold and hug me now? Who's playing the songs I hear in the club I used to know? How can I wed desire with the real thing? Who was Michael Jackson and why did he have to suffer? I really want to know it all, or at least how Nov. 3 will turn out. Oh man, I'm heading down again, so better end this now. Up again.

10. "**Billie Jean**," Michael from *Thriller* in a world of time ago, or 1982, whichever you prefer. Once, I thought I had heard it too many times. Now I wonder if I ever heard it clearly at all. My brother had the record and used to play it on his self-bought system. I recorded it on a cassette, back when mix tapes were harder to pull off. When we could agree on pop hits. When he was the one. Try to remember where you were when you first heard this, and what it could have done to you, for you, if you could have known then, if you could have everything now. I do that a lot.

Been keeping up with the news lately? No? Did you know that "Schitts Creek" swept the Emmys? That was so last week, you say? Well, I mention it for two reasons. One, I forgot to mention it last week and after all, it's one of my all-time favorite shows (rivaled by "**Twin Peaks," "Six Feet Under," and** "**Fleabag**"), and two, whatever absurdity the Rose family brought to us each week—or in those binge moments when nothing else would do—could anything Johnny or Moira, Alexis or David, or Stevie, Bob, and Roland and even Twyla have done or ever think of, make you think the world is crazier than whatever that was that we witnessed last Tuesday night?

Actually, I didn't witness it because I knew better. I knew that if Biden fucked up, I didn't want to see it, and if the other guy—the Orange Plague—was merely himself, well, I didn't want to witness that either. I read the news the next day, oh boy, and I felt as contaminated as if I had been Chris Wallace sitting there like the world was normal, or was supposed to be; or even if it wasn't, that we would somehow get through this together, we and Chris.

He later admitted that "things could have gone better," a line that reminds me of the Lusitania, the Hindenburg, and the Cleveland Browns (who actually won a game yesterday), all wrapped into one.

Chris also revealed that the T***p family did not follow mask-wearing protocol at the debate. They refused to listen to Cleveland doctors' medical advice—that makes the Browns look better, but everybody else???

Oh, hindsight!

One of my neighbors asked me Friday if I thought that the plague that hit the Orange Plague was a hoax (not Covid itself, but that "he" actually had it)—a way of grabbing attention and playing on our sympathy because though I didn't see the debate, I have gleaned, like so many others have, that the orange one didn't fare so well. So, sympathy can do wonders, sure.

But I think we all know now that neither the plague nor the OP is a hoax, or at least 70% of surveyed Americans think that way. The rest? I just don't know, but I'm betting that there's a certain Supreme Court nominee who, like me, just saw a photo from Saturday before last of her young son sitting in the White house on a bench next to Sen. Tillis of North Carolina, where neither of them is wearing a mask, and you could maybe set a plastic truck in between them. Like the master he serves, Tillis is quarantined right now, prognosis uncertain.

Such is life in crisis mode.

So what music do you have for us today to ease our worried minds?

Well, glad you asked.

AMERICAN CRISIS PLAYLIST #18

1. "**Instant Karma**," John Ono Lennon, from a 1970 single on the green Apple label. It beat out "**Let It Be**" for number one at least one week on Dick Clark's **American Bandstand** Top Ten countdown. I remember how dark and haunting it sounded, Lennon's voice seemingly coming from a beyond I had never thought about. It might seem low, or lowdown, or even on the "downlow" to bring this up, but the orange buffoon did ridicule Biden for wearing a mask, and just yesterday, T***p campaign official Justin Miller defended his boss. Go ahead man. "Why on earth are we here?" To live meaningfully and without fear, I thought.

2. "**Walk Away**," James Gang from *Thirds* (1971). Seems to me that when you engage in a mob on an occasion where no one is wearing a mask, and you embrace people because now you think you can pack the Supreme Court with people who value faith over science, you might want to take some responsibility for your actions. Seems to me, you don't wanna talk about it, Mike Lee. I wish you well anyway.

3. "**Let the Mystery Be**," Iris DeMent, 1992, *Infamous Angel*. I could quote every line of this beautiful song and apply it to the mystery that is today. The mystery of how we've gotten to this point, where a sick man has to take a drive to get yet another moment's adulation from a few fanatical well-wishers, likely infecting his guard in the process. No one knows for certain, do they Iris, of where we're going or even where we've been. I notice that he wore a mask then. Too little?

4. "**Jump Into the Fire**," Harry Nilsson, from 1971's *Nilsson Schmilsson*. Even I think I'm overdoing it here, though I had to hear Harry's weird chanting laughter, and I wonder just how he and his partner were making each other happy? Or if they could. What other crazy thing will we jump into before the year, the month, the day's over? Will we even be here next week for **American Crisis Playlist #19**? Do you think we'll be dancing, jumping, or will there be another kind of fire breaking us down?

5. "**Ventilator Blues**," The Rolling Stones, *Exile on Main Street*, 1972. I'm feeling shameless. I'm trying to remember my emotions when I got the news last Friday. Worried? No. Sad? No. Elated? Not exactly. I'll stop there before someone accuses me of being heartless. I didn't come up with this, but I will appropriate it: what if he recovers, and then dies after he loses the election? Would Pelosi be President then? We'd get a woman for a few months and then ol Joe? How crazy would that be? Nothing so crazy like that could happen, right? Right?

6. "**Shut Up and Let Me Go**," The Ting Tings, from 2008's *We Started Nothing*. Speaking of Uncle Joe, isn't this what he shouted at the Orange Plague once or twice during the debate the other night? What if he had said, "You know Donald, you remind me of that Ting Tings song?" Wouldn't that have caused the last remaining Bernie supporter to come over to Biden's team? And imagine what T***p would have heard when the Ting Tings' name was used. Only imagine, but not for too long. Show some respect, after all.

7. "**Close to You (They Long to Be)**," The Carpenters, 1970, from *Close to You*. A song from another administration for this one. Yep yep yep. If you've ever heard this song, you'll never hear it the same from here on. I don't know how to explain it either. I could see longing to be close to Eugene or Daniel or Sarah Levy, but to...him? Remember when Iris sang let the mystery be? That's really hard. I have this single, by the way.

8. "**Dark Days**," Local Natives with Sylvan Esso, from a single released this year. Did they know? Did they foresee it? In the summer, they say, but right now in the early fall of October, it couldn't be brighter from my porch as I see nothing but blue skies, with a bit of breeze reaching my weary mind. A song with such a title can actually be a feel good song if you let it be. And I am, while my dog lies by me giving us both more comfort than we've had all day. I so love this song, and my dog. Have I told you this lately?

9. "**The Ground Walks (with Time in a Box**)," Modest Mouse from 2015's *Strangers to Ourselves*. Another band I want(ed) to see live. Are they still around, and if so, how do we tell? So danceable and so happy. I feel like the ground is moving under my feet, or is that the earth, and if it is, sorry Carole. Modest Mouse makes all things possible and reminds me of "Future Mouse" in Zadie Smith's life changing

novel **White Teeth**. Read that one if you haven't and think about what happens when you're so sure the world is ending. And listen to more Modest Mouse as you do. (It's not, by the way).

10. "**How Long?**" Ace, from *Five-a-Side* (1974). Such a tease, if you remember the story's subtitle. My graduation year, and no, I don't know the answer. A few days? A week? Four years? It depends on who you are, in your "fancy persuasion, [not] admit[ting] that it's part of the scheme." Yeah, it really does. For some, nothing's so wrong; for others, it always has been so wrong. Are we as dumb as we seem? What say you, Ace? November 3 is coming quickly.

Yesterday I discovered that when he was in school back in Syracuse, my therapist knew Delmore Schwartz and Lou Reed quite well. In fact, they sat at a bar called The Orange one night when a tune came on the jukebox that made them jump up and clap and eventually sing along once they learned the words.

That song was something about wanting to hold someone's hand back in the winter of '64. Kennedy was dead and everything, and four years later so would be another Kennedy, because in order to get a punk band called The Dead Kennedys....

But I'm losing my place here. I am being analyzed by a man who was good friends with Lou Reed, and I'm not sure how to process that information. Not that I'm struggling through any angst or pain because of it, but finding out that I am two degrees from what was once the **Rock and Roll Animal** is truly heady stuff.

I think of "**Coney Island Baby,**" as well as *A Coney Island of the Mind*. From beat to Beat to Beatle, the world drips in funny patterns.

Drop, Drop...drip...DROP

I saw Lou once near Lincoln Center as I strolled up Broadway. He stood next to a payphone, and standing with him was Laurie Anderson. I stared, and they, of course, knew why I stared. Instead of snarling or sneering, they smiled back. I wish I had more than a mental picture of that meeting, but the one I have will have to do.

I could have walked up to them and asked why "The Bells," or how "O Superman," but my shyness and certainty that I'd drool kept me walking away.

Over a decade later, I saw Laurie do a show at Georgia Tech, and near the end, she brought Lou on for a couple of numbers. My friend Mark was with me, and some of our students. I wonder if any of them remember?

Of course, Lou is dead, I'm still in therapy, and according to my therapist, our American crisis won't be ending anytime soon.

I love it when my therapist tells me he's going to burst my semi-optimistic bubble and then does so.

He also says Lou's record *The Blue Mask* is his best. I say "Hell yeah," even if I don't agree. It's a moment I could have longed for, and now it just went past, like Lou and Laurie watching me pass that fall day in New York. Maybe they wanted me to stop. And why not? I'm pretty cool, I think.

But as to our music, let's walk, though not necessarily on the wild side.

AMERICAN CRISIS PLAYLIST #19

1. **"Kimmi in a Rice Field,"** Mr. Twin Sister, from 2011's *In Heaven*. Honestly, I have no idea where this band came from or how they got into my library. Who let them in, anyway? If it's you, give me a shout out because I want to hug you and kiss you and tell you how much I love you and them. I don't know why Kimmi is in that rice field, but Kimmi, I'm standing there with you and I don't know what we're looking at, or feeling, or how long we'll be here, though it might be longer than we think.

2. **"I Ain't Ever Satisfied,"** Steve Earle and the Dukes, back in 1987 on *Exit 0*. If you think this is your theme song, who am I to argue, except that it must be mine. So you go your way and I'll go mine. When I saw Steve at The Orange Peel in Asheville a few years back, I'm

sure he didn't do this song, though I'm really not sure. He didn't do "**Transcendental Blues**," and I'm still upset or...not satisfied, so maybe all this is worth it. I thank my friend Les for one day back in 1986 asking if I had heard of this kid Steve Earle. I hadn't and a few **Guitar Towns** away I did. How has the time passed and will it keep on?

3. "**Ghosts**," Bruce Springsteen from his upcoming release, *Letter to You.* When I heard this song last week, I immediately thought of Steve's song above. Don't ask why. I find Bruce's voice so soothing, and we're going on forty-five years now. I wonder if my therapist and Lou wrote letters to each other after Syracuse? I'll ask, but why wouldn't they have? I used to write letters to everyone, including an old college friend named Anne, who died on me at some point after our letters stopped. It's a shitty way to discover from your alumni bulletin that a friend has died. Are there others like me that turn to the death section of the bulletin first? Anne lived in Mobile, on South Ann Street. No shit.

4. "**Paranoid**," Black Sabbath. 1970. *Paranoid.* Because why not? I mean, aren't you? 3 weeks away, and what can I do now that I've voted? So easy to turn an absentee ballot into a smiling poll worker. I assume someone will count it, too, and the fact that I use the word, "assume," validates Ozzy and the boys' spectral vision from my 14th year alive. That Ozzy is still alive is just as miraculous, I think. Can Ozzy vote? Does he?

5. "**The Community of Hope**," PJ Harvey, from 2016's *The Hope Demolition Project,* and in that year, a more aptly titled LP doesn't exist, even though she was a little off in the projection. I gotta say that if I walked by PJ while she was standing at a phone booth, I **would** walk over and not past and ask her who she was calling and why and if she needed a dime or a quarter. What I'm saying is that I adore her

sound and wonder what she was doing back when my therapist and Lou were dancing with Delmore to the Beatles? Yeah, she wasn't alive then, but she is now. I would definitely write to her.

6. "**Here We Are in the Years**," Neil Young, from his live *Tuscaloosa* record, recorded in the year of our lord, 1973. Found originally on his first solo, self-titled album. My first love. I was there, in Tuscaloosa, with Freddy and Jim and Jimbo and Jane. "Time itself is falling so, spreading fear of growing old..." The fear is real and it's happened. We were sixteen/seventeen then. We had not heard of D****d Fu**ing T***p, didn't know he existed. Do we know now? Can we "relate to the slower things that the country brings?" Whatever they are? Subtle faces.

7. "**Till Victory**," The Patti Smith Group, from 1978's *Easter*. Nothing subtle here, though I can't believe this was '78. Thought it was earlier, but that's Patti, who surely walked past Lou on uncertain days in the Village or The Bowery. You know what I mean. I want to hold your hand until the damn election is called and then we'll worry about what comes next with the militias and Q'ers and all the sordid stuff going on in what passes for people's minds and hearts.

8. "**Positively 4th Street**," Bob Dylan, echoing out of a *Greatest Hits* album lost in my downstairs collection somewhere. I thought about using the no direction home "**Rolling Stone**" song, but I didn't want to be that obvious, less positive than this. So much happens when Dylan plays and I can't keep up. But I feel better and realize that in 1964, *Highway 61 Revisited* was still a year away. And "**I Want to Hold Your Hand**" was a year back. And Kennedy was dead.

9. "**Sharkey's Day**," Laurie Anderson, from 1980's *Mister Heartbreak*. Strange dreams. Later on the record, William S. Burroughs chimes in for "**Sharkey's Night**." I never saw Burroughs or Ginsberg or Kerouac, but there's Laurie, living for me day and night. Strange and desolation angels. Inner demons abounding. Mr. Twin Sister Heartbreak.

10. "**My House**," Lou Reed from *The Blue Mask*, 1982. Delmore Schwartz taught Lou and my therapist Joyce's *Ulysses*, my favorite novel. Schwartz was the model for Saul Bellow's "Humboldt," and in my first year of teaching at the college, I taught Joyce and *Humboldt's Gift*, and didn't know my therapist but did know Lou—though I hadn't seen him yet—and wondered about how we walk so steadily over ground that others could never walk freely on, in, about. "A mist is hanging gently on the lake/My house is very beautiful at night." And so it is in all its machinations and cardboard dreams.

I sit in the mountains of Virginia, a relatively blue state, though where I am, there are more Orange Plague signs than not. I passed a sign a couple of days ago that said:

"Jesus is My Savior

Trump is my..."

The car slid past, and I couldn't read the rest. I didn't back up because I don't need the bullshit. Equating Jesus and the Orange Plague, believing that they share guiding moral principles, feels like believing that a soap opera, the Kardashians, Jerry Falwell Jr, and Franklin Graham represent models of true love and sanctity.

Or sanity.

We've taken long hikes over the past few days and looked at houses that we're considering for our mountain retreat—a place to be near our older daughter and son-in-law as life continues to unfold.

It's less than two weeks to the election, and I keep reminding myself that it's likely that we'll never see an aftermath like the one that's coming. Will someone have to lead the Orange Plague away in shackles and bonds? Will he head down to the bunker that he claims he "only visited" when protestors took to the streets back in the summer? Will he emerge looking like the tieless, bearded Saddam Hussein after he hid from his own undoing? Will he watch The Clash documentary, **Rude Boy**?

So much to contemplate, and still much to worry over.

So he has a bank account in China?

So he thinks Bin Laden is still alive?

So he continues to cozy up to QAnon?

And dis Lesley Stahl?

What else will he do before we listen to scientists and psychologists and admit that he has...a problem? A DSM-IV (or is it V now?) variant of some kind of personality disorder?

Having raised such questions, I must now admit that I have no answers, but then I consider that according to Jewish sages, the answer to every question lies within the question itself.

And while you think on that, let's have some music to soothe our savage beast inside as we await the twilight or new dawn of our democracy.

AMERICAN CRISIS PLAYLIST #20

1. "**That'll Be the Day**," Buddy Holly, from 1958's *That'll Be the Day*. A plane crash in Iowa on a lonely winter's night amidst a driving snowstorm. That's one way to end it all. The title came from Holly's abiding impression of John Wayne in **The Searchers**. What would Wayne or Holly think of these days? How would they vote? Yeah, I know Wayne was a Republican, but would he, could he, countenance Cadet Bone Spurs, that All-American he-man? More questions, and herein, the Jewish sages might have to rethink something.

2. "**Paper Planes**," M.I.A. from her record *Kala* (2008). During that snowstorm, the plane Holly rode in surely seemed such. This song, which samples The Clash's "**Straight to Hell**" (*Combat Rock*), has found its way into commercials, movie soundtracks (*Slumdog Millionaire*, for one), and Lord knows what else. One of my students quoted it as she turned in an essay last week: "All I want to do is..." I missed the reference and felt stupid afterward. Guns and money, but where are all the lawyers? Still thriving in the swamp?

3. "**Times Like These**," Steve Earle, from his upcoming as yet untitled release. I just don't know how to describe these times, but I'll defer to Steve who wonders how we'll overcome, whether we'll be set free, and if love is really all we need. If love isn't all we need, though, can we get a little more of it at least. And speaking of which...

4. "**Gimme Some Lovin'**," The Spencer Davis Group, from somewhere in 1967, though you can find it on 1985's *The Best Of*. Spencer himself died yesterday, and I felt such a pang. For almost all my life I've known this group and their big hits, and though I've often been a stranger in their midst, I feel that much more alone in these years, now. The sentiment is stronger than ever, if we even know anymore what he means. Or as The Jackson 5 once put it, "**Stop, the love you save may be your own.**"

5. "**You Know I'm No Good**," Amy Winehouse, from *Back to Black* (2006). "I cheated myself, like I knew I would. I told you I was trouble; you know that I'm no good." I find it hard to add anything to Ms. Winehouse's lament. Well, what did we know? What do we know now? Nothing? Anything? Someone else whose voice I miss and who could have done so much for us, given us so much more, if she only would have, if only she had known. You were so much better than you knew.

6. "**Don't Want You No More,**" The Allman Brothers Band, from their self-titled first album back in 1969. Isn't it fun to find songs and titles that sum up how we are feeling, might be feeling, depending of course on who we are? I feel this way, though I hasten to add that I never wanted you, Mr. Orange Plague, in the first place. Never will, never can, no way, no how. How would Duane and Gregg have voted? Gregg supported Jimmy Carter once upon a day, so.....I love how this song seamlessly segues into "It's Not My Cross to Bear." Makes you think they saw something coming.

7. "**Shut Up and Kiss Me**," Angel Olsen from 2016's *My Woman*. Nothing so very thematic here; I just love the song and felt like adding it, though I can imagine a post-election scenario as we celebrate and scream and drink more champagne or bourbon that I'll say this to my wife and even to my good friend John who wonders where I am right now. Maybe I'll say it to you, too, if you want me to.

8. "**Put Your Money on Me**," Arcade Fire from their amazing 2017 release *Everything Now*. Likely, Vegas isn't giving good odds anymore, because you just can't bet on a guy who thinks dead dictators are still alive and living within himself. Not that he said that, but I've always said he pouts and puffs his chest like Mussolini. Remember when he knocked state leaders out of the way to get to another photo op? Remember when he sat in the White House with President Obama during the transition, thinking, "Oh shit, what have I done?" Yeah, good question there.

9. "**Dog**," The Bottle Rockets, from 2015's *South Broadway Athletic Club*. As my dog lies beside me on my kids' leather couch, I listen to him breathe, and I love him so much. Sometimes life is really just this simple: My dog, he's my dog, is a better living creature by a trillion times (and I'll never be able to count as high as I want) than the creature sitting in the Oval Office. No contest. NO DOUBT. "If you don't love my dog, that's okay. I don't want you to. He's my dog." Words to die by.

10. "**Signed, Sealed, Delivered (I'm Yours)**," Stevie Wonder, from the 1970 album of the same name. My wife's and mine were done two weeks ago. As we await the confirmation, affirmation, and dedication of what we hope is a fresh start, I want to be hopeful. And when I hear Stevie sing, that's it. Hopeful, and on this same record is his cover of The Beatles' "**We Can Work It Out**," and the hit, "**Heaven Help Us All**." More bang for the buck. More words to live by, and no question about it.

Back when I used to listen exclusively to AM hit radio—some fifty years ago—there was this hit by The Grass Roots:

"Sooner or later, love is gonna get you

Sooner or later love is gonna win...

It's just a matter of time...."

So that was a love song, and while in Birmingham it got played constantly, I'm not sure if anyone in the rest of the American world heard it or got it. I'm thinking this was the spring of 1971, and if so, think about the election season on the far horizon then, that great 1972 contest between Richard Milhous Nixon, the sitting President, and Sen. George McGovern. McGovern would have to replace his VP nominee, Thomas Eagleton, with Kennedy family member Sargent Shriver. Eagleton had suffered some bouts of depression, and I don't know about you, but I find it rather quaint that a major party would want to lift a former depressant from its ticket.

We might want to ask "How come?" and these days we might be forgiven for asking, considering what we've put up with for the past four years. Not that the Orange Plague suffers from depression, but he's sure as hell made many of us suffer. I mean, I got back into therapy almost exclusively because of this degenerate refugee from a slumlord's table.

To be fair (right, fair!), Nixon, who of course won the election, also had to replace his running mate, Spiro T. Agnew (aka "Ted") because the Maryland prodigy had gotten into some hot water over something to do with bribery and organized crime. Ted pleaded "Nolo contendere" to federal charges and so resigned in disgrace. Or relative disgrace. Or obscurity.

Ask any twenty year-old person today if they've ever heard of Spiro Agnew and see how they look at you...or how they run.

Even Agnew's failings fail to compare to the lunacy of these past four years. Yesterday, the Orange Plague claimed to have defeated COVID-19, and people are still willing to vote for the jerk.

I am quite sure that I would vote for an Eagleton/Agnew ticket any day before I'd vote for this cretin or anyone associated with him. But then, I've already voted and had my vote confirmed, so what else do I do now except compose the last **American Crisis Playlist** before the last votes are cast? Don't worry, we'll have more music likely before the final count is in. Don't know how many lists, but definitely more music.

So, VOTE if you're going to vote for Biden, and if not, I'm not sure why you're following me.

AMERICAN CRISIS PLAYLIST #21

1. **"So We Won't Forget,"** Khruangbin, from 2020's *Mordechai*. So we won't forget, the Orange Plague has led us into an authoritarian nightmare. People are so afraid of his tweets that they are allowing him to foment riots in the name of white supremacy. This is such a pleasant song, though, that it alone should remind us of our better instincts, our whole selves. We don't have to lapse or be eclipsed by the darkness. This band has worked its way inside me pretty deeply. Definitely one of my faves from an otherwise disastrous year.

2. **"Port of Morrow,"** The Shins, from *Port of Morrow* (2012). I keep trying to think of what this song reminds me of. I'm seeing a dark avenue on Birmingham's southside, somewhere beyond the old Angry Revolt record store and some other place called The Purple Mushroom. Birmingham has this racist and conservative reputation,

and that's true, but looked at more closely, there were stranger places, days, and people, and they were worth knowing. But you had to get out more and search yourself, too. There still is a park called Avalon, and when you think of that, how could any town be so bad? A distant port in some troubled storm.

3. "**Lovin' Her Was Easier (Than Anything I'll Ever Do Again)**," Kris Kristofferson, from 1971 again and *The Silver Tongued Devil and I*. Another 1971 hit on AM radio, and if you played it next to the Grass Roots, you might wonder at the taste and recklessness of those of us listening to and buying such records. I had an inkling while listening to this song that there was a world of music in my life that I hadn't wanted to know, though I did know it was there. For what's the difference in liking this and in liking a Johnny Cash or Merle Haggard ballad? And man, I loved this song. Still do.

4. "**Numb**," Linkin Park from 2003's *Meteora*. I was never a Linkin Park fan, or I should say, I never gave them much of a chance. True Confession: I first heard this song as one of the after-commercial lead-ins to Paul Finebaum's radio show back when he broadcast exclusively from Birmingham. I'm a sports junkie, or rather an Alabama football junkie, and shit, poor Jaylen Waddle. Anyway, I feel pretty numb these days, and maybe that's a better feeling than the downward alternative. So thanks boys, I owe you that.

5. "**Mirrorball**," Taylor Swift, from 2020's *folklore*. I'm wondering if this will be my favorite album of the year? I keep playing it and finding new songs to love. Of course, I felt that way about Haim's new record, too. I suppose it's hard to lose when the music's this good. What song do you imagine Joe and Jill, Kamala and Doug dancing to when the count is in? I might pick this one, but who'd understand? Who understands anyway? Apparently, Taylor does. Power on.

6. "**Bluebird**," Miranda Lambert, on *Wildcard* (2019). Another artist my daughters turned me on to. Notice how ending sentences in prepositions makes WORD go crazy? We played this last week at my daughter's place during a poker game. Each of us put up $20 and my wife walked away with it all. She kept getting weird, straight flushes even when she wasn't dealing. My son-in-law wants to take her to the craps table soon, and I might like to watch that. She's a bluebird in my heart for sure.

7. "**Brand New Day**," The Mavericks (2017), *Brand New Day*. Okay, this is the song I'm dancing to in mid-November, or earlier, depending...We saw the Mavericks at *Austin City Limits* back in 2018, though it seems longer than that now. I wrote in some other story about their covering "**How Can You Mend a Broken Heart?**" and how my wife and I cried because ours were. Anyway, Raul has it right, and I hope he's ready to mend and melt my heart soon.

8. "**I've Been a Long Time Leaving (But I'll be a Long Time Gone)**," Waylon Jennings from *Dreaming My Dreams* (1975). Well, that says it better than I could Mr. Orange Plague. So, get to packing and don't worry about Melania: she'll be packin' too, though maybe not a plush bag. And please stay gone. No one will miss you a few minutes after you're gone, though some of us have been missing you ever since you got here. Missing in that sense of "Please get out of my life."

9. "**MisAmerica**," The Legendary Shack Shakers, from *The Southern Surreal* (2015). Blast this one from the rooftops any old time and right now would be a good start. I bet Waylon would have covered this tune had he lived long enough. And it has everything to do with the condition my condition is in. My dog is sleeping right by me, and for him, this is a hymn of sorts, a holiday tune wherever stockings are laid by whatever chimneys you care to choose. Can you tell that I'm just making shit up now?

10. "**Walk, Don't Run**," The Ventures, from 1960's *Walk Don't Run*. Though if you haven't voted yet, then do the opposite and the same goes for the OP as he exits, stage right, and I do hope he takes a wrong turn in Albuquerque. That'll be me playing surf guitar and pointing down when he walks by. I'll turn my back on him, as I've been doing these last four years. In 1960, we should have been rid of Nixon, by the way. Bad pennies.

I write on Friday morning just as Pennsylvania has tipped over into the Biden camp. When that tipping point happened, I said to my wife,

"Look, Pennsylvania has gone blue! This is it."

And she said,

"But look how divided the country is!"

I don't know at what tipping point in our marriage I became the optimist, but there you go.

"It's all about fear," she laughed when I suggested that whenever our dynamic had played over these last forty-eight hours, she brought up the divide after I raved with positive news.

Of course, we're both right. My therapist has warned me not to get too hopeful about the state of our national state, for challenges, lawsuits, and chaos still cloud our horizon.

Not to mention the tantrum-thrower-in-chief.

I am not wise enough to explain, much less fully understand, why anyone, or so many people, sadly, take this guy seriously, this Orange Plague. I know that Race/Caste/Gender play a great role, as they always have in our republic. As one-hit wonder band, Ace, once said, "How long has this been going on?"

Much more pertinent, how long will **this** be going on?

Maybe some of us can have the conversation about why we fear each other, whether that's red or blue, white or black. Maybe.

I've been wrestling with which songs to add this week to the ever growing crisis playlists I've been compiling over 22 weeks now. I can't begin to match themes to songs in a coherent way this morning, and so let me just put together some old favorites that might soothe some fears, or rev up some latent desires. Desires to love and dance and play everything loud, in hopes that we can pop some champagne later and at least celebrate ridding ourselves of the occupant in the White House. And yes, I know he's not going far away, but here's hoping anyway.

(Oh, and that dynamic just occurred again. I quoted Eugene Robinson who said that if we are getting rid of "this horrible person in the White House, it's a great day for the country." And my wife said, "Yes, but there's still so much work to do." True, but...)

1. "**Sunny Girlfriend**," The Monkees, from 1967's *The Monkees' Headquarters*. My good ol' brother Mike was the Monkees fan in our household, and he had this record early on, when he was only seven years old. Michael Nesmith wrote and sang lead on this little ditty, letting us know then—though how could we really see?—that he was more than a guy in a toboggan hat who filled a role on a made-for-TV pop band. The song is buried on the album, but here it is now, dedicated to my sunny girlfriend/wife!

2. "**Take the L (Out of Lover)**," The Motels, from *All For One* (1982). I am not ashamed to say that I LOVE pop songs like this one. Maybe it was the video back then, in heavy rotation on MTV, that caught me, or maybe it was simply the power of the chorus, crescendoing relentlessly and speaking in its punny way to heartache and loss and what we all experience at some point in our young/old lover lives. Where I used to hang out in those days, that's gone, too, as are the former lovers who hosted us all.

3. "**Mississippi**," John Phillips, a single which you may find on *Creeque Alley—The History of The Mamas and the Papas*, 1991. The song came from the red/blue 70's, pre-Watergate. I feel like I included it on some earlier list, but so what? It always feels good to hear it, despite what

Mississippi or John Phillips have proved to be. I think my Dad even liked it, and that was a feat I hardly thought possible. "Down on the bayou while you never know what you're doing." Or anywhere else.

4. "**I Believe in You,**" Neil Young, *After the Gold Rush*, 1970. It's a close call, maybe closer than the vote count in Georgia, but I'll say that this was the one song that pushed me over into the "Neil Young is my favorite rock artist camp." A slow, dirge-like ballad (what a redundancy that phrase is), it spoke to the same sort of woebegone heartache I mentioned in The Motels' tune above. But how different. Neil and the Motels, Conservatives and liberals. We all win and lose and believe in what we think is best. "Finding that what you once thought was real, is gone, and changin'...am I lying to you when I say that...."

5. "**Photograph**," Ringo Starr, from 1973's *Ringo*. So this is the last semi-happy song this week. Happy in the sense that we can love and remember loving even if we're hurting now. "Every time I see your face it reminds me of the places we used to go." Hard to think of another line that so nostalgically reminds us of how it feels to remember the past when things seemed better. What is our picture of America? What do we see? What will we remember? This entire record is pretty strong, if you want to play and think about how Ringo was always the peacemaker.

6. "**Conversation 16**," The National, from 2010's *High Violet*. I might be some kind of sicko, but this song still grips me. I wrote an essay a few years back using its lyrics to frame a story I knew about a former girlfriend who had been raped. I knew her rapist, too, and when I dated this girl, she was still in shock from her rape, though I had no idea then exactly what had happened to her. The full story would take me another forty years to discover, in a private Facebook conversation we had. Of course, she's lived with the story all along. She never revealed the guy's name to anyone but a very few of us. And yes, he's EVIL.

7. "**Psychopath**," St. Vincent from 2014's *St. Vincent*. Way down the track-list on her record, this song rewards something—patience, endurance, revenge? "What can we do now," said the beggar to the thief? He is what he's always been, and why it's so difficult for so many not to see the truth is beyond me. If I win, everything is cool; If I lose, it's all fraud. I hate to besmirch the good name of "Charles Foster Kane," but there is no "fraud at polls." The fraud has occupied the oval office for the last four years.

8. "**Another Brick in the Wall/The Happiest Days of Our Lives/ Another Brick in the Wall Pt. 2,**" Pink Floyd, *The Wall* (1979). You gotta hear them all and not cherry pick what you want. Like votes in certain states. So the OP did build a wall all right—right in the middle of America. Hallie Jackson is reporting at this moment that "No one in the White House wants to be the one to reveal to King Lear that the party's over." And Dandy Don died a while back, and so did Cosell. Who's left? James Baker says all votes count, too. "We don't need no education...." Well????

9. "**Psycho Killer**," The Talking Heads, from *The Best of*...(1977). Man, did you see NBC's Jacob Soboroff following that former DNI official in Las Vegas, asking about why he thinks there's fraud and if there is fraud, exactly where is it? And the mobs trying to get into the voting centers in Vegas and Philly? It's gonna get scarier, too, and that's not my wife talking. Better run run run run, run away......

10. "**Ring of Fire**," Johnny Cash, found everywhere but certainly on 1969's *Live at San Quentin*. Fiery rings, down down down, wild desire. The flames should grow higher, and if they're feeling the heat in the Pennsylvania Avenue fortress, then they have some choices. Keep on descending; pour more oil on; or maybe, maybe, douse the fire with water or CO_2. Life is about choices, and while there is division, one choice is becoming increasingly clear. We'll have a new president in January. What else we'll have is entirely up to us.

Well, the year finally ended, but not without Rudy Giuliani's hair dye, more senseless and baseless accusations of voting fraud, and a few too many people believing that the vaccines were hoaxes, too. Mike Pence got one, anyway, and then my daughter told me to watch *The Queen's Gambit*, and I thought she was making a political joke until I found the series on Netflix and loved it beyond reason. I bought the novel by Walter Tevis and loved it, too.

Movies seemed to appear, too, and so we watch Borat, and Rudy, and then turned back to Netflix and *The Crown*. Life, politics, and people of class sure can get weird, especially when matched to music from The Eurythmics, Gillian Hillis, Herman's Hermits, The Kinks, Cut Copy, Siouxie and the Banshees, Otis Redding, The Balkan Beat Box, Arlo Parks, Yes, Tame Impala, and The Traveling Wilburys.

Did Hanukkah and Christmas actually happen? Did anyone celebrate? Did Georgia really turn blue, and did The Black Keys notice? I'm sure Alabama's Mo Brooks didn't because he was too busy wondering why no one wanted to have him over for turkey.

Oh, and college football actually had a season and Alabama, in this case, represented us well.

I wondered if our national crisis was abating, if I would have to end the Crisis Playlist earlier than I expected. It's funny to consider what was about to happen, how Jan. 6 would be another date that lives in infamy for us—at least for those of us who fear authoritarian insurrections!

It's been nearly a week since all media outlets projected Joe Biden and Kamala Harris as the winners in the 2020 Presidential election. The moment is large and maybe one of the best internal moments occurred when old Rudy stood at the 4 Seasons waiting to be landscaped while he delivered more false proclamations.

Reportedly someone informed him that the election had just been called.

"By whom?" Rudy reportedly asked.

"By everyone," went the response.

Even Trump News, as Chris Hayes calls Fox.

But don't let the results get you down, Rudy. Someone in our neighborhood just today re-posted her Trump lawn sign:

"For God and Country,"

leading me to ask,

"Which God and which country?"

As the Orange Plague keeps floating ideas about how he might, maybe, possibly, and in some far-out alternative-fact-universe still win, the Corona Virus keeps raging. Maybe the new vaccine will be here by summer. Dr. Fauci, at least, seems encouraged by that news, and so am I. Regardless of the OP, Fauci keeps working and reminding us to stay indoors, wear masks, and listen to music. Or at least I think he said that last part. He should have, anyway.

So while the OP keeps railing at even this positive news—you know they came up with the vaccine after the election just to get him, don't you?—let's focus on some upbeat tunes to help us move through another Friday the 13th, just 69 days before we're done, for now, with the latest incarnation of the "Know-Nothings" in the White House.

AMERICAN CRISIS PLAYLIST #23

1. "**Runaway**," The Traveling Wilburys, from 2007's *The Traveling Wilbury's Deluxe Collection*. Maybe I've written about this somewhere else, but ten years ago, we were having a party—remember those?—at our friend John's house, and he played this cover of the Del Shannon classic. It sounded so good to me, and while I knew it was the Wilburys, I was blanking out on who was singing. "That's Jeff Lynne," my friend Al told me. Oh Jeff, oh Al, oh John. I love you guys so much, just as I love this song beyond reason.

2. "**The Less I Know the Better**," Tame Impala from 2015's *Currents*. Should I take a cheap shot here? Oh why not, for I've been taking them all along. Did the White House really think that holding a mask-less election night party was: a) going to provide a celebratory night? b) going to allow the dueling Trump women to show off more gauche finery? c) going to allow Eric any sort of platform? and d) not going to encourage the Corona Virus to spread like wildfire? I'm sorry, but stupid is just stupid. Tame Impala, though, quite smart and oh so very smooth.

3. "**Someday, We'll Be Together**," Diana Ross and the Supremes, a single from way back in 1969, or on any *Greatest Hits* package you can name—a song that jumped to number one faster than a Georgia recount. We're so split right now, that I thought I should play the hopeful optimist and encourage togetherness. When that violin intro starts, I don't know about you, but I want to hug my dog and dance around and try not to pull my hip out of joint. This was their last dance together, and if you have to end on something, it's hard to imagine anything better. I believe it's true.

4. "**Conspiracy Theory**," from Steve Earle's *Jerusalem* (2002). "Hush now, don't you believe it. Go back to bed now, don't you cry." I wonder who that could be written for? I hear that the Q from QAnon has gone quiet, living in some bad bunker somewhere. There's internal fighting in those ranks, but they'll likely emerge to reinstate the Illuminati again. Or the Protocols of the Elders of Zion. Or maybe they'll be telling us that Paul is dead. Or that Generalissimo Franco is cadaver diving still. Steve is my God.

5. "**Brain Matter**," St. Paul and the Broken Bones, from *Sea of Noise* (2016). I got to see this Birmingham-based band live seven or eight years ago when we still had a decent music venue here in Greenville. White soul from a group that finds ways to make me feel decent and good about my home area. Our brains seem to have been dormant for the past few years. Let's wake em up and give em a good stroll through the park or even just down the street. Love to love you baby.

6. "**Take the Fifth**," Spoon from *Girls Can Tell* (2001). So after he leaves office, what's the OP got waiting for him in the southern district of New York? Can you see him ever taking the fifth? I would so love to see him on the stand trying to explain why he's so rich, so bankrupt, so successful, and such a loser. Maybe this song can play on an endless loop in the background, and we can even import some "dancers" from that club next to where Rudy was delivering his fraud speech the other day. Something to see, and report on.

7. "**Steeeam**," Shelly, from a recently released single. Pop at its best, and what I wonder here is how much of that vapor has been wafting off the OP as he sits alone, watching TV, and tweeting out vast and grand conspiracy theories about how he really won, and maybe wondering why the universe has finally conspired against him? He shouldn't worry, because SC's own Sen. Graham is still out there waiting to

play golf in the steam heat of this 76 degree Friday. Gonna get cold tomorrow, Lindsey, so strike now while the irons are hot. Yeah, I did write that.

8. "**Kiss Them for Me**," Siouxsie and the Banshees, from 2002's *Best Of*, though clearly from the 80's New Wave era. So, please Mr. Donald, say goodbye to all that, and feel free to shed some moisture on all those in your peculiar orbit. It doesn't matter to me whether or not you wear a mask while doing so, because it's your life, your only life, and I'm so sorry about that because I do practice radical love when I can. Kiss them for me. Where's my dog? Gotta dance to this one.

9. "**Hope You're Feeling Better**," Santana from 1970's *Abraxas*. No, not you Donald, or even you, Corey, or even you Mr. Meadows. No, I'm talking to all my dear friends and family who lost sleep and years to our collective fears and worries and existential angst. Not that we're out of the woods, but here's to better days and more wild guitar and more Gregg Rolie, wherever he is, singing with such mysterious gusto. Question: which Trump family member can name one Santana song? Which one has even heard of this "Mexican" band?

10. "**Na Na Hey Hey (Kiss Him Goodbye)**," Steam from 1969. "He'll never love you, the way that I love you." I clearly have no shame. "He's never near you, to comfort and cheer you, when all those sad teardrops are falling baby from your eyes." Go on, and kiss him goodbye.

I don't know what it is about grown men and their hair. Hell no, I'm not proud or glad that I've grown increasingly bald way up top. Nor am I happy that my hair has thinned and turned from a reddish/auburn tone over the years into a duller gold. But short of peroxiding it back in the sixth grade (just once and to no real effect), I've let it do what it naturally wants to do.

I don't see myself shaving it down to be totally bald, and so as long as I don't see a rear view shot of my head, I'm good.

And so No, but Hell No, to combing over, dyeing, or treating what I have left with any chemicalized reproduction of something alien to my head (and notice that I have not mentioned any form of rug).

All of this to mark yet another distinction between me and the OP and, of course, Mr. Giuliani. Honestly, don't these guys ever ask anyone else's opinions?

Heard it before I finished writing it.

The New York Times interviewed several Manhattan hairdressers about Rudy's dye-do, and they had mixed responses. But whether they said yes it was dye, or no, it was mascara, they all screamed,

"Quit, for God's sake, doing anything like this."

That might be a loose interpretation, but I stand by it.

Last night, my wife and I watched the new **Borat** movie, and we've been debating this morning as to whether Rudy did lie on that bed and begin to consider practicing some form of self-love with Borat's daughter. I don't know, but at least his hair was natural. It was actually the daughter who had hair issues which, if you've seen the film, you understand.

I don't know what Rudy was thinking as he agreed to participate in this film. My wife is convinced that it was all fake, kind of like Rudy's hair color. And I wonder if the OP is still gray? It's at least a more honest tone, and I never thought I'd use the word "honest" in any connection with Mr. OP who, last time I checked

LOST THE ELECTION.

One more thing about the Borat film:

LOVED THE MUSIC.

Ahhh, the Balkan sound.

So here's to authentic hair, honest politicians, and **Sacha Baron Cohen**, whom my wife thinks is awfully weird, but I say, compared to what?

AMERICAN CRISIS PLAYLIST #24

1. "**Keep 'em Straight/Hermetico**," The Balkan Beat Box from 2007's *Nu Med*. I told you I like Balkan music. I like Klezmer, too, because my people came from "over there." I want to attend a Beat party with the BBB, because I feel like it's a place that would allow me to wear my hair any way I wanted to. And keepin'em straight is important these days as the OP keeps inviting poll folk to the WH to get that special brand of trump hair tonic, something to inject, though as of this writing, people enter and leave maskless but at least they're not bending over for him.

2. "**If You Knew What She Wants**," The Bangles, back from 1986's *Different Light*. It's hard to riff off this title, because no man ever knows what "she wants." I mean, if we did, would we ever consider combing our hair over? At least with a comb-over, we understand that the man in question is experiencing some inferiority complex so deep that no woman could ever figure out what he wants either. The

best question for any man is, "If you knew what she wants," would you accommodate, or pretend you hadn't heard? A lot of that creeping around the White House these days.

3. **"Livin' Thing,"** ELO from *A New World Record* (1976). Well, just to pick on Rudy one last time in this week's list, when he appeared on camera the other day—the follow up to his 4 Seasons appearance (**"Walk Like a Man"**)—tell me: Didn't you wonder for a minute if *Nosferatu* was real? The Willem Dafoe movie from the 90's, *Shadow of the Vampire*, asked the same question, but I swear, Google the 1920's version of *Nosferatu* and put it alongside Rudy's dye running. And then swear they're not the same "person."

4. **"I Am the Walrus,"** The Beatles, from *Magical Mystery Tour* (1967). I went to bed last night thinking about this song, singing it, actually, which made my wife rethink her questions about Borat. Who falls asleep to words like "I am the egg man?" Songs like this one always make me wonder not if the Beatles knew more than everybody else, but rather, how much more they knew than we mere mortals? Or at least John and George. Paul makes me wonder about other things, mainly because I'm sure he dyes his hair. "Man you should have seen them kicking Edgar Allen Poe."

5. **"Gunshot,"** Lykke Li, from 2014's *I Never Learn*. This entire record makes me want to sing, so once I learn the words, look out. The album's title could be the epitaph for many of us, and something to think about when 2024 comes calling and a certain orange man asks us to consider him again. I'm not one to worry excessively, so I'll leave it alone for now. But at the rally Borat visited, the homogenous section of Americana who turned out to support trumpism, made me want to pull out a civics book again and ship it to someone.

6. "**Sparks,**" Beach House, from *Depression Cherry* (2015). Well damn, I got myself depressed again thinking about the future. I can't be happy in the moment, even though I did yoga a while ago and felt so relaxed and peaceful. This band is the absolute best to write to. I remember sitting in Iowa City, listening to them on my iPod and writing the hell out of a scene for my writing class that night. My teacher from that time has disappeared on me. Sent him an email and it bounced back. Shit Jim, I hope you're okay. I remember how you helped me and gave me hope when I never knew I could. Write.

7. "**The Adults Are Talking,**" The Strokes from this year's *The New Abnormal*. They did this one on SNL a couple of weeks back, and they remain on my list of bands to see before I turn 70. Still a few years. They've been around for a good long while, right Al? Anyway, this seems like a good one for our age as we try to figure out not only who the adults are, but why they dye their hair. And by the way, have you noticed that those most likely to call someone or something else a "fraud" are also the ones who truly and best understand/live the concept? Question: if two adults from the trump administration were talking, would anyone know it?

8. "**Instant Crush,**" Daft Punk from 2013's *Random Access Memories*. One song truly leads to another, right Julian? So, I have/had an instant crush on MSNBC's Nicolle Wallace. My wife knows about it. She has a crush on Obama. I heard her listening to his interview with Jimmy Kimmel and laughing like a woman who has a crush on someone famous. Fortunately, we both like the other's crush and aren't too threatened. Also fortunately, we tend to crush on smart people. Which is also why we've crushed on each other for 36 years. And danced together for all that time, too.

9. "**Turn Blue**," The Black Keys, from *Turn Blue* (2014). And so Georgia has turned blue officially after a hand recount, certification from the secretary of state and the governor, both Republicans who, I know, shudder about all things blue. Play this one over and over deep into the midnight blue hours, and hold someone close. You'll thank me later, though since I'll be doing the same, I'll already know and understand. My favorite band of this decade. And their best record.

10. "**Time Has Come Today**," The Chambers Brothers from 1967's *Best Of*. No more time on the clock for Donny and Rudy. The game is over. Tick-tock. Tick.

Metals are everywhere today, or at least here within my sanctum. First, we have the silver anniversary of the **American Crisis Playlist** which, even though federal courts keep shooting down challenges to the election (remember? the one that trump LOST?) and even though virus vaccines seem ever nearer on our horizon, must go on until I, for one, feel safer.

Second, today's the yearly renewal of the **Iron Bowl**, and though I expect my beloved Crimson Tide to win, Nick has Covid and won't be on the sidelines, and I'm slightly more nervous than usual. At least the game's in Tuscaloosa, because down on the plains, awfully stranger things happen (by the way, is the Netflix series returning? Anyone???).

Maybe there's other metal around, and no, I won't be listing any heavy metal here. In my youth, it was termed "Hard rock" anyway, and in a past list, I did pay homage to Black Sabbath. I forget what else constituted 1960's Hard Rock, and maybe you'll remind me. What I remember sounds more bluesy these days, like Alvin Lee and **Ten Years After.** Oh, and Hendrix. Always Hendrix.

The game's not till 3:30, and I need to stay sane until then and not while away the hours either. So here's to more music, and I hope, as usual, that you find something to take home—something to wear well and keep humming through the increasingly long, almost winter nights.

Oh, are you watching **The Queen's Gambit,** also on Netflix? You should, you know.

1. "**The End of the World**," Herman's Hermits, from their *Greatest Hits* (1973). I should have mentioned or listed this song, done originally by Skeeter Davis, in an earlier playlist. But I forget the Hermits and how well they could sound. On episode three of *The Queen's Gambit*, this song has a special moment, an emphasis that music so often provides for a storyline. Haven't we all felt this way at some point? Mostly we move on, except for those who can't, and those we've lost too recently.

2. "**Cold Water**," Cut Copy," from this year's *Freeze, Melt*. I don't know if Biden's naming John Kerry to his cabinet as environmental czar will make a grand difference in what's so clearly happening to our natural world, **to us,** but at least it's something, compared to what we haven't had these past four years. I'm relatively new to this band, but I'm a fan already. All I need is you in the midnight sun. A little electronica for your Saturday soul. Calming, naturally.

3. "**Black Dog**," Arlo Parks, from her upcoming release, *Collapsed In Sunbeams*. So I'm a sucker for any song mentioning a dog in its title. But this one continues the mellow flow, and damn her voice drips right into my heart. I'm so looking forward to the rest of the record. "Let's go to the corner store to buy some fruit. I would do anything to get you out your room." I remember days when walking to the store was easy and convenient, and someone always dropped by to suggest we do so. And the black dog isn't always your friend, as those of us who know him, know.

4. "**Lifetime**," Romy, from a brand new single. Still no hard rock in sight, but we can dance, can't we? Once a groove, always a groove. I started stirring roux for my post Thanksgiving gumbo to this song yesterday. The stirring got a bit excited, but man, the minutes oozed

by, and by the time I got finished, I had such a chocolate-y roux, and hours later, with the turkey and shrimp and spices, it tasted like Romy sounds. Smooth, rich, and leaving me, at least, wanting more. Once in a lifetime, something matters.

5. "**Cha Cha**," Balkan Beat Box, from their self-titled 2005 record. I'm so glad I remembered them. I know, I used them in last week's list, but so what. Sue me, take me to court. Or listen to these crazy sounds, the infectious beat, and Orson Welles, as **Charles Foster Kane**, chiming in every now and then amidst the trumpets and sax. Where can I go to hear this music live? Please help. I think they appeared at The Orange Peel in Asheville once. Figures. Missed it. DANCE.

6. "**Walk Like an Egyptian**," The Bangles from 1986's *Different Light*. So might as well reprise another band from last week, and if you play this one right after the Balkans, you'll have an amazing segue, or at least I thought so as I was adding the onions and celery to my roux yesterday. Clearly un-politically correct, and back in 1986, no one knew or used such terms. Anyway, it's The Bangles, so let it go. Please. Or keep walking.

7. "**The Great Divide**," The Shins from a new single, which makes me so happy. The Shins themselves make me happy, and if this song reminds you of hair bands from the 80's then so be it. It's funny, but as we were rewatching *Schitts Creek* the other night, Jocelyn, Moira, Twyla and the ladies were headed to a casino to see Poison perform. But Poison canceled on them and poor Jocelyn was momentarily devastated. Can you imagine Poison doing that to anyone? They recovered with some champagne and special cookies. As we knew they would.

8. "**My Girls**," Animal Collective from 2009's *Merriweather Post Pavilion*. So, my lost friend Owen hated Animal Collective, and Owen was the type of guy who prided himself on keeping current in musical

trends and liking the outre, and the otherwise thumping sounds of bands like LCD Soundsystem. I don't know why AC couldn't turn him on. He never fully explained, and while I understand that they're not for every taste, still, it seems like a fine line to be drawing in your own personal sand. I miss him.

9. "**Jealousy**," Chicano Batman from *Freedom Is Free* (2017). I wonder what he would have thought of this band. I wonder so many things about Owen and our lives. He would have come over for Thanksgiving supper, and he would have been here this afternoon watching the game and opining about how scores and turnovers and everything else tend to even out over the course of four quarters. Words to live by, I know, and so we keep on lighting the lights and reminding ourselves of what we used to have and what we still do. My daughter is here to watch, so never fear.

10. "**Disco Fever**," GOAT, from 2012's *World Music*. I caught my wife dancing to this song on our porch yesterday. The sound appealed to her and as she swayed and did her Persian steps, I realized again just how good I have it. I get to cook and watch football and play good vibrations and watch people I love dance. All is certainly not lost, but I do feel for the ones who aren't with us and who have suffered so much. In our town, we have the **Harvest Hope Food Bank**, which I affirm is a worthy place to volunteer and to donate needed funds and goods. Anyway, Disco Fever is one that's allowable.

All eyes continue to stare at Georgia. Staunch Republicans there don't know what to do. They'd like to keep believing that somehow, some way, the Orange Plague is still in contention to win back his presidency. And yet, no one in the state, most especially the staunch Republican officials who have certified the state's votes and, to their dismay, admitted that Joe Biden and Kamala Harris won Georgia by 12,000 votes, can provide any hard or damnable information that would confirm fraud or change the outcome.

So is it that Republicans are their own worst enemies?

In Valdosta, GA, Saturday night, while everyone should have been at home watching Alabama avenge itself on the artists formerly known as the LSU Bengal Tigers, many attended a rally where their infamous leader pounded the podium and proclaimed that everyone knows he won Georgia and the rest of the states. He lukewarmly mentioned the two senate races coming up in January and to some degree advocated that people get out and vote.

He said next-to-nothing about the pandemic, only that he was right about it.

And of course he was, at least last January when he admitted to Bob Woodward that the virus was far worse than anyone realized.

And so here we are. MAGAs are rallying without masks; Christmas is looming; and the most popular gift this year is the copper-infused mask available at **Nufabrx.com**. I got mine in a three-for-one sale on Black Friday.

I also started thinking about a long-forgotten genre of rock music, well, at least long-forgotten by me. So inspired by the anti-OP forces in our midst, I remind and give you...

Progressive Rock.

I can't lay claim to know the first moment when a synthesized chord launched this genre, or which band came first. But I have tallied all the votes, certified the genuineness of this product and pronounced these fine artists and songs to be the winners.

And I didn't need a rally to do it.

So get your mellotrons out; your beaded vests and elephantine plaid bell bottoms, and ready yourselves to remember intricate variations on certain dark themes matched with lyrics that no one, including Eric Trump, could possibly understand.

🔲 AMERICAN CRISIS PLAYLIST #26 🔲

1. "**Pictures of Matchstick Men**," Status Quo, from 1968's, get ready, *Picturesque Matchstickable Messages from The Status Quo*. Is this progressive rock, you ask? I have no idea, but I figure that it was surely the precursor of something. This band was incredibly popular in Britain and in Germany. I remember being in Heidelberg in 1974, and the only band anyone wanted to listen to was Status Quo. I could be exaggerating just a bit, but isn't that the point of progressive rock? A Birmingham, AL, DJ named Jim Batton once tried to convince his listeners that every Status Quo song sounded alike. I repeat the question above.

2. "**Legend of a Mind**," The Moody Blues, from *In Search of the Lost Chord* (1968). As you'll hear, the song invokes Timothy Leary, who might have been the true originator of progressive rock, what with his "tune in" mantras and astral planes. The song progresses and switches moods, tempos, and rhythms over and over, sounding both British and slightly far eastern as the Moodies find instruments that rock bands, short of The Beatles, normally eschewed. Yes, I said "eschewed,"

because this is progressive rock we're speaking of. Listen for the flute riff. And notice how I stayed away from the title since I don't want to be making fun of anyone.

3. "**America (2nd Amendment)**," The Nice, also from 1968 and their record, *Ars Longa Vita Brevis*. Now you understand that progressive rock is in full swing because a rock band is titling its record in Latin. That's progressive, right? Or bombastic. And speaking of bombs, does our second amendment guarantee us the right to own bombs? Not that I want to, but I'm trying to get a handle on the buzz these days from the QAnoners. The Nice is otherwise known as Keith Emerson's first band, and if you don't know Keith, just wait. He'll be reprised in an alternate reality coming up. It's a fact, alternative or otherwise, that you can't spell progressive rock without Keith Emerson and his synthetic sounds.

4. "**The Knife**," Genesis from 1970's *Trespass*. Of course you realize that progressive rock songs need to clock in at around nine minutes as this one does. I don't know why, but in order to prove that rock music is serious, we need to turn short stories into novels. This, of course, was not the Genesis of MTV days, but it does have the keyboards of genius, and it continues our second amendment theme, the right to wield knives. I see basements in Valdosta, GA, and ten-foot high speakers, and old sofas where guys with headphones are sitting stoned out of their minds wondering how anyone could be listening to CSN&Y while this is happening inside their heads.

5. "**Empty Pages**," Traffic, 1970, from *John Barleycorn Must Die*. Now there is no doubt that these guys knew how to put over a song. And this one runs only 4:35. It's ornate enough to qualify, but still straightforward in its mix of rock and blues and jazz, not to mention Steve Winwood surely understanding that he had a career

in front of him. I love how this song announces itself and refrains the announcement. We so over-rate density. And they hadn't gotten to the low sparks yet, either.

6. "**The Endless Enigma, Part 1**," Emerson, Lake, and Palmer, from 1970's *Trilogy*. This is hard for me, because back in high school, and for a little while in college, I loved ELP. Not so much the afore-mentioned Keith Emerson, but certainly guitarist Greg Lake. I started to list "From the Beginning," my personal favorite ELP song, but it's so acoustic, and doesn't provide the "range" of true ELP progressive sounds. Besides, look at the title and try to tell me that it alone shouldn't qualify this band for one of the center spots in the progressive rock movement. I say "movement" as if it were and as if I know something more about it. I don't, but I did see ELP twice, though the first time in Tuscaloosa almost allowed me to see God, or at least know that my hearing had found some decibels it didn't know it had or could possibly lose. This was one of those stoned evenings where, by all rights, I shouldn't have been driving home, forty-five miles away.

7. "**Astronomy Domine**," Pink Floyd from 1967's *The Piper at the Gates of Dawn*. The oldest song on the list, but even then, can we say that this one kicked off the genre? It's only four minutes long, but if you want something more massive, further down the album is the nine minute "Interstellar Overdrive." Sometimes I just don't know what to do with myself, to quote Jack White who is progressive in another way. I so wanted to list my favorite Floyd songs, "Us and Them" and "Wish You Were Here," but again, too ballady.

8. "**Yours Is No Disgrace**," Yes from 1971's *The Yes Album*. Okay Fred, you knew I was coming to you; you knew I wouldn't let you down, because you know I know that Yes is the other centerpiece of the progressive rock movement. Now, sadly, I parted ways with them once they got to *Tales From Topographic Oceans*, because I was too

impatient to follow concept albums that were three discs along. But this song I still find very listenable, just as I will always adore "Close to the Edge." On a sailing ship to nowhere, leaving any place..." This version was pre-Rick Wakefield, though his run of it on *Yessongs* is pretty brilliant, too.

9. "**Buddha**," Manfred Mann's Earth Band, from *Messin'* (1973). In all seriousness, I was seventeen and boxing jewelry in my Dad's old store, listening to progressive FM station WJLN (later WZZK) in Birmingham, and "my friend" Bob Gilmore played this song, and I wondered why I had been listening to CSN&Y. Why do some songs simply carry you away with a sound and words that maybe you'd already heard, and maybe shouldn't have made that much of a difference to you, but they did. They do. I love how MM kept "progressing." I loved that radio station, too, though boxing jewelry left something to be desired. Still, my Dad gave me that job and let me listen to such tunes. Life was very rich.

10. "**Cirkus**," King Crimson, from *Lizard* (1970). Apple Music calls this progressive and "ART" rock. Well all right. Robert Fripp was my God for the 90 minutes that I saw him and the band play live back in Birmingham at the Boutwell Auditorium, named for a former mayor who was anything but progressive, and I wonder if he knew about King Crimson and what they were doing on a stage in a hall bearing his name? This is my favorite KC song by far (check out the clarinet, oh my god), though the Schizoid Man comes in a distant second. Fripp played this one and Fred and I looked at each other and sealed what was already one of the friendships of my life. Ah life, I go forward now....

First, I should have included The Staple Singers' "**Respect Yourself**" in this week's list, because when it comes to 126 Republican members of the House, and sixteen state attorney generals, "respect" is just another word for believing you've got nothing left to lose. And now, all we're losing is thousands of more lives every day while politicians of the red kind keep sucking up to the loser in charge by insisting that they are protecting democracy while he is clearly subverting it.

Respect yourself and the rest of us.

The election is over. There was no fraud.

So thanks Staple Singers, because it takes musicians to help us see certain lights.

Honestly, and now there are members of congress, like my birth state Alabama's Mo Brooks, who will try to challenge the election once more on Jan 6 when Congress meets to affirm the electoral college's vote, which is occurring tomorrow. I mean, what the f**k is wrong with Alabama? Neil Young asked almost fifty years ago, and while that offended Lynyrd Skynyrd and a few others, no one has ever fully addressed what's going wrong with Alabama. Maybe if your favorite football team is winning, that's all you really care about.

Well, I care about the football team, too, but it's only a minor joy in the midst of so much sorrow. And shit, Mo, how are the Covid cases in Alabama doing and the non-mask wearers? You doing anything about that? No, just go ahead and waste everyone's time by posturing about an election that...

Trump Lost.

And you who backed him, you lost, too. **And thanks for making the rest of us lose so much since 2016**.

When my candidate and I lost four years ago, yes, I whined and complained and redoubled my therapy, but I also accepted the outcome. I hated it, but accepted it, and I don't necessarily think that my attitude and grip on reality make me a better person than Mo or the OP, but they don't hurt.

Oh, and The Proud Boys are hanging on, taking unscheduled (or so they say) White House tours and fomenting chaos on city streets. Proud of what, by the way, boys? And why "boys" and not "men?" Or does that say it all?

Maybe I'm just bitter because my fantasy football team got kicked out of the playoffs, but at least I can decipher fantasy from reality.

And actually, the bold roast coffee blend helps. Real Men drink bold roast.

Whether I am bold or not, proud or not, I feel like a better person when I let it all hang out and when music finds me and I, in turn, find and repurpose it.

So here you go, #27 with no apologies.

AMERICAN CRISIS PLAYLIST #27

1. "**Show Biz Kids**," Steely Dan, from 1972's *Countdown to Ecstasy*. Lost wages. Tell me this song doesn't get inside your fiber and make you want to dance in ways your body no longer knows, if it ever did. "They got the booze they need, all that money can buy." I wonder what stars come out "while the poor people are sleeping with the shade on their light?" I wonder what the trump kids will do when they see that show biz has wrung them dry and we "don't give a fuck about anybody else" in their world?

2. **"Do Ya,"** ELO, from 1976's *A New World Record*. I've already stated my love for all things Jeff Lynne. In college, I adored this band, and maybe one other guy I knew, who also loved Queen and K.I.S.S., loved them, too. The lyrics here are quite simple, and you could apply them to the loser in the White House who'll be leaving us soon, but I'm not sure he really wanted anyone's love. Our pure adoration and worship, but I think "love' is an abstraction in his world, merely a theoretical concept to make others think there might be a heart in there somewhere. Remember when Elaine said to Jerry, "Maybe there's more to Newman than meets the eye?" and Jerry responded, "No, there's less. I've looked into his eyes and they're pure evil." Kind of like that.

3. **"Stop Your Sobbing,"** The Kinks from 1964's *Kinks*. So, if you read last week's playlist, you might remember that I professed love and adoration and out and out worship for the Netflix original, *The Queen's Gambit*. My wife and I have been stringing this seven-part gem out. We have one episode left, and I can't stand it. Can't stand to finish it. I don't want it to be over, and yeah, that's me sobbing over my MacBook Pro. Anyway, in episode six, two songs popped up on the soundtrack—one I knew, this one, though I didn't immediately recognize the artists. Actually, I'm not sure I ever knew who did this song originally, because I know and like a later cover version of it better. I was only eight years old in 1964 when the Kinks were so very young. What will they leave us this time?

4. **"Tattooed Love Boys,"** Pretenders, from *Pretenders*, 1980. Notice that this song doesn't use the adjective "proud." I noticed. You might not know that I and every other straight, and maybe even many gay, men in 1980 wanted to love Chrissie Hynde. I was only twenty-four, and when she and the band broke out, I had a hard time finishing my Shakespeare seminar paper (I got a "B"). Well, to be honest, I

would have had a hard time finishing that paper even without being distracted by Chrissie. I might have even gotten a tattoo for her. Yet another of the bands I would kill for love to see live. Isn't this a good one, though?

5. "**Circle the Drain**," Soccer Mommy, from 2020's *Color Theory*. Here's a new one to try on, as we find our Comet and Ajax and Bon Ami to clean the drain that has been so dirtied in the supposed swamp of our collective dream/nightmare. SM has been on my radar since 2018, and she's getting better all the time, as an artist should. She's making some best album of the year lists, or at least she did on NPR, you know, one of those ultra-liberal places that actually deeply considers our reality instead of firing from our orange comb overs whenever we can't stop our sobbing.

6. "**Tut, tut, tut, tut**," Gillian Hills, from *Twistin' the Rock, Gillian Hills, Vol. 9*, maybe from 2002, but who really knows? This is the other song from *The Queen's Gambit* I heard in episode six, and I'm not going to explain its content, or try to describe the scene it's in, because that would be sacrilegious. I didn't know the song or the artist, and I would also tell you something else that happened to me last night when I played this song, but I'm not that kind of person. And as I recollect it all, I'm smiling, not ….

7. "**Jaguar**," Victoria Monet, the title song to this year's release, *Jaguar*, another record mentioned by both NPR and ***The Bitter Southerner*** as one of the best records of the year. Listen without judgment, or at least do the best you can. I can't wait to give the rest of the record a better listen as I count the days until Jan. 20, when the White House will finally be fumigated and made safe for two dogs, a cat, and the new president. Meanwhile, thanks Victoria for adding to my personal fave list!

8. **"The Hardest Button to Button**," The White Stripes from this month's *Greatest Hits*, though originally found on 2003's *Elephant*. I can't believe that this album is seventeen years old. What was I doing or thinking in 2003? I don't remember, except that I was discovering the Stripes and wondering where they had been all my life. Do you think they mean that little button in the back of a man's collar that he tries to fasten after setting his necktie in place? Another button? Where? All interested parties apply below. This song just gets better as I age. My dog wants to dance with me now, so hang on....

9. **"Psychedelic Shack**," The Temptations, from 1970's *Psychedelic Shack*. You'll know it if you see it. C'mon and show me what you mean. "People, let me tell you about a place I know. To get in, it don't take much dough." The Temps were trying to get next to all of us, and pushing white kids who didn't quite understand soul to consider that soul was expansive, as are all people. Anyway, this song makes me think of Randy Ford and Ray King, two guys of different stripes whom I attended eighth grade with. They might not agree on much except this song. And I'm with 'em. "That's where it's at."

10. **"I've Been Loving You Too Long**," Otis Redding, from 1966's *The Very Best of Otis Redding*. I finished reading a book last week about a famous disc jockey from Birmingham, Shelley Stewart. Except he was more than a DJ, and the music he played was more than most of us could comprehend. The book is called **Mattie C's Boy,** as told by Shelley to Don Keith who, in a former life, was also a DJ. Keith broadcast from WVOK, an AM hit station, and Shelley from WENN, WJLD, and finally WATV, all playing Soul music. Shelley helped the movement for Civil and Human Rights in the Magic City, and almost boarded a plane with Otis one cold, winter night. A voice told him not to. I'm glad he didn't board and so wish Otis hadn't either. It's been too long, really.

Hanukkah has passed, and Christmas is upon us. My phone app tells me that ours might be a White Christmas this year, and unless I'm forgetting something in these past sixty-three Christmases, this would be my first. Not holding out any real hope, and not even sure I want it, because this year, what I truly want is to be rid of this crisis.

Don't worry: when the crisis ends, I will come up with other playlists, but until then, there are certainly some woes to address, as this passage from today's *New York Times* attests:

"**By this weekend, the president was considering naming a conspiracy theorist as special counsel to investigate voting fraud, for which there's no evidence, asking his advisers about instituting martial law and downplaying a massive hack his own secretary of state attributed to Russia**" (https://nytimes.com/2020/12/20/us/politics/trump-republican-party-future.html).

And, apparently disgraced, though pardoned, General Michael T. Flynn wants the military to stage an election do-over.

It's astounding and not in a good way.

Fortunately, we now have two vaccines on the go, and even Mike Pence has gotten himself immunized, though I have to wonder about the long-term effects of his close and daily exposure to the Orange Plague. It's like standing too close to a microwave while it's operating. You have no idea the damage it can do. And maybe you don't care. Or maybe you want to be sterilized in all the wrong places.

In our lovely village, we are chancing a Christmas with our children. I know that there are warnings against doing so, but we're willing to keep masks on and distance in check, and they are willing to hole up with us for days on end.

We'll see what happens, which is what I've been saying for a long time about literally everything.

I also want to say that one of the things I've most enjoyed lately is the camaraderie I've found with the other writers on **The Riff**, and with the ones on **One Table, One World**, another cool Medium publication. Building communities is essential, even more so these days.

But so is checking out new, and a bit of old, music. So here we go in our 28th consecutive week of defaming and admiring.

▭▭ AMERICAN CRISIS PLAYLIST #28 ▭▭

1. "**A Hero's Death**," from Fontaines D.C., off of their 2020 album, *A Hero's Death*. "Life ain't always empty," even when you think you're about as down as you can be. But again, I have certain privileges, and one of them is a friend named Les, who said I needed to check this band out, especially the cool guitar work. And so I did and fell in love with the excitement, the bravado, and the attitude of "this is who we are, what about you?" We've definitely lost a few heroes lately, even if we didn't know they were heroes when we had them, like...

2. "**A Girl I Used to Know**," Charley Pride, from his 1968 release, *Make Mine Country*. My wife would kill me if I linked the picture of her that I've saved on my iPhone. Not that it's sordid or dirty, but she'd be embarrassed by her youth and beauty. Should I do it anyway? I'll think about it as you and I appreciate how gorgeous Pride's voice is and what a legend in Nashville he was the minute he stepped on the Opry stage. I remember seeing him on TV—on **Hee Haw**, and whatever other country and mainstream variety shows came on back then. This one kills me—so country, it hurts.

3. "**Apologies**," Brandy Clark, coming to us from her most recent record, *Your Life is a Record*. "Sorry I'm not who I was when I met you..." Hhhhmm. I don't want to think about who I was when I met my wife, though she remembers that I was a guy with the sides of my head shaved, wearing a French-cut t-shirt proclaiming "**No War**," a shirt she's saved in her special box of collectibles, hidden somewhere beneath our stairs. She didn't save that haircut, so....Brandy puts over these songs with an instrumentation that reminds me of Pride's era. I'm not afraid to love Pop, never have been. No sorrows here.

4. "**Oh Lonesome Me**," Chet Atkins, found on the 1996 compilation, *The Essential Chet Atkins*. Now Chet is essential listening, and when I hear him, I think of my grandmother and the grandfather I never knew and wonder if they'd ever go two-stepping out. He never drank, nor did she. Neil Young did a bang up version of this one on *After the Gold Rush*, and when I first heard that back in 1971, I had to wonder what I was missing in these musical synapses. Something was going on and I wanted to know about it, or at least why it was that the lonesome songs always spoke so softly and profoundly.

5. "**Welcome to Hard Times**," Charley Crockett from his 2020 album of the same name. New country that sounds so old, kind of like **Jerry Lee** when he slowed it down and let you see the lantern on his piano. This one is making a bunch of year-end Top 20 lists, and I see why. Some are always living here, but most of us know it now, except the OP who so strangely thinks more about his burgers and fries and staring either at his ceiling or rifling through pages of random periodicals looking for his name. Or at least that was true when he left Ivana or Marla or whomever.

6. "**Trouble Sleeping**," Corinne Bailey Rae, from 2006, a self-titled record. Who is sleeping well these days, and please tell me, if you are, what you're taking to do so. If I'd just listen to Corinne as I'm lying in

bed, maybe she'd help. Probably would beat those mystery thrillers I insist on going to bed with. Smooth Soul and she deserves more recognition, but sometimes searching for these beautiful sounds makes the payoff greater. Hope you think so, and hope you sleep well, too.

7. "**Love is a Stranger**," Eurythmics making lives better back in 1983 with *Sweet Dreams (Are Made of This)*. We're almost done with season four of **The Crown**. And while we were viewing the penultimate episode the night before last, I heard this song playing in the background as Diana was practicing her freestyle ballet. Sleeping or waking or dreaming, it all started to make sense to me. We do the best we can until we can't, until we discover that who we are is not who they want us to be. No sleeping then...or living.

8. "**We Made It**," Cedric Burnside, styling the blues on his 2018 record *Benton County Relic*. Maybe I'm premature by eleven days, but y'all, 2020 is almost gone. I learned of Cedric through his progenitor, RL. And if you haven't listened to RL, then stop reading (no, don't yet) and go find you some. This is stompin' music, don't you think? I could listen for days and then sleeping wouldn't matter so much. I want to be in a club, listening now. Where oh where?

9. "**Dead, Drunk, and Naked**," The Drive-By Truckers from *A Southern Rock Opera* (2002). It's a funny concept, but of those three words, it's always "naked" that will set the demon posse on us. My younger daughter and I were supposed to see the Truckers at the Ryman last April until, you know, "The Covid" hit. Never been to the Ryman, or at least its insides, but I did walk by a bit drunk one night with some pals from the **Southern Jewish Historical Society**. You would have had to be there, but you couldn't unless you were a member of the tribe. And only one of us was orthodox.

10. "**Things Change**," Dwight Yoakam, from *A Long Way Home* (1998). Maybe my favorite song of Dwight's (I call him Dwight like I know him, but I so wish I did). It's a sad one, but when you get to the edge, just listen to that guitar and we're right back where we started. For my generation, it was always going to be the guitar, even when my daddy told me to listen to a house band on TV and pointed out a guy named **Johnny Gore**. "That's an electric guitar," Daddy said, and it was red, and I was only three in that year, 1959. And I never forgot. "Don't go passin no blame, because you know..."

I never thought I'd see a coup attempt in America, or at least in the US part of North America. The cult of celebrity is alive and well, though even from this later perspective, I just don't get why anyone reveres, could revere, the former president (#45). The images from Jan. 6 still inflame, what with the members of Congress, old and new, who encouraged the dumbing down of our country and the enthusiasm of some for authoritarian dictators.

Still, we finally inaugurated a new President and VP, the vaccines were being administered more often and regularly (my wife and older daughter got their first in this period), and somehow, we crowned both a national college football champion (Roll Tide) and a Super Bowl Champion (gotta give it to Brady).

The greatest sign of life looking healthier was that Dr. Fauci looked like 20 years had been lifted from his life. Can you imagine?

There were still cultists out there who questioned whether space beams were controlling us, or whether People who were forced to wear masks were being treated like Jewish victims of The Holocaust.

I also began a new semester, teaching a course in Film And American Culture, which got me to watching some classic and then new films (*I'm Your Woman* being a highlight), some of them musically-inclined like *The Bee Gees: How Can You Mend a Broken Heart?*, and *Jimmy Carter: Rock and Roll Presidency*.

Oh, and my younger daughter began baking sourdough bread from starter, and we all baked and cooked and danced to music from Kacey Musgraves, Bowie, The Black Pumas, Bleachers, London Grammar, Lana Del Rey, Neil Young, The Clash, The Talking Heads, Aretha, the Delfonics, The Black Angels, The Black Keys, The Weeknd, and Blondie.

I have no idea what Billy Joel meant when he wrote that song back in the forgiving 1970's. Listen to it for a rave-up if you want, and consider it a bonus for this first crisis playlist of the year.

On Jan.6, [**Ed. Note: Who could have known?**] Sen. Hawley from Missouri plans to force Republicans to vote on declaring Pres.-elect Joe Biden the President. This is like that note you likely passed to someone you liked back in the fifth grade. Like.

"I like you. Do you like me? Check yes or no."

So, the OP is very clearly going to check Sen. Hawley's yes box, and I hope that allows Josh to sleep better and have one of those nocturnal events that forces him to get up and take certain measures to get comfortable again.

I hate to mention the variant strain of the virus that has been discovered in Colorado and California, but it's here and no matter how hard I close my ears, it will be a force we have to account for, though many are saying that our vaccines will cover this strain too.

And in unrelated but also good news, music is being released now and next week, and on and on and on. I have a sample of something new for you here, and a few that came out last week. A couple of old ones to consider, too, because as I hear them, I pass them on, as if I and they are contagious. Some contagions are clearly worth the risk, so since it costs nothing to listen and since your ears, minds, hearts, and soul might be nurtured and strengthened, why not?

So, while Hollywood is struggling on some level, this is a goodbye only to all things wretched that plagued us in 2020 and in the three years prior, and as we wait for the grand goodbye on Jan. 20, let's crank up the volume and dance.

1. "**Lonesome in My Home**," North Mississippi All-Stars, from the 2019 release, *Up and Rolling*. It seems forever and a day since I saw these guys live, right here in Greenville, SC, in the old Handlebar listening room. My friend Al joined me then, and I'm guessing this was fifteen years ago. Deep electric blues, and if the title says too much, then I can tell you that if you hit this one at maximum volume in your own home, lonesome won't be your first or central emotion. These guys kill it and always have.

2. "**Everybody Knows**," Leonard Cohen on 1988's *I'm Your Man*. I first heard this song as it kept refraining in Atom Egoyan's 1994 film **Exotica**. I was obsessed with the film for a time, because Egoyan has a way of peeling layers of film truth as if he had a hard piece of garlic in front of him. The song haunted an even more haunting film, because grief and loss lead us to forbidden places sometimes. Anyway, "Everybody knows you're in trouble. Everybody knows what you've been through....take one last look at this sacred harp before it blows."

3. "**Atomic**," Blondie, way back in 1979 on *Eat to the Beat*. Everybody knows that Blondie was an underrated band and when you allowed yourself to dive deeper into their albums, you could find gems like this one. Believe it or not, it found room on episode six (or was it seven) of HBO/Max's limited series, *The Flight Attendant*. Yet again I want to know who on that production team found this song and said, "Yeah, gotta have it. It goes right here." Blondie scared one of my grad school friends, and while I loved that friend, I discovered that I loved Blondie more. Another rec is to watch Debbie Harry in David Cronenberg's crazy **Videodrone**. Crazy is strictly relative, even more so now.

4. "**National Anthem**," Lana Del Rey on *Born to Die* (2012). Naming your song "National Anthem" is like naming your novel **The Great American Novel**, which means only that we all wish we had done it

first. "Money is the reason we exist," she says, which is maybe why I fritter mine away on old cookbooks from Bessemer that I'm finding with increasing regularity on that most American of outlets, eBay. I know I'm late to the game, but man, you can find literally anything you want on that great American flea market. Lana proves that pop can be angst-ridden, though I think it has always been that way, as listening to many old Supremes songs could also prove.

5. "**Space Cowboy**," Kacey Musgraves on *Golden Hour* from 2018. Every now and then, I put a song in simply because it's too beautiful, and while I could make some shit up, I really want to just listen to her voice and that steel guitar that mournfully wails in the middle. It's the kind of country song that the genre has been so famous for all these decades. Makes me think of home and days before I knew too much.

6. "**Someday**," Neil Young from 1989's *Freedom*. When my wife was pregnant with our first daughter, I made a birth delivery mixtape, since we were using a midwife and going through labor in an alternative center. I loaded the tape with Neil's ballads, and no, I did not include the "**Down By the River**" type cuts. I did put this one on and even sang it to her as she was eating ice chips and getting ready. I also swear that when "transition" started, all music went off. I remember our midwife, who was also pregnant, chewing on soda crackers to combat her own nausea. And in the end, we had a healthy baby girl, owing, of course, to Neil and my mixtape. Someday.

7. "**California**," Mina Caputo from this year's *The Mones*. Learned about this one from Rob Janicke's great story on **The Riff**. Man, I love this song, and poor California. Did you know that the ritual playing of The Rose Bowl has been moved from Pasadena to Arlington, Texas, this year? And that's the least of California's troubles, but at least this song helps in the sense that beauty is still beauty.

8. **"Willow,"** Taylor Swift, from this month's *evermore*. One of my students texted me when Taylor's latest arrived and I downloaded it immediately. Turns out that my younger daughter had already memorized this one, and as she created her first sourdough starter a few days ago, she played this album over and over, and I thought that life surely is interesting and wonderful and worth it all even in the plagues days we are so desperately trying to cope with and escape. Call some old friends now, see how they're doing, and beg them to listen to this record. And bake some bread.

9. **"Baby It's You,"** London Grammar, a single just released from their upcoming record, *Californian Soul*. I've been listening to this band over the past year and find their sound...infectious. I expect this song to find a place on a limited series soundtrack soon. It's a good one to hear on rainy days like this, before a semi-wet walk with your dog, which is before making New Year's Jambalaya, chocked full of meats and spices. I'll make the peas and collards, too, as I record my own sound memories. No matter how many times someone uses this song title, it all comes out the same.

10. **"Is There Something in the Movies?"** Samia, from 2020. A single, and a lament. The answer is yes, but what you find is what you put in. I miss the movies, though I'm teaching an online course in Film and American Culture this coming term, which focuses on FEAR (**Rear Window**, anyone?). Is there something in the movies that's better than fear, or my love? I'll be watching online, too, which, while not perfect, at least means I'm still alive and kicking and anticipating with love, 2021. What about you?

Holy F**k!

I might still be in shock. And it doesn't help that the variant strain of Covid is raging and scientists warn that we'll be blindsided if we don't act. Fortunately, a responsible set of adults will be taking leadership soon. The question is: can we wait for responsible leaders for another thirteen days, and, during that wait, will the cretin-in-charge destroy what's left of us?

I have almost laughingly referred to T***p as the Orange Plague, and plague, he is. But let me be even more clear:

He should be impeached, arrested, thrown in jail as an inciter to riot, as a subverter of the Constitution, as a traitor to our country. This should happen now, and while we're at it, the Hawley's and Cruz's, and Tuberville's need to be exorcized from the Senate. Treason is Treason. Tyrants are Tyrants, and what we have had for four years is a drift and then a locomotive toward Authoritarian Dictatorship.

Why anyone would invest so much in one mortal man, I'll leave to the historians and theologians.

I have never seen, nor imagined I would see, what transpired at the US Capitol yesterday.

Donald J. Trump is unhinged. He is a psychopath, and to believe anything else is to continue believing that the world is flat and that QAnon conspiracists are playing with a full set of brains.

I remember this summer seeing the bunker of Q, Trump Train, and Don't Tread On Me beachcombers set up in a compound near us on Edisto Beach. They drove trucks with Trump banners and were raising children in their mold. They looked normal and very very white, even in the sun.

They aren't normal, though. I understand that they believe that they are victims, are aggrieved, and somehow see their world slipping from them.

However, I have no sympathy for them, no bond with them, and I do not share, support, condone, nor am willing to tolerate any longer their delusion.

That doesn't mean I'm up for physical conflict, but that I'm tired of mincing words.

I have written before that I want music to be my saving resolution for this year. Music, sadly, will not save us. But maybe it will sustain something of our collective sanity and help our better angels to appear and serve us.

The crisis continues; it worsens, and so...here's coping.

▱ AMERICAN CRISIS PLAYLIST #30 ▱

1. "**The Man Who Sold the World**," David Bowie, from the remastered version of *The Man Who Sold the World*, a record that originally appeared in 1970. How on earth could so many believe such a charlatan, such a huckster, such a lying cheat? How has he sold his followers such a distorted nightmarish vision of us? Why are so many still following him as if he's Jesus or something? And make no mistake, many Christians somehow believe he is.

2. "**Tell Me Lies**," The Black Keys from 2019's *Let's Rock*. Widespread fraud: "We won in a landslide and everybody knows that, The other side knows that?" Really? **You lost, you keep losing, you keep lying, and no punishment is too severe for you**. You will, however, go down as the worst president the country has ever seen. No lie. And I'm glad. I hope you know it, and I wonder just what Kellyanne

Conway, and her "alternative facts," is feeling now? They're only lies and always have been.

3. "**Burning Down the House**," Talking Heads from 1983's *Speaking in Tongues*. I watched six straight hours of news yesterday. I had intended to answer some mail, to dust and vacuum our house, but I was mesmerized by history. At the point I started watching, it was certainly possible that someone was going to torch the Senate chamber, or set off a bomb, or be caught up in a mass gunfire exchange. I couldn't leave my TV and felt like a prisoner of events that both did and did not seem real. **The People's House**: that's what I kept hearing. Those thugs on camera seemed like the undead, though, or the guys back when I was in high school who terrorized the corridors of my sight and mind because they hated longhairs, and black people, and anyone who didn't share their stupid and limited testosterone view of manhood.

4. "**Armagideon Time**," The Clash, from *Black Market Clash* (1979 or thereabouts). "Remember to kick it over...no one will guide you...not Christmas time, but Armagideon Time...Lotta people won't get no supper tonight...no justice tonight." This is when I fell in love with The Clash. It still ranks as one of my three favorite Clash songs. And it's the first song I thought of last night as I watched Washington stumble into darkness. It resonates this morning, too, as I wonder if those who want to "just move on," who say "Nothing to see here" are crawling out from their caves again.

5. "**Only a Pawn in Their Game**," Bob Dylan, from 1964's *The Times They Are A-Changin'*. Thirty years after he shot and killed **Medgar Evers**, Byron de la Beckwith still walked the streets of Greenwood, Mississippi, a free man. Imagine that, in America. A member of my institution just wrote that he believes ANTIFA infiltrated that "peaceful" mob yesterday, so of course, blame yesterday on black

people. White people can't be wrong or misguided or lying killers, right? Until we confront racism and our legacy of coddling racists, right here is where we'll rot.

6. "**The Silver Tongued Devil and I**," Kris Kristofferson, from *The Silver Tongued Devil and I* (1971). Except T***p isn't exactly silver tongued. He uses words like "tremendous" and "sad" over and over. You know, empty words from an equally empty head. I mean, the guy has a vocabulary of about thirty words anyway, but maybe that's America right now: sound bites, clips. I think I heard Josh Hawley use the made-up word "irregardless" last night. Not a word Mr. Stanford and Yale graduate. But don't let inaccuracy stop you.

7. "**What's Going On**" Marvin Gaye from 1971's *What's Going On*. Oh Marvin, what is going on right now? I have such high hopes for this year, despite the plagues and chaos. Am I crazy? Have I been smoking again? Do I remember a time when AM radio was a sanctuary for the music of my life? Do I want to go back, way back in time? Is reading the news healthy anymore?

8. "**Love Train**," The O'Jays from 1972's *Back Stabbers*. I could have used the title song, because after all, Brutus, no one knows how it feels to have your country "insurrected" like we do right now. Do I call my T***p friends and ask them "How does it feel...to be a complete unknown?" Anyway, my daughter played this song as we counted down the New Year last week. She's only twenty-six. This song predated her by twenty-two years. And yet she has it hot on her playlist. So now, I have it on mine.

9. "**Tubthumping**," Chumbawamba from 1997's *Tubthumper*. She also played this one, remembering it from her childhood. Don't you love that? My daughter remembers my playing "Tubthumping" as part of

her childhood nostalgia. Hell yeah. We get knocked down but we'll get up again. They're never gonna keep us down. Democracy does not include authoritarian dictators, Donald. Please. Leave.

10. "**Keep on Rockin in the Free World**," Neil Young, from 1989's *Freedom*. This one seemed an easy choice, back when some feared Jesse Jackson. Imagine. Everyone says they want freedom, but clearly, what we mean by it isn't the same. What will our world look like next week, or even tomorrow? Or January 20? I still have faith, somehow, though my psyche feels beaten up right now.

A Long, Slow Climb Upward

Two days after the Inauguration of a normal, sane President and highly competent Vice-President, I feel like I have been dazed and confused into semi-oblivion. My wife keeps dancing around the house, and I want to dance, too, but after four-plus years of creeping into each day, I might have forgotten how to dance and how to express relief and joy.

"I'm happy and hope you're happy, too."

So says Bowie in a song to come a few moments from now. If I say it often enough, will I believe it? I'm happy, I'm happy, I'm happy.

And I am, but there is so much to worry about still, so much fear and trouble and depravity, all rolled up into Ted Cruz and Josh Hawley. Get rid of a major creep and all its tentacles keep writhing and trying to squeeze the life out of us. Even if the OP is convicted, we still have these guys preying on our collective refusal to understand history and denounce fascist bigots.

Hey, I got a Ph.D. from The University of Tennessee, guys, and your credentials don't impress. I'm not sure mine do either these days when Dr. Jill Biden is somehow blamed and chastised for wanting to be referred to by a title she earned and deserves.

But really, I am happy. A dark pile of crap has been ushered off to a state I used to visit every summer. Does Florida deserve this? Well, for a few summers some shysters down there tried to sell my parents some swampland. It's a sordid story, but one the OP would appreciate since what he sold us over the past half-decade is worth as much as the underwater world my parents naively wanted to own.

Even winter has moderated a bit here in South Carolina, where our greatest contribution to the post-OP era is to offer up a lawyer to defend the OP in his trial which will occur sometime in February, it seems. Maybe on Valentine's Day. Wouldn't that be lovely or nice or appropriate? What cards would Hallmark produce then?

So, since I'm feeling so good, I've come up with a few tunes to find a balance between happiness and crisis, whatever that means or looks like.

I'm trying and working and like our new President (thank God), I'm putting my entire soul into this list.

AMERICAN CRISIS PLAYLIST #31

1. "**Under Pressure**," Karen O and Willie Nelson, from a recently released single. Seems unbelievable until you hear it. After all, if a country music legend and the lead singer from the **Yeah Yeah Yeahs** can face the pressure and sing like this, melding their talents, what can't the rest of us do? "I sit on the fence, but it don't work." No fences, no badges, except when violent mobs try to overthrow a country. "Why can't we give love that one more chance?" I'm listening, and loving.

2. "**Oversharers Anonymous**," Wild Pink from *A Billion Little Lights* (2020). Though there were only 400 lights lit the other night around the reflecting pool at the Lincoln Memorial, it felt like a billion. Check out this band—solid all the way through, playing with an ease and competence that we can only hope translates into defeating this virus. Thankfully, there's a plan and more vaccine distribution on the way. And did you see Fauci yesterday? The guy looks two decades younger and even more energetic, which is good news for all of us, though the numbers will keep building. He thinks we might have plateaued now, and here's hoping. Those billion little lights come with masks, too.

3. "**La La Means I Love You**," The Delfonics from 1968's album of the same name. I fell in love with this song somewhere around 1971 when it played on a Solid Gold Weekend over the airwaves of WSGN-610 in Birmingham. There's a certain kind of Soul Music that has always found me, and while this one might sound sappy to the cynics, I keep hearing those higher notes and keep wanting to reach them. Lyrics don't have to be profound; they simply need to move us into what we feel matters most. During all the years of the Pop era, it always comes down to this, doesn't it?

4. "**Ashes to Ashes**," David Bowie from *Scary Monsters and Super Creeps* (1980). I bet you could ad lib here from the title of this album, so I think I'll just let you, knowing full well that we'll be sharing the same sentiments if not the exact words. Aside from the "**StaggerLee**" lyrical myth, is any story in rock/pop more legendary than **Major Tom**? If there is, jump on in with your selections. Ah, those rumors from ground control "I'm stuck with a valuable friend..." actually, I'm "stuck" with many, including the voices who appear in response to these lists. Thanks Steven Hale, Kevin Alexander, Jessica Lee McMillan, and Jim Whisenhunt.

5. "**Birthday**," The Sugar Cubes, harkening back to 1988's *Life's Too Good*. Bjork might be all things to everyone, but on this song, her growling angst works perfectly. I had only recently moved to South Carolina when I found this song and band, and man, it hit just right, explaining how I felt almost daily in a new world where I was so young that hardly anyone else in my job environment had heard of MTV. I'm so glad to have rediscovered this song, and after three decades and more, I'm happier and freer, and haven't watched MTV for almost as long.

6. "**Dear Prudence**," Siouxsie and the Banshees, from 2009's remastered *Hyaena*. I know that I risk much goodwill by listing a Beatles' cover. Yes, yes, yes, I know that no one did it better, but come

on. Siouxsie and her mates do this one justice, and "the sun is out, the birds still sing," and it really is good "to open our eyes and look around" on this brand new day. Let me see you smile, and if for no other reason, go back and listen to **Amanda Gorman**'s poem again. The sun really is up..."it's beautiful and so are you." Look around.

7. "**Bohemian Like You**," The Dandy Warhols (2000) from *Thirteen Tales from Urban Bohemia*. Nothing sinister here, just fun and pop and being/feeling so like you. I do remember first hearing this song accompanying old Nate from *Six Feet Under*. Not to dwell on what happened to him, but he did have a good car. Play this loud and try not to dance too long, because it ends too soon even for me. Let's all feel good for at least 3:32.

8. "**I Wouldn't Be Surprised**," Bobbie Gentry, *Touch 'Em With Love* (1969). This song opened the new film *I'm Your Woman*, starring Rachel Brosnahan from "Mrs Maisel" fame. Gentry had more famous songs, or at least one famous song, though "**Fancy**" also charted. When I heard her voice again, I couldn't place her though I knew I knew her. What would surprise us these days? Did you know that a Republican lawmaker had his gun confiscated yesterday when he tried to enter the Capitol building with it? He also tried passing it off to another member who refused to take it because he didn't have a carry license. Such is truth in the post-trump era.

9. "**Mario's Cafe**," Saint Etienne from 1993's *So Tough*. "Everyone is dreaming of all they have to live for." Don't these words simply mean more today than they did even last week? This band is growing on me all the time. So glad they showed up in my inbox, almost as if by magic (go ahead and take credit, you who offered them to me). I long for a cafe somewhere, like the one in Prague that summer when, wearing my Yankee cap, I was mistaken by an American couple for Steven Spielberg. I steered them toward **The Golem Cafe**, because they needed someone to watch over them.

10. "**Cinnamon Girl**," The Gentrys from 1970's *The Gentrys*. I mentioned this cover in my new series of perfect tunes, and so I thought I'd add it here just to prove to myself and everyone else that I can stand covers of my all-time favorite artist. So maybe the guitar riffs aren't as strong, but you get the picture. "Ma, send me money now, I'm gonna make it somehow. I need another chance, you see, your baby loves to dance." What else is there left to say?

The state of South Carolina has the first two reported cases of the South African variant of Covid-19. No one knows how it got here, or if they do, they're keeping mum. Of course, our governor, Henry McMaster, continues to allow restaurants to serve indoors, with "restrictions." This state is very sick with Covid, one of the two hottest spots in the country. Unemployment rates have gone down, and so the state is reluctant to restrict businesses.

I realize that take out isn't the same as relaxing in your favorite cafe or bistro and partaking of a several course meal. I'm not sure how anyone totally relaxes these days anyway, but I'd rather go ahead and double mask, walk to the take-out window and head on home. I'd also rather cook, too, as my blog over at One Table, One World attests.

So I can wait out this aspect of the crisis, and also, while waiting, I get to sample and play more music.

I found some gems and old faves this week, as I was trying, and usually failing, not to pay attention to the other craziness plaguing our land. Just because the OP has headed to gaudy Mar-A-Lago doesn't mean his pin-headed minions aren't still spreading good cheer and conspiracy theories out there. **Someone, for instance, believes that former California Governor Jerry Brown used lasers from space to cause the California wildfires, with what end in mind I leave up to you.** That's a new member of Congress from Georgia spreading this insane idiocy, and I'm not going to repeat the racist and anti-Semitic and traitorous words she's also been spewing, because that would give her even more room here and further distract me and then I'd have to list some rage rock, which I'll do some day.

But not today.

So while I'm waiting for one of our favorite local eateries—**Fork & Plough**—to post their take-out supper menu, here are those promised tunes, from a land whose promise is wearing too thin these days.

⟨o-o⟩ AMERICAN CRISIS PLAYLIST #32 ⟨▣⟩

1. "**Jive Talkin**'," The Bee Gees, from *Main Course* (1975). Have you seen the HBO documentary, *The Bee Gees: How Can You Mend a Broken Heart?*" I can't say that the Gibb brothers were favorites of mine, though I appreciated many of their hits and their songwriting prowess. My brother and I bought some of their singles, and I had to get *Saturday Night Fever* when it exploded into our world. I was a college guy then, and had plenty of friends that had been frequenting discos in Birmingham at least twice a week. So there's a moment in this film where a NY DJ explains the anti-Disco movement, and I won't give anything away, but that anti-movement's most strident adherents would find themselves extremely comfortable at a MAGA or QAnon rally. Not that you have to love Disco, but publicly burning records usually leads to other forms of hatred. Not a disco song, but to be kind, there's been a lot of jive bullshit emanating from those OP pinheads. And now, I love the Gibbs.

2. "**Leave Me Alone**," I Don't Know How But They Found Me, from 2020's *Razzmatazz*. Giving Jimmy Kimmel credit again, he had this band on the show a week ago. I had never heard of them. The name alone makes me happy, and listening to this one last night as I made breakfast for supper almost caused me to scorch the hash browns. My dog wondered why I seemed so high, and so he grabbed his football because, why not? Of course I didn't want him to leave me alone, but getting that ball away from him defies my wavering strength. Anyway, there's more to hear on the record, so be ready to go clubbing, in your mind at least.

3. "**Here Comes the Night**, Them (featuring Van Morrison) from 2015's *The Essential Van Morrison.* It's sacrilege, I know, but I can take Van only in medium-sized doses, but I'll put this song up against most of its era's peers, whatever they may be. I remember too often longing for the night because that was the time we could all go a bit crazy, seemingly unworried about the trouble we'd find. You know, those days when, if you were living at home or home from school and you'd get ready and head out the door around ten, one or both of your parents would wonder who had spawned you. I'd usually tell mine where I'd been the next day. Usually.

4. "**Oblivion**," Grimes from 2012's *Visions.* Nine years is a long time in a person's life, and I won't attempt to chronicle where I was back when I first heard this tune, or all that's happened since. I think of my daughters, though, who in that span, graduated from college, and one from grad school, got well-paying jobs, got married (one of them again), and now the one who isn't married is about to buy her first house. So much for oblivion, but my other thought is my friend Owen who called this to my attention back then. So so so love it.

5. "**Sleepyhead**," Passion Pit on their album *Manners* from 2009. And this one is even older, which makes me crazy because I'm looking at the spot where I was sitting with my younger daughter and her high school friends when I asked if they knew this band, and they all said, "Oh yeah...'Sleepyhead!'" Then we listened, and it felt like we had all turned a corner, and we had. So that daughter loves 70's music now, and I'm trying to get her to listen to the crazy stuff I'm finding, and then we bond over Taylor Swift, Billie Eilish and Hot Chocolate. Life is sure funny.

6. "**Reflektor**," Arcade Fire from 2013's *Reflektor.* Are you still dancing, or dancing yet? Please explain. My daughters don't seem to connect with this band, but you can't have everything, musically speaking.

We're connected in so many ways, and besides, Arcade Fire makes certain demands. I like to think that The Bee Gees could appreciate what's going on here, as would anyone who wants to get lost outside of K-Tel's party hits. Time for another record from these guys, I say.

7. "**Spirit in the Dark**," Aretha Franklin from the 1970 album of the same name. Did you see Aretha on CNN's documentary of *Jimmy Carter (Rock and Roll Presidency)*? It made me remember how Aretha blew other singers away just as easily as butter melts in a hot biscuit. What spirit is holding us these days? I love how this song so slowly builds, always controlled by that voice. I can't wait to see the new Aretha film coming soon. We should be remembering all of her records, and the times she captured.

8. "**Since I Met You Baby**," Sam Cooke from 1961's *My Kind of Blues*. Back to my cooking last night. I had this one going and my wife, who was listening to a book on tape while standing next to the fire, began swaying and moving, and I wish I had been videoing her. Some music just penetrates your soul, and Cooke has a way of making us stop everything and wondering how his voice does it and why can't we have some more, please. Which we can if we want it.

9. "**Stay Gold**," The Black Pumas from 2020's *Black Pumas*. A good bridge between the eras of Cooke, Franklin, and so much that we often overlook today. I so hope that when I do feel like I can go to a club again that I'll be able to spend an evening with these guys. Soul, and heart, and a band that has no inhibitions about bringing us home. And the falsetto—something else linking so many singers, black and white, and reminding me again of The Bee Gees and those who inspired them.

10. "**Don't Play With Guns**," The Black Angels from *Indigo Meadow* (2013). So that same Georgia Rep plagued one of the survivors of a school shooting, calling him a coward for advocating gun control. Her

message was that if more teachers carried guns, this wouldn't have happened. Would I have learned more about verb conjugation had Mrs. Norton been wearing a gun strapped to her waist? Would I have mastered binomials, whatever they are, had Mr. Hicks been packing a Glock? What we're told in one generation gets obliterated in another. Saw these Angels in Asheville a few years back, with my wife and Owen. We got it.

So much going on in this week leading up to our collective commercial property, Valentine's Day (which I wrote about over at PS I Love You, but don't tell anyone in my family yet). Tonight is the Super Bowl. Friday is my late Mother's birthday. Still celebrating **International Clash Day** over at my house, and, oh yes...

Someone has a conviction trial starting on Tuesday, though one of his lawyers can't work past Friday evening at 5:26, I think it is, because that's the beginning of the Jewish Sabbath. He could get a special dispensation to continue defending the OP, but will he? Should he? I'm all for honoring someone's wishes, but maybe this should have been considered before the OP fired his other lawyers because they didn't want to use as a defense the OP's notion that he really did win the 2020 election.

If you're feeling a bit delusional at this moment, well, so am I. Apparently, the smart money is still on no conviction, especially since members of her own party gave MTG(Q) a standing ovation after she allowed us to rest easy in her own affirmation that 9/11 actually occurred and was not some George W. Bush inspired plot to keep the World Series from going on that fall (I'm making that World Series part up. Could you tell?).

I'm going to watch the Super Bowl tonight, and all apologies to **Frank Bruni** and my good friend Ali, but I'm pulling for the Chiefs. Probably not a hard pull, but Mr. Brady is a supporter of the previous administration, or so I've picked up, and I can hold a grudge with the best of them. Still can't believe that the Chiefs are getting away with that nickname, but it's likely on the chopping block.

Life is sure funny.

My wife got her first Pfizer vaccine on Thursday and feels good. She came home and went immediately to work building her second Adirondack chair from Yellawood. I celebrated by downloading more music, and so, here's what I came up with to entertain you on this sunny Sunday, though it did snow here last night. So beautiful, and since we have nowhere to go...

AMERICAN CRISIS PLAYLIST #33

1. "**Just Like Me**," Paul Revere and the Raiders, from 1965's *Just Like Us*. The first band other than the Beatles that I truly loved. They were the house band for Dick Clark's weekday teen music show, "**Where the Action Is**," and I raced home from fourth grade every day to watch and see my favorite pseudo-American patriots in their three-cornered hats and garish revolutionary garb. This was their first hit, followed soon by "**Kicks**," but listen to that organ, and know that I used to pretend sing with a hairbrush in front of my mirror to this song, and I wanted so badly to be Mark Lindsay, with his ponytail, and when I got to be a man, I got the ponytail, just like Mark.

2. "**Rock and Roll, Pt 2**," Gary Glitter from *Glitter* (1972). I know. College football teams and god knows who else have appropriated this song for cheers and revivals, and whatever else they can make a buck off of. In 1972, it was an enormous hit on AM radio where I first heard it. I didn't know much about the "glitter" scene in England and the bands hovering around Bowie, like **Mott the Hoople** and others. I remember watching a coworker named Phyllis dancing to this song in the old jewelry store where we worked. The boss was gone, my Dad was holed up in his office somewhere, but Phyllis let loose. I've never forgotten that moment. Or her.

3. "**Up the Hill Backwards**," David Bowie from *Scary Monsters and Super Creeps* (1980). Doesn't it feel like that right now? "While we sleep, they go to work...it's got nothing to do with you, if one can grasp it...I'm okay, you're so-so, up the hill backwards, it'll be all right." I suppose it all comes down to what we mean by "all right." I read today that some believe that Michael Flynn might be Q. I just don't know what to do with myself sometimes. I do wish Bowie were still here, but at least these guys are...

4. "**100,000 People**," Kings of Leon, from their forthcoming album, *When You See Yourself*. "Nothing makes me feel the way you do..." and that kind of says it all when I think about the holiday on the 14th, and my wife and my daughters, and Max. And the Kings. Everything these boys touch turns to golden sounds as far as I'm concerned. I love love songs that have such power and come from sources I wouldn't have imagined. Imagine is the operative word, and as long as we can do that, we can keep coming back from the last four years when America was made horrible again.

5. "**Chinatown, featuring Bruce Springsteen**," from a new single by **Bleachers**. I don't know...if you told me this song was first cut in the 1980's, I'd have no problem believing that. Not that it's too excessive with its electronic keyboard background, but I see an MTV video with singing heads amidst a sundown-y backdrop. Another love song, and that's how I'm rolling in this moment. Bruce doesn't even seem to be wearing his real age. Maybe I'm not either. We'll see. Check out the video, live on the rooftop of **Electric Lady**.

6. "**She's Lost Control**," Joy Division from 1979's lost treasure, *Unknown Pleasures*. I'm teaching a great novel right now in my Southern Gothic Lit class: MO Walsh's ***My Sunshine Away***. Speaking of love and obsession, the narrator goes through a dark music period where he, and the girl he adores, obsess over Joy Division. I played

some for my class. Two people liked it, but even they admitted that they didn't really want to hear any more. The novel is definitely a mystery, and Joy Division, I have to say, is the least gothic part of it. It's one of those stories where you begin chanting early on, "Don't go into that room." But of course, eventually you do.

7. "**Wallflower**," Sevdaliza from 2020's *Shabrang*. As part of International Clash Day, I heard this song on Seattle's KEXP, and I have to say that whatever I was doing, I stopped and listened harder and wondered again where I had been and what else I'm missing. So much out there, and maybe songs, like people, come when you most need them. I'm a sucker for oddly-formed sounds from distant places, and there's enough warning here about who we are to keep me thinking and wondering long into my night.

8. "**One More Time**," The Clash, from 1980's *Sandinista!* One of my favorite songs from this record, showcasing the various Clash sounds in one song—the dub version that follows on the album continues the groove, but the ghetto continues too. I finished reading **Prof. Eddie Glaude**'s recent study of James Baldwin last week, *Begin Again.* Glaude urges us to quit apologizing for the misguided rust belters who went OP and to focus on all the black and brown people who are still victims of American bigotry and policies that keep them from feeling whole and human. That's more important stuff to know while the Repubs are still trying to sneak guns into the chambers.

9. "**Save Your Tears**," The Weeknd, from 2020's *The Highlights*. Back to romance, and this voice and the attending rhythm section make me feel happy and ready to dance the night away (apologies to **Van Halen**). I'm so glad that R&B lives on, and even more glad to have discovered The Weeknd, and I repeat typing that just to mess with my spell check. And the notion, "save your tears for another day..." yeah, maybe till Friday when we see how the conviction is going.

10. "**New Day**," Night Beats from their forthcoming *Outlaw R&B*. I love this sound, again from a band I know nothing about. I'm ready to learn more, and since we're only two weeks into this new American day, here's hoping that the number of those fully vaccinated will catch the number of those infected sooner rather than much later. J&J is coming as is, I hope **NovaVax**. I'm waiting patiently. And listening.

.

Interlude VI

In the cold winter nights, where could we find relief? Oh yeah, in a vaccine called Pfizer. So while my wife got her second dose, I got my first and felt like I did on that Christmas when I got my first football helmet.

Politically speaking, things were still chaotic if you followed the former, losing president as he kept embracing flags and portraits of himself. For Valentine's Day, what do you suppose he got himself? I discovered that many of my neighbors were still hoisting T***p signs and flags and slightly more subtle messages like "An Appeal to Heaven."

My wife and I continued watching a lot of late-night TV, because Jimmy Kimmel rocks, and to a lesser extent, so does Colbert. Each night they continued mocking the Loser of Mar-A-Lago and then showcasing some of the best new music around, from Best Coast to Phoebe Bridgers. And when we weren't viewing these new gems, we'd find ourselves rewatching Schitts Creek because something about Daniel and Eugene Levy, Catherine O'Hara and Annie Murphy works as an antidote to the pompous foolishness of anything in the so-called Republican sphere of consciousness. Still wondering why there was so little music in the series.

And speaking of music, artists like Jimmy Ruffin, Gordi, Deerhunter, Gladys Knight and the Pips, Santana, Kris Kristofferson and Rita Coolidge, Uriah Heep, Sam Cooke, The Killers, Keane, Silver Convention, and Elvis kept heartening me and providing as much viral antidote as my vaccine (in theory anyway).

More rumblings from the dead of winter. The impeachment/ conviction trial will now hear from some witnesses who will tell us what we should already know. What so many of us have known. Our former president fomented, incited, a coup, and he did so not because he had a sinister plan in mind, but because he enjoys chaos, enjoys watching people do his bidding. Enjoys the world on his tiny string.

Last night, in preparation for Valentine's Day, my wife and I watched the 1956 Don Siegel version of **Invasion of the Body Snatchers**. It's a creepy film sometimes, though wasn't so when I first encountered it back in the 1980's. Then, it seemed like just another odd, black and white monster film from a decade when the monsters were often teenagers who transformed before our eyes into werewolves or zombies. I laughed while watching the odd gender circumstances and sly sexual innuendos. I noticed the rather open ending, a device that stifles mainstream audiences and Hollywood itself, but shakes the rest of us with the nods and winks of a world where anything is possible and the "good guys", whoever they might be, don't always win.

Someone is always the good guy, and if you peek back over your own life journey, you might discover that the badges or licenses or formulas for determining good from bad have changed.

So as we all know, "the Body Snatchers" were really commies, not planetary others. They looked like us; spoke like us; drove cars and ate like us. They were all incredibly white, too, and so the "us" in question had to make us wonder about whom to trust, what side to take. The commies could be anyone in the 1950's until that decade changed, and suddenly, or so we were led to believe, the commies started darkening and turning into the Civil Rights champions.

So as I think of the film now, I think of how Russia has interfered in our elections and the powers that be didn't believe it or take this threat/reality seriously. I think of how we term them our "adversary" now, but not adversarial enough to condemn the OP's love affair with them; not that I want us to relive the Cold War, but I find the semantics so strange, unnerving. Like someone has taken over someone else's body, mind, and soul.

As I watch the Republicans on the Senate floor doing their best jive and shuffle to convince somebody that this trial is unconstitutional, I wonder what soundtrack they're listening to. What words and what music?

In the film, we never quite learn who has administered the pods in the first place: which planet they're from, and what they plan to do when they take us over. So, I ask now, who's calling the Republican shots and for what? Have they not seen what I've seen, heard what I've heard?

Is making America so very white again worth it? Is the great Q conspiracy actually solving anyone's problems? Helping us through Covid? Healing our racial divide?

I'm also rereading **Danzy Senna**'s first novel, *Caucasia*, and I remain stunned at how good it is, how well it captures that in-between world of racial identity that many of us live in and that many others of us have never seen, much less believed. It's funny and sad what we say, what we talk about, what we call each other when we think no one else is listening.

These are moments of crisis that so often go unheard, or unremarked if heard. No wonder a former president can equate Nazis with anti-fascists and get away with it. And wink at us while he's speaking. Such a sad little monster.

And so, on to the soundtrack for this week.

1. **"I'm Ready,"** The Black Pumas from 2020's *Black Pumas Deluxe*. A funky beginning to this week's list—a song about needing love in the city, reminding me lyrically of an old Turtles' song from 1969, **"Love in the City."** I'm loving everything I hear from the Pumas, especially that lead guitar that chops me in half. I knew nothing of this band until about a month ago, and now I'd follow them anywhere, city or country.

2. **"Car Jamming,"** The Clash from *Combat Rock* (1982). Whenever I feel frustrated, I find myself getting soothed by The Clash. "Car Jamming" gets lost in this album's more mainstream sounds, but the rocky rhythms and Strummer's lonely, plaintive singing bring me back to the first moments I heard this, lolling about my local record store, wondering how to disentangle myself from someone I didn't like as much as I once thought I did. Car jam indeed. The place was called *The Last Record Store*. Where are you now Mike Procter?

3. **"Hollywood Boulevard,"** Big Audio Dynamite from *No.10, Upping Street* (1986). Another record I don't listen to as much as I should. The star-studded sidewalks of the glittering world keep us from noticing all that lies behind the scenes, just as in the film I watched last night. Doctors were the gods of this film world, and while reverence doesn't wear so well, I keep thinking of how we weren't paying enough attention to those who researched the science of disease. Maybe we never do. Someone reminded me that Rand Paul is a doctor. Uh huh.

4. **"Pledging My Love,"** Johnny Ace, from the 1973 *Memorial Album*. I felt the need to throw in a gushy romantic Valentine's song. Okay, maybe I'll add a few more. I swear I'm not pissed off all the time; it just gets hard when you know someone is a lying thug and you can't do anything about it. And then there's my wife, sweating over repainting our kitchen cabinets while I type away in endless distraction. I got her a really expensive box of chocolate truffles and am cooking some crab bisque for us tonight. No more alien movies either.

5. "**What Becomes of the Brokenhearted?**" Jimmy Ruffin from 1967's *Jimmy Ruffin Sings Top Ten*. I remember a Valentine's episode of TV's "**The Wonder Years**" where adolescent Kevin Arnold walks along the sidewalks of his neighborhood while his crush or love or whatever she was, Winnie Cooper, walks along on the opposite side of the street. This song accompanies their journey, and even though I didn't know how their love or the series would end, I understood everything from this song. It still makes me wonder about teenage love and how real and devastating it is.

6. "**For the First Time**," Best Coast, from 2020's *Always Tomorrow*. "I'm trying even harder than I ever did before...on Friday nights I don't spend too much time lying on the bathroom floor as I used to. The demons inside of me must have finally been set free." I have a feeling I'll be listening to this song long after we've all said good night. I feel about this band like I do about my noon cup of coffee: how would I get through the rest of the day without them/it? Sometimes "I do feel like myself again, but for the first time." Another homage to love.

7. "**Extraordinary Life**," Gordi, as found on *Our Two Skins* (2020). Do you ever feel like this—how extraordinary life is? And I don't understand how we've managed to lose sight of how it isn't and can't be for so many. I have it so good, and I try to give back, but it's never enough. Gordi's voice should calm us down, so maybe at the next Q club meeting, they could fire up a joint and give this a listen, and really just calm the fuck down about their crazy shit and help us all out because no one is plotting against them. At least not yet.

8. "**My Pledge of Love**," The Joe Jeffrey Group from 1969, but found on 2010's *Super Hits Scepter/Wand Pop, Vol 1*. I remember afternoons of riding in my mother's car as she did her errands at the grocery store, or even more exciting, at K-Mart. I had just discovered AM radio, or at least had discovered that she'd let me listen to it in the car as much

as I wanted. This song would hit the waves, and I had no idea who Joe Jeffrey was or where he came from. And then I saw the 45 at K-Mart and knew slightly more.

9. "**Breaker**," Deerhunter from 2015's *Fading Frontier.* When my late friend Owen recommended Deerhunter, I had to listen. He so rarely steered me wrong, after all. I don't know if this song ever hit him as hard as it does me. If you check the count of how many times I've turned to it on my Apple chart, you'd think I keep it on repeat play. Well, even if I did, I'd stand behind it and ask, so what song do you repeat until you know every note and chord? "Jack-knife on the side street crossing. I'm still alive and that's something. And when I die, there'll be nothing to say except I tried not to waste another day trying to stem the tide."

10. "**All About You**," (featuring Foster the People), The Knocks from a brand new single. Just found this song a few hours ago, and I want it to be my soundtrack, please. It reminds me of Saturday afternoons in the raw sunshine of winter, the afternoon waning, and maybe there's still time to head outdoors to some park where love is always flourishing. See you there.

"Why can't we be friends? Why can't we be friends?" So sang **War** back in the early 1970's. I didn't know why then, and I'm not sure I know any better now.

"I didn't know we were still speaking?" Jedediah Leland says to Charles Foster Kane.

"Of course we're still speaking, Jedediah...you're fired."

Friendships form and are torn asunder for too many bad reasons. Even good reasons make me wonder why, and if, after enough time, we can't mend our broken hearts and minds. And so, I dedicate this playlist not to the national crisis, but to my old friends from **Bessemer** who, shamelessly, I will be naming below, as I remember and honor our relationships through the following set of songs. Hoping they remember...

AMERICAN CRISIS PLAYLIST #35

1. "**We Just Disagree**," Dave Mason from 1977's *Let It Flow*. I heard this song again on Sirius-XM's "**The Bridge**" this past Sunday as I was driving to my wife's office. When was the last time I heard it? Had to be a couple of decades, and I was surprised not at how good it still sounded, but that I remembered almost every lyric. In 1977, I was in college again, after having returned from work in DC. Much of my free time on weekends and in that summer was spent with my friend **Jack Griffi**s. He and his then wife were living in his grandmother's basement apartment. It was often more of a scene than you'd think. Jack had loved Dave Mason since his Traffic days, and maybe he could explain why we both loved this song. Jack was a rock and roller who, along with his brother **Steve**, played in a band whose various names

were "The Trojans," "Night Wind," and "Mother Savage." Manning the drums, Jack understood the backbone of The Beat. I'm betting that this song is on his rapid play tune list. Hope so anyway.

2. "**Kentucky Woman**," Deep Purple from *The Book of Taliesyn* (1968). It takes a certain kind of "hard rock" band to cover **Neil Diamond**, don't you think? Jack and Steve loved Deep Purple, and together might have founded the Deep Purple fan club, Bessemer chapter. In my view, this was "Purple's" finest record. I don't know if that really says anything today, but though the band, once singer Ian Gillan replaced Rod Evans, could screech with the best of them, I preferred this more melodious sound, in part because, truthfully, I once loved Neil Diamond, too. Don't wince, Jack and Steve. I also once wrote about finding the album in an unlikely venue: I think that this was the story that caused **Noah Levy** to ask me to join The Riff.

3. "**Evil Ways**," Santana from 1969's *Santana*. **Steve Griffis** and Night Wind band mate **Russ Guyton** were also in our high school's Key Club, a fraternity of sorts. In 1972, for our school's annual variety show, "Tiger Talent," they led the Key Club band in the talent competition, playing this Santana hit. Steve was lead guitar, Russ on bass, and singing was a combination of vocalists led by my friend and neighbor, **Joe Terry** (mentioned more directly later on). It was a rockin' good time as the light show mesmerized an audience of Alabama kids still trying to negotiate youth and rebellion. I can still see Steve's red guitar, and I still know that the Key Club band did not win the competition that night. They were bested by...

4. "**If I Were Your Woman**," Gladys Knight and the Pips, from 1971's *If I Were Your Woman*. As sung in Tiger Talent by a sixteen year-old girl named Joyce Williams, a girl in my class whom I hardly knew because she was African American and I, Caucasian. We had some classes together, and while she didn't speak much, when she did you

understood, even if you didn't really, what the word "sultry" could mean. I promise you that when she sang that night, dreams arose, only to be crushed by the grimness of life in Bessemer, circa 1972. I had this single, still have it actually, in my collection of old 45's down in the basement. And while I rooted that night for my friends, it was clear to me that Joyce was everybody's star. And besides, when I tried to pledge the Key Club, they turned me down—me, and my friend **Jimbo Mulkin**.

5. "**Where Is the Love?**" Roberta Flack and Donny Hathaway, from 1972's *Roberta Flack and Donny Hathaway*. Jimbo was my acting friend. Well, let me put that another way: Jimbo loved to act, and so he organized us one night in high school to do our own dramatization of ***Jesus Christ Superstar***...in his bedroom. I think we stopped before the nails got hammered into Ian Gillan's hands. Jimbo's tastes in music ran along a slightly different stream than mine, and so when I jumped in his old Buick Skylark one afternoon, I noticed the RF/DH eight-track tape lying on his floorboard. "Is this what you're listening to now?" I asked, because I was a little stunned that something so mainstream filled him with joy (forgetting for the moment my Neil Diamond fixation). "Yeah," he said. "It's fabulous." And you know...it really is.

6. "**Friends**," Bette Midler from *The Divine Miss M* (1972). Yes, I remember, Jimbo. You once added a soundtrack to a Super-8 film you made of all of us, and this song formed the heart of it all. I remember how we all grabbed each other, falling and laughing (3 Musketeers?) somewhere in your old house. The other song from this record that was an AM hit, "**Do You Want to Dance?**" was my favorite, but I wouldn't have thought anything about Bette back then if it weren't for you. Bette will never be my favorite, but I'll also hold this record close because for a bit of time, it defined us. And only you could have brought it so closely to us.

7. "**High Priestess**," Uriah Heep, from 1971's *Salisbury*. Stop me if you've heard this one before. A man walks into a bar...Actually, **Joe Terry** called me over to his house across the street one day so that he could play this record for me. I picked this song because it was number one on side A. Somehow in the remastered version, it's moved down into the middle, but I'm losing you, I know, in esoterica. Uriah Heep cancelled while we were at their show, so fuck'em still. But I'm glad Joe took the time to make me listen to a different sound, that he cared enough about me, a guy two years younger which in high school time is really eons, to expose me to worlds far away. And I can't tell you about our explorations on the south side because my daughters might be reading this.

8. "**Laughing**," David Crosby from 1971's *If Only I Could Remember My Name*. Love, and always will, this album's title. So David, right? The only person I knew who actually owned this record back in '71 was my friend **Fred Wallace**, Bessemer's optometrist. Fred had vision, surely, and while we kind of made fun of Crosby's "**Almost Cut My Hair**" on *Deja Vu*, when CSNY did their solo albums while still together, Crosby's venture was the only one Neil Young played on. And Neil, as you know, was truly our rock god, Fred and I. Neil sings on this tune, and maybe helped write it, too. "I was only a child, laughing in the sun." I have photos, and so does Fred, of us playing together as tiny babies. Only I wasn't so tiny. Laughing....

9. "**Running Dry**," Neil Young from *Everybody Knows This Is Nowhere* (1969). I wonder which Neil record Fred would select as his favorite? Maybe he'll respond below. This might be mine, especially for the 10 minute version of "Cowgirl in the Sand," which follows this song. I picked "Running Dry," though, for two reasons. One, I used to sing it alone in my bedroom almost every night back then, when I was fifteen. I also stopped the needle countless times as I wrote the lyrics in blue

ink on the album's inner sleeve. My friend **Jim Whisenhunt** borrowed the record once and thought that I had actually written those lyrics. He put them to music, too, he said, though he never played his creation for me. God, we could have been stars, had potential plagiarism not gotten in the way.

10. "**I Never Had It So Good**," Kris Kristofferson and Rita Coolidge from 1973's *Full Moon*. Hard to believe that though I was born and raised in Alabama, and so grew up with country music as my background soundtrack early on, I refused its charm until Jim played this record for me, and especially this song. These lovers' voices mesh so well, and though I was older than Jim by almost a full year, I wondered what else he knew that I didn't—what else he dared to listen to that I thought I couldn't. We still learn from each other here and in other musical sub-spheres. Like all of my old friends, really. So true.

I keep saying that next Tuesday will feel like Christmas again... because I'm getting my first vaccine. My wife has both; our older daughter has both; and like me, our younger daughter will get her first dose this coming week. Love in a vaccine—a year ago, all I was thinking of was seeing **Sturgill Simpson** live in Charlotte with my girls and son-in-law in tow. Little did we know all that would happen, and that Sturgill himself would contract Covid a few days after this show.

I'll write more about the concert at another time, but yes, it has been a year, and loss would go on to underscore our days, numbering out into more grief. Yet, what we experienced then is barely a candle's glow compared to the experiences of so many others and their relative nightmares.

With over 500,000 dead from the virus, it's hardly a celebratory time. And then, there's the CPAC from last week where the OP once again embraced the American flag as if he loves that piece of cloth and the country it represents so much better than he loves himself. As **Jimmy Kimmel** shouted last week,

"He doesn't love any of you!"

Why is that so hard to understand? Love is a four-letter word, and it has nothing to do with crowd size, walls, or the massive ego of a petty little man who will always be a scar on our nation's history with his brand of bullshit.

So, what happened to my Christmas again?

Here at **The Riff**, we believe in music and its power to heal, to bless, to inspire, and to challenge us to find our way out of this and any other crisis that comes our way. I love the stories being generated on the site by Gary Chapin, Jeff Goodwin, Steven Hale, and Reuben Salsa among so many others, and always feel better once I've read about even such forgotten odes as Neil Diamond's "**Jonathan Livingston Seagull.**"

So, with all due homage, respect, and inspiration, I offer these gems to get you through your night, week, and windy month.

Have fun, and as always, play them LOUD.

▱ AMERICAN CRISIS PLAYLIST #36 ▱

1. "**Private Idaho,**" The B-52's, from *Wild Planet* (1980). It was B-52's week around here, self-proclaimed, and I kept seeing visions of older men at dance parties trying to figure out how to move to these sounds. Who wears a tie and business suit to a student party, and what do you do with your coat once this song begins playing? Is this the state song of potato land? It should be, because Idaho isn't honored every day, or year, with such a testament to partying out of bounds. Dance dance dance to you're dead.

2. "**Fly Robin Fly,**" Silver Convention, 1975, from their self-titled first album. Did they have a second? I went to college with two sisters, **Millie and Robyn Rushing**. I wonder where they are now? Millie once gave a dramatic reading of one of the more S/M parts of Judith Rossner's *Looking for Mr. Goodbar* in our Oral Interpretation (I swear) class during my sophomore year. You can never forget your own, or your professor's, face when a frank and open—and beautiful—young woman intones the "F" word over and over for a grade. Her sister Robyn once danced solo to this song at a friend's pre-wedding party. Certain images linger.

3. "**Smile Like You Mean It,**" The Killers, from 2004's *Hot Fuss*. My older daughter used to play this song on our way to her high school back in those days when I drove her everywhere. I kept wondering how she found a band like this and why I didn't find them first. It didn't

matter so much except I understood how life was changing so quickly, almost imperceptibly. She, finding her way to adulthood, and I, trying to let her do it without too much aid. I found that some of my college students loved this song, too, and that cinched it for me. Still sounds worthy of all of us, too.

4. **"Everybody's Changing,"** Keane, from *Hopes and Fears* (2003). This CD I actually swiped from my daughter, put it in my to-go carry case, and left it in my car so that I could listen to it whenever I wanted, which was at least twice daily as I made the 90-mile round trip to my college. I think she was okay with that once she learned what I had done and why. I'm sure she remembers this song, a pop hit from her thirteenth year and my 47th. Listen to the lyrics please. "So little time, try to understand that I'm trying to make a move just to stay in the game, I try to stay awake and remember my name, but everybody's changing and I don't feel the same." I love the ambiguity.

5. **"Black-Hearted Love,"** PJ Harvey and John Parish, from *A Woman A Man Walked By* (2009). You know how I love PJ, and I remember hearing this song the first time somewhere somehow someway standing in our den with the TV on and PJ making me feel wrapped up inside. I also remember a critic from that time reminding everyone that PJ just wasn't to everyone's tastes. Got that right. I wouldn't want her to be, either, though I will say that when I was grading AP Lit exams in Louisville a few years back, I met two diehard PJ fans, also grading. The essays were about a **Vicar in one of Thomas Hardy's novels.** How many AP students, we wondered, know what a Vicar is? How many know what a PJ Harvey is? Or a black-heart? Is that the OP crying? Watch the video, too. Oh Dave.

6. **"Do You Wanna Dance?"** Bette Midler from *The Divine Miss M* (1972). Were we really this innocent back when I was sixteen? This sensitive? All of my close friends in **Bessemer, Alabama,** swooned to

this song, or at least I like to think we did. Back then, no one knew how to pronounce her name, but that would change. I think of my friend Jimbo's car, the lake near his house where we swam and tried to avoid touching the gooey bottom, and still Bette could stop us cold in our Schlitz beer when this song came on the radio. True true true.

7. "**House of Cards**," Radiohead, from *In Rainbows* (2007). This one's for you Noah (Noah Levy). I loved Radiohead before I heard this song. After? Have you ever watched that last second of light melt away from your own back porch as you try to figure who on earth will understand it, you, them, all of us? In these moments, understanding merges with love. And the whole record resounds, but not as much as the moments here. One of my math colleagues at school digs Radiohead, too, and in different moments, we both were affiliated with the University of Montevallo. Strange days.

8. "**Hearts Content**," Brandi Carlile (2012) on *Bear Creek*. Last week, my younger daughter was preparing her sourdough starter while I finished up the pasta carbonara for her mom's birthday, and she put on her own playlist. This is the song that grabbed me, and of course, I couldn't name the artist. Another learning moment. The sourdough crusted perfectly; the carbonara found the right blend of pancetta and cheese, and Brandi sang us to red wine bliss. My daughter selected the vintage, too.

9. "**Hold Yourself**," Tune-Yards, from their forthcoming album *sketchy*. It's the vocals that always get me with this band, and I'm struggling to remember who they remind me of. Kind of like **Blood, Sweat, and Tears** in that brassy/bluesy vibe, but I know that isn't it either. **Phoebe Snow**? Colbert had them on a few weeks ago, and they amused him in what I hope was a good way, but you can check that out for yourself. Lots of promises still to come. "Parents are children, all of the time," indeed.

10. "**Punisher**," Phoebe Bridgers from 2020's *Punisher*. I seem to recall that someone wrote about her attempts to smash her guitar on **SNL** a month or so ago. Seems like David Crosby was upset at her. Wild, right? I record SNL every week, but we had an unexpected snowstorm that night and our satellite dish didn't care for those conditions and so blacked out, and so I missed Phoebe and have to take everybody's word about her supposed transgression. I feel punished for sure, but not as much as Crosby's been for his particular views. We should remind him of his own absurdities, but let's listen to Phoebe instead.

The time changes again tonight, and I was almost caught off-guard. This is why, I assume, clocks spring forward and back on late Saturday nights. People like me who don't attend the church of their choice—if we forget about time, we'll just have an extra or less hour to do whatever we do on Sunday: walk the dog, write for The Riff, or in this season, finish up taxes.

Anyway, yesterday my chiropractor literally had my back, and so I am ready for whatever one less hour means tomorrow.

Also, **I had my first Pfizer vaccine last week**, and so in another three weeks, I'll be fully vaccinated and ready to resume normal life, whatever that will look like. I wonder if I'll still recognize my town, Greenville, and if I'll notice what has transpired in my absence? I've been strangely content since President Biden was inaugurated, and have loved the calming influence. I've also been reading more prompts and challenges by my fellow writers. Last week, Harry Mule wrote a story about playlists and food. I thought I'd follow with a list dedicated to an orb that has guided me all of my life, the beautiful and exotic moon.

I'll ask right from the start that you don't scream about the songs not on the list. Sure, I thought about "Moondance," and "Mr. Moonlight," and even considered "**Moonbeams and Bluejeans**," but I sang these songs to myself and didn't like my own sound. So I sang the others and felt much better. It's cloudy here today, if that influences anyone's reading or contemplation. Yesterday, it was 82 degrees; today, almost 20 degrees cooler.

I hope you and the Moon understand.

And please accept the challenge. You don't have to be as obvious as I might be, either. But keep in mind that my original home state's GOP just passed a resolution naming our former cretin-in-chief as "one of the greatest presidents in our country's history." So no **Alabama moons** here.

1. "**Mr. Sun, Mr. Moon**," Paul Revere and the Raiders, from *Hard 'N Heavy (With Marshmallow)*, 1969. A happy little ditty from the band I loved the most back in the 60's. I kept wanting someone else in my guy group to love and appreciate them, too, but songs like this—happy feel good numbers—just didn't appeal to angry, surly tough guys (you know how 13 year-old boys are, right?). At least it made it to #9 on Dick Clark's *American Bandstand's Top Ten*.

2. "**Moonlight, Feels Right**," Starbuck from *Moonlight Feels Right*, 1976. Apple Music classifies this as Disco. I don't see it, nor am I sure how I managed to hear and remember it. In 1976, I was a junior in college and considered myself above Pop. Of course, I loved Disco, so I don't know who was fooling whom. This isn't Disco, and I'm sure I heard it on my mother's AM car radio. And whatever else you might think, it was the first song that came to my mind when I conceived this list.

3. "**Moonage Daydream**," David Bowie from *The Rise and Fall of Ziggy Stardust (and the Spiders From Mars)* 1972. It felt transgressive, somehow, to receive this record for a Christmas present from my friend Jimbo in that year when he and I were sixteen years old. I had read about Bowie in various music mags, and I think he even made it to *Time*. On a first listen, I didn't know what to think, how to feel. There I was—alone in my darkened room, the glow of the stereo receiver the only shining glimmer near me. And then I heard this song, and life changed forever—at least musically.

4. "**Moonshadow**," Cat Stevens, from *Teaser and the Firecat*, 1971. I understand that he didn't turn out like we planned, which might be as much on us, given that we seem to think that we own the artists and that they

should continue following some script we've agreed on with, or for, them. I don't pretend to know what all went on in Cat's head, or why he decided to follow the more radical notions issued out of Islamic Iran. What I do know is that this is the only song my wife and I have ever sung karaoke to. We sounded so gooooooood. Just ask our daughters.

5. "**Harvest Moon**," Neil Young, from *Harvest Moon* (1992). So sue me: I'm a Neil junkie or freak or addict. Believe it or not, this isn't my favorite song or album by far. I felt it was a revisit of a better record from the early 70's, and I had put it out of my head until **Poolside** covered it. I always appreciated the hard-rockin' Neil the best, and if I had to go for the ballads, then *After the Gold Rush* satisfied me more. But I played this for my babies often enough—a lullaby of sorts to soothe all of our troubles. It's still soothing, too.

6. "**Moonlight Serenade**," Glenn Miller, from many records all over your favorite music service, but first released in **1939 on the Bluebird label**. Miller was one of my Dad's favorite musicians, next to **Benny Goodman**. I don't know if this was Dad's favorite Miller song, and I wish I could ask him. I also wish I could tell him how much I love this tune; how much I love Miller, too; and how much I appreciate his exposing me to the Big Band and small combo swing music of his youth. Dad had tons of 78's. We kept them for a long time, but their condition deteriorated to almost nothing. One of many regrets. Listen, though, and understand what beauty and artistry are.

7. "**Moonlight in Vermont**," Stan Getz, which you may find on *Getz for Lovers*, released in 2002, but clearly all over the Getz library. The first two CD's I ever bought were a Benny Goodman release and a Getz compilation, where, to my memory, I first heard this song—a song I consider THE most romantic song I've ever heard. When you think sultry saxophone, how could you not think of this one? Please play this for me when I grow old and am ready for my own lullaby again.

8. "**Blue Moon**," Elvis Presley, from 1956's *Elvis Presley*. **My brother Mike** would kill me if I didn't include Elvis on this list. This album, from my birth year, used to sit in the front of his album collection. Everyone in our household

loved Elvis, and even my Dad would have grudgingly admitted that "The King" was something else. I think of the changes, yet the consistency, of what appeals to us about the music of our lives: mellow notes, the intensity of someone who knows that when he sings or plays, no one has or will ever sound like this.

9. "**Dancing in the Moonlight**," King Harvest from 1973's *Dancing in the Moonlight*. Why do I associate this song with the bands I loved back in this era, from Neil to The Eagles to America and The New Riders of the Purple Sage? The folkiness, the alt-country vibe? Such a one-hit wonder, though, and I know there have been covers, but for me, this song screams driving around in my friend Jim's mother's wide Chevy and us singing to our vocal heights. And then the following spring, we'd graduate and go on to even greater heights.

10. "**Moon River**," lyrics by Johnny Mercer, composition by Henry Mancini, sung by **Audrey Hepburn** in *Breakfast at Tiffany's*, and made even more popular by Andy Williams—his theme song which he intoned every week on his TV series in the 60's. That was a mouthful. I always liked this song when my parents played it or when I heard it on Williams' show. But I didn't love it until I finally watched *Breakfast at Tiffany's* four years ago. I swear, if they hadn't found that cat...but they did. I wondered if I had ever heard anything more beautiful, and also why it had taken me so long to appreciate this Capote work and Hepburn's acting.

Am I the only one to get that Matt Gaetz and Marjorie (Taylor) Greene have the same initials? Am I the only one to get nauseated at the prospect? Is this the best even the Repubs have to offer (heard it while I was writing it).

So yeah, Rep. Gaetz had some moments in the sun over this period of our Crisis Playlist Series, and maybe I am the only one to compare his hair to that of Jack Nance's "Henry," in David Lynch's apocalyptically weird *Eraserhead*. Sometimes people just look like they would be sleazy and worse in real life. Like, who doesn't look at Manson and Hitler today and wonder what the hell? Not saying Gaetz is even remotely there, for sure, but what am I saying, and where exactly is he?

To ward off any other demons, I got my second Pfizer shot during this period, and felt, if not invulnerable, then at least worthy of shopping at our local grocery without a mask. I still refused to eat indoors, which caused a ripple among old friends, but we moved forward, enjoying takeout Thai food on our deck and reliving simpler times, like giving birth to our first children and when we met each other in Lamaze class.

Major League Baseball decided that it could actually start and try to get in a full season, though players were still running afoul of Covid, but at least fans like Kathryn Dillon, and me, were happy.

We were even happier turning again to music, and artists like Taylor Swift (who was releasing her own versions of older records), Todd Rundgren, Big Audio Dynamite, Young-Holt Unlimited, Japanese Breakfast, Foxygen, Haim, Rostam, Valley Maker, Warpaint, Jade Bird, Radiohead, Dire Straits, Tom Tom Club, Gorillaz, and Tai Verdes.

Another mass shooting has filled our skies. I haven't had the heart to read about all the "thoughts and prayers" sent out to the victims' families from people who oppose any form of background checks, any checks period on buying deadly weapons. A white man killing Asian Americans: just another violently horrible iteration of someone who believes his world is lost and overwhelmed by people who don't look like him.

The thing that always seems to get lost—or I should say, ONE thing that always gets lost—is that when we examine the looks of those we see in our immediate world, hardly anyone looks like us or me, though once I was told that I resembled closely the teacher, "Gary," on that TV series from the 90's: "**Thirtysomething.**" That was back when I had long hair, and I do have to say that my hair was once halfway down my back.

Thoughts and prayers to my former hair.

The subtleties of the ways we do and do not look like each other leave us grasping and gasping. The desperation that white skin must be preserved; that fair-hair must be silky and fluffed and passed on to one's children—these are the things that drive me crazy (echoed later on in the list).

I remember wondering what my Middle Eastern wife's hair must feel like before I actually touched it. This is where bias and prejudice can grow. Her hair couldn't possibly be as fine, as soft, as soothing to the touch as mine, or as that of the dyed red-haired girl I crushed on back in high school. No, it had to be rougher, coarser, maybe even scratchy.

Of course it wasn't any of those qualities. It was hair, different from mine, but ultimately the same.

And as many of you know—and I want to scream this out too—it is very possible to live in a household, to LOVE in a household, where two or more languages are spoken. True, not everything will be understood immediately or even after a few hours, but I ask you: whom do you understand immediately or ever?

For God's sake, I speak the same language as Mitch McConnell, Ted Cruz, and he-whom-I-will-never-name-but-is-the-former-occupant-of-the-WH, and I often have no idea what they're talking about and if they even know, themselves.

"Seasons change and so do I

You need not wonder why."

With all apologies to **The Guess Who**, we do have time in this changing season to scream, to change, to do both and wonder why we keep seeing the same horrors and somehow tolerate the same bullshit from tired old white men who think America is one thing, one experience only.

And while I don't pretend to be a big fan of Cardi B and Megan Thee Stallion, it distresses me to hear all the complaints about their Grammy performance from, again, tired white men like Tucker Carlson who somehow believe that this act is a harbinger of the decline of the American Empire. As Jimmy Kimmel offered this week, **Yeah, and that experience on January 6 must have been just a farmer's market stroll.** Though I credit the stroll to my daughter.

So easy, right, to blame the Black women as if they're our real problem.

So, the songs I offer here are both complaints and panaceas; fuel for our outrage and our aesthetic engines. Use them wisely, let that music play, and try to understand the magic men and women of all backgrounds who so clearly color our world.

1. **"Love of the Common Man,"** Todd Rundgren from *Faithful* (1976). "The simple things in life/Seem so hard to learn sometimes/And it takes so long, catch it while you can.../cause everyone needs the love of the common man." For over sixty years I've been watching and trying and waiting for the people in my world to quit calling each other names and stop believing that one's birth heritage is the truest marker of acceptability and worthiness. My mother, quoting Lincoln, I think, used to say that "the Lord sure loves common folk because he made so many of them." To me, this is one of Todd's most overlooked songs. It reaches long.

2. **"I'm Doin' Fine Now (without you baby),"** New York City, from *One Hit Wonders, Vol. 7,* and dating back to 1974. "I remember the day you up and left/I nearly cried myself to death." The lyrics, though not very original, work well in this soulful arrangement. Though I never owned the single, when it came on the radio, I always turned the volume to LOUD and sang. Heartache, loss, betrayal, the lovelorn. These are realities that strike all of us and are our common denominators. Trust the music, even when the love vanishes.

3. **"Soulful Strut,"** Young-Holt Unlimited (1968) from *Soulful Strut.* **Kevin Alexander** got me to remembering this song on his Heavy Rotation story this week. He mentions **Barbara Acklin's "Am I the Same Girl,"** which is really another version of "Soulful Strut," a song I first remember hearing as the background music on Dick Clark's *American Bandstand*, when Dick would talk through the rules of the yearly AB dance contest, a contest, I should mention, where couples of any color could compete. I loved the song and it took me a while in those days before Google to identify it. That piano will always be my touchstone for romantic sunsets on the west side of town.

4. "**Californian Soil**," London Grammar, from their forthcoming record, *Californian Soil*. A new song from a band I love. "I left my soul on Californian soil." I have felt like that recently, as my recent essay, San Francisco Dreaming, on *Literally Literary* testifies. The vocals and strings tell me that I've always longed for that land, and I truly haven't felt the same after imagining and experiencing those San Francisco nights.

5. "**Thursday's Child (Rock Mix)**," David Bowie from *hours—'Expanded Edition'* (2004). "Sometimes I cry my heart to sleep" and stumble upon an album by an adored artist like Bowie, and wonder why I close certain doors and stop taking chances. Kevin, put this one in your next heavy rotation, or just listen to it and chat with me what your thoughts are. I was a Sunday's child, so look all that stuff up and consider friending me. And me, you. Bowie keeps giving and you know what the right-wingers thought about him.

6. "**Seeing Other People**," Foxygen, from 2019's *Seeing Other People*. Yeah, so it was their San Francisco song that first lured me to them, no wonder, and I've kept them on my radar, though not always upfront near head's edge. Do we? Do we? For my sixty-first birthday a few summers ago, Owen bought tickets to see Foxygen for us. They were playing here in Greenville at a downtown amphitheater. Then Owen had to back out for a vacation with his girlfriend. Then Foxygen canceled. **Then Owen died**. I see him and other people in my dreams every night, and in waking hours, too.

7. "**BAD**," Big Audio Dynamite, from *This Is Big Audio Dynamite* (1985). "Bad life, bad language, bad news...." As sorry as I was that the Clash split, I was electrified when I heard about BAD and then put this one on my own heavy playback in the mid-80's, in the days just after I married my wife. We'd dance alone in our old Victorian house-apartment in **Knoxville's Ft. Sanders district**. Just us and

30,000 other students climbing over the hilly terrain. "Jesus Christ got crucified so the empire of Rome could get gratified." That about says it all, speaking of things that drive me crazy. Jesus Christ = Megan Thee Stallion in Tucker's fantasies.

8. "**The Park**," Uriah Heep from 1972's *Salisbury*. When my across-the-street neighbor Joe called me over to his room in his grandmother's house, just to play *Salisbury* for me, I didn't see Jesus or have any particular sort of revelation that afternoon, but since at that point I didn't know this band or the literary reference from whence they drew their name, I thought of how life changes on a notion of shared music. Joe did me a good turn then and gave me a joint not long after. So if you listen to this one, go ahead and light up. You'll heal quickly, or think you have anyway.

9. "**Don't Wanna**," Haim, from *Women in Music Pt III* (2020). For my daughters, who love Haim. For me, who loves them, too. For us all, because women have been rocking for a long time and still don't get the justice—though sadly, they do get the knocks from many of us. "I don't wanna give up on you, I don't wanna have to." I feel that way about the US. And I AM getting that second vaccine in ten days, so no giving up. Imagine a day when live music can be experienced without streaming or zoom as the normal option. I hope Haim is one of the first acts I get to see/hear!

10. "**Road Head**," Japanese Breakfast, from 2017's *Soft Sounds From Another Planet*. A beauty to end with this week. Shimmering sounds on the last day of winter. The blue skies make me feel like we could live peacefully forever, and so happy spring. Happy Persian New Year, and happy lands with people of all sorts, especially those who don't look like me. The road ahead is still long and worth the drive.

Last Wednesday our daughters left town again after spending a week with us. We had fun: cooked, played dominos and **Chick-A-Pig**, and listened to tons of music. A day later, my wife left for three days at the beach with her sister as they face the one-year anniversary of their mother's passing. Max, my dog, and I have maintained good spirits, walking and playing with his nerf football in our lower yard near the creek, where creatures and waters pass by, waving or not.

When you're basically alone, you might dream that little creatures wave at you while passing downstream amidst thunderstorms and the occasional tornado warning.

Still, this is a much better scenario, fate, than driving to Hilton Head on your anniversary and being killed in an act of road rage, a horrible story I read about today, amidst all those others of angry men firing guns or wearing body shields and packing assault rifles in Atlanta area Publix Markets. I also read about a preacher who's declaring an impending civil war where he might have to take up arms against all the liberals which include his own children.

You know we liberals: we're the ones who want sensible checks on gun ownership; who believe in voting rights for all; who support equality in marriage for everyone; who want all of us to earn a decent living wage; and who think about Jesus as a social activist, that is, if we think about him at all.

As I write this I realize again that liberals aren't uniform believers; that we differ on many things, too. I support, for instance, a woman's right to control her own body, including having an abortion if it comes to that.

And, if you don't want to get Covid-vaccinated, that's your right, too. But I'm getting my second one on Tuesday night, and I sure wish most would follow suit.

All of this might be the result of my having too much time on my hands to ruminate. My wife will be arriving home this afternoon, and among all of the other reasons I miss her, our house is so quiet without her, not that she's a big talker. No, we both "lean introvert," and so it's more that my head isn't such an echo chamber when she's here, and at certain moments we find time to ask how the other's doing.

So I'm doing fine, could be better, but as I turn to this week's music, I hear good things coming, including baseball, **Kathryn Dillon**! Buy baseball tickets and not assault rifles with that hard-earned cash!

▣ AMERICAN CRISIS PLAYLIST #39 ▣

1. "**No One is Missing**," Valley Maker, from their 2021 release, *When the Day Leaves*. Maybe I don't fully understand this song, but my thoughts wander to why no one is really missing. My mind and my memory keep everyone here, before me. "Time slips," the singer sings, and that's true, but then, a moment's glance and I am standing again in my mother's house on a rainy Sunday, as she asks me to order us some lunch from **The Bright Star in Bessemer**. She doesn't feel well; the road is short now. I get the lunch, and the restaurant owner, Jimmy, will be a ghost soon, too. But when I see these scenes, they both are there, making sure it's all been paid for, that all orders have been rendered accurately. A taste and a memory like no other.

2. "**Headstart**," Jade Bird, from a 2020 single. I love the way the song builds here and she helps us fold on into the momentum. I'm having a hard time compiling my list of artists I have to see once I can venture into a club or hall again. But Jade is someone I think my wife and I would love to see and dance to. Just a short piece so we

don't lose each other, our breaths, or our late-night stamina. That was what happened when our girls were here: we made it to 11:30 each night. Wow.

3. "**Stuck in the Middle**," Tai Verdes, from another 2020 single. "She said, are we exclusive or not?" I remember the days when dating was this tentative. What was the longest-term, on and off again romance you were ever stuck in? I had one that went on for three years. Long distance though it was, I couldn't understand how it kept reviving when, to be honest, we had so little in common except love for the person who brought us together. Such was college romance, and I got stuck between her and her old boyfriend, and then she got stuck between me and my new girlfriend. And still it took another year to end.

4. "**Forever**," Haim, from 2013's *Days Are Gone*. My daughters are big fans of the Haim sisters, and so I realized that I hadn't listened to this record in a while. I love how our roads, lives, keep intersecting over music, especially music this good. There are certain constants in life, and being in one's den or living room with music supporting a dice roll, or the placement of a double eleven domino so that the next move is more expansive, seems like a scene that I have been living in forever. The pile of dominoes that we draw from is called "the boneyard," or so said my **beloved Nanny**.

5. "**Sometimes I Don't Know How to Feel**," Todd Rundgren from *A Wizard, A True Star* (1973). Yeah, I've been in a real Todd mood lately, and this song strikes my other mood—that stuck in the middle with or without you mood—that paralyzes my emotions. I find Todd's music, songs like this one, "**Hello It's Me**," "We've Got to Get You a Woman" to be more romantic, in that late-night longing, listening alone in your room and staring out a darkened window into nothing kind of way. Some find him to be too over-produced. But his echoing effect, the overdubbed voices and the keyboards make me lose myself. And it

oddly feels pretty good. I thank my friend Les for making me listen to this record so long ago.

6. "**I Might Be Wrong**," Radiohead, from *Amnesiac* (2001). Radiohead has been a popular entry on The Riff lately, which caused me to want to dive back into their heady mazes. This song appealed to me early on, and yes, **Noah Levy**, I know I'm selecting a single song off an entire record, and I understand and even agree with the desire to listen to a complete record. Though I could be off or even wrong, this song seems to fit into my muddled mind's playlist today. And it's pretty damn pretty, too. I love its relentlessness, and of course, Thom's voice.

7. "**Hurdy Gurdy Man**," Donavan, from 1968's *The Hurdy Gurdy Man*. So I'm cheating here, or at least double-dipping, and you would know if you read my story on **Zodiac**, elsewhere on *The Riff*. I don't remember this song from the year I turned twelve. Did it make it to the radio? Did Dick Clark play it on *American Bandstand*? And if so, did I hide under the covers when I heard it, not even trying to pretend how weird it was and how much I wanted it all—whatever it was—not to be true? The season of the witch and of the looming Manson family. Remember?

8. "**Blunt Force Concussion**," The Dirty Nil from *F*** Art* (2020). Not sure what I think of his voice, but I do like the way the song kicks my ass and makes me feel happy in that way rock and roll has always seemed to. I've never had a concussion, but that Clash concert in 1983 made me think I had experienced the head-on onslaught of something bruising. I appreciate the knocks, too, because when something hits this hard, it's hard not to feel pushed, alive, and unstuck from whatever middle you or I might have landed in (**Cautionary note:** I don't feel as if I'm making any sense today, but you understand, right?).

9. "**Skateaway**," Dire Straits, from 1980's *Making Movies*. In 1980,

I was starting my second year of a Master's program, and my friends—Les, Mary, Crafton, The Beach-Man—we loved this record, and I see us walking down the campus strip, anticipating Friday nights at whichever local bar might accept us. I keep thinking of how I understood Faulkner well, or so I thought, but couldn't quite figure out what I wanted to do, whom I wanted to love. These were happy days, and yet I'd feel lost at the end of the evening. Which way was my place, and would Friday please come again soon so we could start all over? "She gets rock and roll, in a rock and roll station, in a rock and roll dream. She's making movies, on location. She don't know what it means."

10. "**I Know the End**," Phoebe Bridgers, from 2020's *Punisher*. Okay, **Jeff Goodwin**, I finally got to watch Phoebe's performance on *SNL*. I didn't know that it was this song she played and then smashed her guitar too at the end. All the way through the song, while admiring its beauty and its shifting tone and rhythm, I felt sorry for her gorgeous black guitar, knowing how it would end. This might be one of my favorite songs of the last two years, even. Poor guitar. "Romanticize the quiet life, there's no place like my room...The billboards say the end is near." Don't they always? But in that circular way that life keeps playing, isn't it only the beginning?

As I sat tranquil after my second vaccine last Tuesday, waiting the required fifteen minutes to ensure that I wouldn't react badly to the serum, I got approached by a young woman wanting to know why her favorite soft drink wasn't in the vending machine. She was looking for a Diet Coke, or a Coke Zero, or something that had maximum caffeine and minimal sugar.

We were cohabitating in a mammoth former K-Mart which was situated in a shopping plaza with a mammoth former Bi-Lo grocery store. Like K-Mart, Bi-Lo has gone under. You don't know Bi-Lo because it's based here in Greenville. I wonder at its passing, because Bi-Lo stores were everywhere in town. A victim of Covid? Of Publix?

"How much do you think they charge for these drinks?" the girl asked, because sure enough, though the machine accepted Apple Pay and any credit card, no price could be found on the various forms of bottled water and flavored sports drinks in it anywhere.

Next to that machine was the food version, where you could buy almost any power bar you wanted, or some baked chips, and even one lonely bag of Chee-Tos. I pointed out the orangey bag to my new friend, but it was a drink she wanted. And then, my time was up, and so wishing her well, I walked out of this place, passing up the chance to grab a package of off-brand saltines, two to a pack.

I don't want to seem all judgey, and god knows that someone might be in need of a salt-upturn after swooning from the shot-in-the-arm and all it means.

Still, such experiences make me wonder. I saw others, mainly singles or pairs, getting their safety shots, and it felt both good to see, and unsettling, as many of the people there were being helped by parents or partners, and they seemed hopeful, and uncertain, and in need of care beyond this facility. A shot, a life. What is safety now?

I had absolutely no reaction to my injection, other than a slightly sore arm, and so compared to many others (and this should be my mantra), I am very lucky. Walking out to my vintage 1998 4Runner, I fell in step with a mother and her daughter. I wanted to ask if they needed some help, if everything was all right. But there I went judging again. For all I know, their life is happier than mine. Their vehicle was newer and better, anyway.

In a rush to get to my appointment—did I seriously believe I would be punished and forbidden from entering had I arrived five minutes late, cutting off my savasana early so as to avoid any penalty—I worked myself up to an almost panic, thus spoiling my beautiful yoga flow. But on the drive home, windows open, sun slowly falling behind the buildings of the Greenville skyline, I felt calmer, freer, and so ready for a nice supper and...

Music.

Peace to all I encountered that evening, and I hope others will follow soon, though I wonder what will happen to the former K-Mart once we have all been vaccinated?

AMERICAN CRISIS PLAYLIST #40

1. "**4Runner**," Rostam, from his new release *Changephobia*. "I used to keep you up all night. You used to drive when I got tired." When our first child was an infant, she liked to pretend she couldn't sleep. Actually, she did fight sleep, and so the doctor recommended we put her in the car and drive around because the tranquil feel of the rhythm of the car would act as a rock-a-bye-baby. We were driving Hondas

back then, but you get the idea. We discovered old roads leading to newly-invented towns, and parts of town that then required locked doors during our midnight driving hours, but which are the cooler venues today. Like Rostam, things keep changing and getting steadier, fear or not.

2. "**New Song**," Warpaint, from 2016's *Heads Up*. Remember 2016? We had never heard of Covid-19; K-Marts were hanging on by a corporate thread; and we either hadn't yet, or just had, elected a man whose sole (not soul, never soul) reason for being was to sow chaos and crisis, and without whom this series would not have been necessary. Does that seem real now? Heads up: my wife saw something, maybe from a Fox News source, suggesting that he is running again in 2024. I keep not finding such info, so I'm choosing tails on this one.

3. "**Tried to Tell You**," The Weather Station from their brand new release, *Ignorance*. "To stand behind the idea that anything matters...I tried to tell you." Think of how many times you've been told such. I heard that line so many times growing up, like the time I thought I would peroxide my hair, or the time I thought shaving the sides of my head would be cool, or the time when I was in fifth grade and insisted that my mother buy me that orange Nehru jacket, which I then wore to church the next day. So hard to be cool in 1960's Bessemer. So shhh, my secret is out: **https://www.amazon.com/Secrets-I'm-Dying-Tell-You/.**

4. "**Aries**," Gorillaz (feat. Peter Hook and Georgia), from 2020's *Song Machine, Season One*. If you aren't dancing yet, what's the matter? I hope I never get too old for dancing, for Gorillaz, or for Nehru jackets. Don't own one now, but there's always eBay, or my local second-hand shop, Bee Hive. Speaking of bees, my dog Max won't let the bumble variety alone, and one got him a little while ago. He looked at me and asked, "Why?" "Don't know, buddy," I said, "but I did try to tell you."

5. "**Interstellar Love**," The Avalanches (feat. Leon Bridges) from 2020's *We Will Always Love You*. A bunch of new tunes this week, and this one, to me, is worth several repeat plays. Maybe it's my mood—good yoga flow this morning—and maybe it's Leon playing along so effortlessly, or maybe it's the idea of love transcending this plane. Or maybe it's the way I feel about Max, who is quite fine now, and looking out the window as his mom has just departed to run errands at what one day will be a former Wal-Mart.

6. "**We Will Become Silhouettes**," The Postal Service, from 2020's *Everything Will Change*. The album titles this week are killing me. Should someone write a free verse poem using them all in order? But for this one, it's the song title that hits the hardest. "We'll become silhouettes when our bodies finally go." Not a happy thought, although since a silhouette is something, the shadow of a dream perhaps, at least we'll still be noticed, and maybe our darker outlines will cause someone else to wonder about all that's missing or lost. That everything will change—that it's changing now, that's it's our only constant—is the one thing I did learn from **Percy Shelley**. No phobia, Rostam.

7. "**Out of the Woods**," Taylor Swift, from *1989* (2014). "If the world was black and white and we were in screaming color, would we be out of the woods, in the clear yet?" I can't tell you, although I tried to, how stupid I feel that I didn't listen to Taylor sooner. I played this for my Southern Gothic Lit class last week, and a student commented that she couldn't believe that this record was already seven years old, which means she was only twelve or so when it was released, and she begged to go see Taylor live and her wish was granted. I understand. Time is constantly changing.

8. "**The Steps**," HAIM, from 2020's *Women in Music, Pt III*. Yeah, I've been listening and playing HAIM in heavy rotation (Hey Kevin Alexander!) lately, and why not? What's not to understand? Do you understand? This entire record could make it into a playlist, and none of us would be the worse for it. Painless, happy, and fit for a romantic encounter of interstellar love, I think.

9. "**It's All in the Game**," The Four Tops, from a 1970 single. If you read this story, **https://medium.com/the-riff/in-the-shadows**, you'll know about my feelings for Levi Stubbs and the Tops. But did you know that Merle Haggard once did this song, and did it well? I didn't, but am so glad I know now. I remember my father telling me that the song was older than I knew, and he was right. I remember his telling me that he really liked it, too. It spoke to him: "Many a tear has to fall, but it's all in the game." It makes me wonder, too, about my dad and all the other tears that fell.

10. "**Pretty As You Feel**," Jefferson Airplane from 1971's *Bark*. Underrated, under-appreciated Airplane, from a record that hardly anyone remembers, if they ever knew about it at all. There was a point in my life when I thought the Airplane beat everyone, that they combined all that was right with rock, with blues, with almost jazzy improvisation. Of course, in 1971, the band was running out of its almost original steam, and I was fifteen, trying to find a place where I could be content in music, in love, and in algebra. I failed the latter, but that's for the best. Should have known better anyway. So stayed away from trig and opted for Shakespeare. Good decision. Wish the Airplane's direction had been as wise.

How many of you knew I would? Come on...tell the truth. How could the **American Crisis Playlist** series not go after the saintly Matt Gaetz. Sorry, I'm borrowing the moniker that our former president and LOSER, the Orange Plague, bestowed on current President Biden.

"Saintly."

Once upon a time when my parents were preparing to visit me in D.C., driving from their home in **Bessemer** (where last week a union for Amazon was defeated), a neighbor asked them if they'd have to drive through Florida to get to our nation's capital.

I hope my parents didn't answer her in the way they told me the story, stating,

"Do you go through Florida to get from any one U.S. state to another?"

But I started thinking about our neighbor's question this morning:

Do all roads lead through, around, by, or over Florida?

And then I started thinking of that greatest of American films: Orson Welles' and Herman Mankiewicz's **Citizen Kane**. At the end of Charles Foster Kane's life, he retires to "Xanadu," somewhere near the Florida Keys. He lives in his "unfinished pleasure dome," distant, aloof, and lost in old grudges, his wife's jigsaw puzzles, and the crazy statues he's acquired from the world, all in an attempt to pay tribute to himself.

Is any of this sounding familiar?

If you don't subscribe to *Politico*'s "*Playbook*," you should. Just today, we get passages like this one, regarding some festivity held in or near someone's private Florida club last night:

"A slew of well-heeled Republican National Committee donors descended on Palm Beach this weekend, excited to be schmoozed, eager for access to the ORANGE PLAGUE and other potential 2024 nominees, but mostly interested in hearing how far their dollars would go toward winning back the Congress and White House.

Trump's speech didn't do any of that.

'It was horrible, it was long and negative,' one attendee with a donor in the room tells Playbook. 'It was dour. He didn't talk about the positive things that his administration has done.' Instead, Trump used the final night of the retreat to talk about himself, his grievances and how he plans to enact retribution against those who voted to impeach him—which runs counter to the donors' main objective of making sure their dollars go toward winning overall" (*Playbook*, 4/10/21).

My family used to vacation in Palm Beach when I was a teenager because Dad "won" a free trip there, if by free we mean my parents had to spend one of our three days in Florida listening to a **land-shark sales pitch**. Our hotel was nice anyway, and it was on the beach. So maybe this is the reason why when someone mentions Florida and how to get there, I think immediately of charlatans who want your money, who almost beg for your money, and then use it to purchase white patent leather shoes, or greater images of themselves.

Playbook also mentions that if the OP decides to speculate on another land deal in D.C., he might choose Florida governor Ron DeSantis as his running mate.

What you won't find at the coverage of the rally is any mention of the afore-mentioned Matt Gaetz. I suppose he was busy driving from Florida back to D.C. Do you suppose he had to cross through Alabama to get there? Do you wonder who might have been with him in the car? Do you imagine her age?

The one person who might find some happiness in all of this is Florida Senator Marco Rubio, just because no one is mentioning him for V-P, or suing him, or blaming him anymore for the decline of western swampland in his native state or in the district he works in when he and his 99 other buddies are in session.

Marco: your state's pretty whacked, and I should know. I used to drive through there all the time from my equally whacked province on my personal road to somewhere. And when I drove, I had the radio on, listening to tunes like these:

▣ AMERICAN CRISIS PLAYLIST #41 ▣

1. "**Genius of Love**," Tom Tom Club, from 1981's *Tom Tom Club*. I'm so sorry and disturbed to know anything about Matt Gaetz's "love life." I hope he hates this song. I hope he's never heard it, and please, don't think of it when you think of him. I doubt he knows what "being in heaven" with **Bootsy Collins** might mean, or exactly who **Sly and Robbie** are. And as for that "Genius" part, well...Anyway, I love this song and as offshoots of another band go, TTC is it, baby. I wonder what **Kurtis Blow** thinks? Not to mention, JAMES BROWN, JAMES BROWN.

2. "**King of Pain**," The Police from *Synchronicity* (1983). "There's a little black spot on my soul today...it's the same old thing as yesterday." Has anyone ever asked, "WWMGD?" He's only 38 years old, and so when this song was released and it "stood here inside the pouring rain," Matt was only zero years old. Really! He was born in this year and how could he have known that this song would lament his later life? His "destiny to be the...," you know. "I'm always hoping that you'll end this reign." Or his.

3. "**Burning Down the House**," The Talking Heads, from *Speaking in Tongues* (1982). **David Byrne** called and asked why I was featuring Tom Tom Club, and also why I was spending so much time talking

about Matt Gaetz when I could be inciting an insurrection somewhere, or strolling into the House chamber with a Holocaust denier? Now, technically, David Byrne doesn't have my number, but Matt Gaetz did bring a Holocaust denier as his guest to the House one fine day. Don't know if that guy was from Florida or not, but damn, they can't have everything down there, can they?

4. "**Fearless (Taylor's Version)**" from the brand new, re-thought-out *Fearless (Taylor's Version)*, a redone collection of her old stuff. I suppose Matt Gaetz thought he was fearless when he drove from Florida to Wyoming to speak against **Liz Cheney**. Liz didn't seem so bothered, though, but then, she hadn't been scoring for her fellow congress-people her sexual conquests, or showing a photo array of the best and brightest and most underage. Not saying anyone really did this, but I did read about it in the news, a place I don't consider fake but definitely fearless.

5. "**Y Control**," Yeah Yeah Yeah's from 2003's *Fever to Tell*. "My winner's out of control." But MG was never "my" winner. Isn't it funny that MG is half of MAGA? I used to be able to add, subtract, and even multiply fractions. Maybe divide them, too, but it's been a long time, and I really am a bit timid to relive those glory days with Mrs. Wilkinson. I think a healthy debate would pit MG against Karen O. She'd kill him, and that Y thing would fade on off.

6. "**A Girl Like You**," The Young Rascals from *Groovin'* (1967). There's so much to write about here, to say to the one you love, right Matt? Primo on the word "girl." Now, I never double-dated with Tucker Carlson, and as far as Tucker seems concerned, maybe Matt didn't either. It's so hard for me to imagine scenarios when I sympathize with Tucker, so thanks for this one Matt. Is anyone checking ID's? I bet the Rascals are regretting their adjective right now.

7. "**Family Friends**," Wild Pink from 2021's *A Billion Little Lights*. This past Friday night, my wife and I gathered with some old friends—people we met in lamaze class 32 years ago, when Matt Gaetz was only six. Are you wondering whether I'm losing my mind? We sat out on our lovely porch and talked about those old days. We showed pictures of our babies, when they were babies, and wondered how so much time has sifted through us. They drove down from upstate New York where they now live on 45 acres of gorgeous land. I won't spill their route down here, but I can promise you one thing...

8. "**Love is a Losing Game**," Amy Winehouse from 2006's *Back to Black*. I know she had addictions and demons, but I think she gave us so much in this song, and really, in the entire album. Listen to how easily she slides along the notes, how her voice expresses what pain really is. I don't profess to know how love treated her, or who treated her in and out of love, but when I listen, I think of all who likely took advantage of her. The "her"; sadly, is ubiquitous.

9. "**Love's Unkind**," Donna Summer from *I Remember Yesterday* (1977). Back in 2008, I was standing on the outside of the inside of the **Prague airport**—a station that both Donna Summer and Kafka would understand. It was 5:30 in the morning, and I was ready to fly home from my first ever Creative Nonfiction workshop. Through the airport's sound system, I caught this tune—a sound I hadn't heard in twenty years or so. I remembered those words quoted, sort of, above, and then when I could get to a computer, I looked them up, Googled them if indeed Google existed then. I really don't remember. Anyway, love is unkind to some, as we know. But really, it's not the love that feels or acts. It's the one who's sporting the **Eraserhead** haircut.

10. "**I Saw Her Standing There**," The Beatles, from *Please Please Me* (1963). "She was just...And you know what I mean." Is this a cheap shot? Only time, Politico, and other news items will tell. We'll be listening, and oh-so-judging, Matt.

Things were looking way up at this point. I gave a virtual reading from my latest book—*Secrets I'm Dying to Tell You*—which had been published the previous Covid summer, and I got to meet many new friends from The Riff online. So much fun to mix old friends and new, and to see them all on my computer screen—the next best thing to in person.

And Derek Chauvin's trial started. The idea of breathing, something we all take for granted, filled me and I hoped for a just and speedy and non-violent period for this trial.

Blake Bailey made some news, too. Sad to think that knowing and writing about Phillip Roth could lead to this, but the company you keep is a thing.

Oh, and Ransomware attacked an eastern oil pipeline and a guy from my home state blamed it on Biden. Sure, right. Who said the crisis was over?

We also reached the end of another school year, and though I chose not to participate in live graduation, I did make a special playlist for the graduating seniors I had taught, dedicating specially-curated songs to them. Feeling fully vaccinated but still not secure, I even met one of these students for coffee—and she gifted me with a specially-curated rock she found.

Rock. And. Roll.

Musically speaking, this period was heavily influenced by The Handsome Family, Canned Heat, Taylor Swift, Kid Cudi, Middle Kids, The Clash, Brandi Carlisle, Led Zeppelin, The Black Pumas, Howlin' Wolf, The Steeldrivers, John Lennon, Patti Smith, Teenage Fanclub, Dead or Alive, Bowie, Billie Eilish, and Against Me!

It used to be that words like "virtually" were considered "weasel words" by logicians, meaning that sentences like "We were virtually there," indicated that we really were NOT "there," wherever "there" is. The weasel is in the "virtually": it masked the reality and most people would read through it as if it wasn't really in the sentence.

For the past year, of course, virtual is the new real, or normal, or whatever life seems to be.

I say all of this because by the time you read this new playlist series offering—#42, can you believe it?—my virtual reading will be done. I've eaten a couple of Gaba Calms this morning, as I try not to let nerves and anxieties interfere with my excitement for the event. But it's about as perfect a day here in upstate Carolina as spring can offer: temp in the 70's, blue skies broken up by the non-threatening clouds. There's still sadness and violence and trials in our land, and a refusal of some to accept ideas of racial/gender equality, of harmony triumphing over perceived, suspicious differences.

And there's still music, bringing us joy, perhaps more sadness of the melancholic kind, and inspiration for writing, cooking, or preparing for a virtual book launch.

I feel sure that this playlist will include a song that's been on the list before—a first, I think—but necessary because in the virtual event tonight, or last night, I will speak/or did speak of some songs that played a core role in the essays about place and friendships and grief that I wrote and am reading from.

So, not feeling so full of crisis today, I offer these ten tunes so our grooves will be perpetual, endless, and for as long as we want or can, in sync.

1. "**Caring is Creepy**," The Shins, from *Oh, Inverted World* (2001). A rediscovery, at least for me. Diving into the backlog of Shins' tunes, I found this one again. Once, an old friend was dating a woman—his first relationship in forever, he said. The four of us took in Jonathan Demme's film *Something Wild* (starring Melanie Griffith, Jeff Daniels, and Ray Liotta). I remember film critic David Edelstein referencing the film as "Blue Velcro," referring to another violently disturbing film that came out shortly before. So my friend, let's call him GEORGE, told me sometime later that his girlfriend didn't care for my wife and me because we were "too nice," and she didn't trust us. I won't name her here, but you know, Katherine, caring isn't so creepy, unless you want it to be.

2. "**By Now**," Danielle Durack from 2021's *No Place*. Forgive me for forgetting which one of you Riffers turned me on to Danielle and her wistful and longing voice (Was it you Kevin Alexander?). I understand how she thinks her loss, her heartbreak, should be over by now. I was corresponding this morning with my former and now retired therapist, and he mentioned his new cat Solomon, but also the loss of three cats in the past year. And it never takes much provoking or evoking for me to remember our beautiful cat Morgan, gone now almost three years. The cat my daughter found/rescued in her high school's parking lot. The good thing: we never get over love, and as my then therapist said, "Animals teach us how to love." So whatever I thought, that I'd be over this loss by now, I'm not, because it's the love that lingers, that comes on so strongly.

3. "**Mainstream Kid**," Brandi Carlisle, from 2015's *The Firewatcher's Daughter*. "Your revolution is in the way of my confusion." Holy F**k can she sing. The mainstream isn't so bad when songs like this one can kick our collective asses. I suppose I've lived most of my life in the

mainstream, though there have been a few tide pools, eddys, or dams along the way that have driven me underground. What do you think: is tripping while viewing *The Rocky Horror Picture Show* for the first time, (back in 1978) mainstream? Damn Kevin (not you Kevin), I didn't know you could wear panty hose and garters so well.

4. "**Immigrant Song**," Led Zeppelin, from *Led Zeppelin III* (1970). I don't have much to say about this song, except that it sounds cool following Brandi's tune, and that my friend Fred Wallace was the first person I know to have the record, back when we were fourteen. Was THIS mainstream? Fred had the most enormous sound system of any kid I knew, and you know, when you want to crank this song up in your good friend's basement bedroom, no one can stop you or tell you anything about how uncool you might be in those days before either of you had tried marijuana or knew about Rocky Horrors.

5. "**Coffin Nails**," Lucero, from 2021's *When You Found Me*. Until this record, I hadn't given Lucero its proper due. I love this song, the singing's rawness, but even more, that lovely piano coming in during the vocal pauses. Sounds like these help us see that trying to define/label genre is a losing game, that is, if you need to be definitive, because can't you hear all the echoes of Blues and Country and Rock and Folk and even sounds farther back? We're so focused on the coffin that we lose sight of what binds and fastens it. And us.

6. "**Fast Car**," The Black Pumas, from 2020's *Black Pumas Deluxe*. It's hard to improve on Tracy Chapman's original, but I think they do it more than justice. I love the pacing here, not so fast, making us consider that we can be calm as life speeds by. Shit, did you know that I'm turning 65 in July? I get offers from Medicare every day. Not there yet, but moving, moving. Slow down, don't move so fast. Have to make this moment last. Anyway, go for it Pumas, and I'm ready for your next record, if that's not too fast for you.

7. **"Pursuit of Happiness,"** Kid Cudi (featuring MGMT) from 2009's *Man on the Moon: The End of Day*. There are moments when I think everything I need to know, I've learned from *SNL*. Not that they get everything right, but they had Kid Cudi as musical guest last week, and I pursued some happiness with him. Using MGMT when they were at their critical height was a good move here, but again, his vocals are so ably supported by the sound, and I want more...happiness and joy.

8. **"Back Down South,"** Kings of Leon, from *Come Around Sundown* (2010). I was talking to my brother-in-law last night about why I love the South—why it feels like my place and my home. "It's all the music, the literature, the folk art and wisdom," we both concluded. He realized that he's been "a southerner" for over forty years now, originally hailing from California. I have barely ever left; depending upon how you think of D.C, you could say that I've never left. I don't love everything about this region, of course: the only way I'm Red is when we're talking of the Crimson Tide, though there were a few moments years ago when I felt red in that hip, commie sort of way. Anyway, this song and the Kings in general mean more to me than I can say. They sing me home.

9. **"My Sister's Tiny Hands"**, The Handsome Family, from *Through the Trees* (1998). I published a piece in our sister pub Songstories yesterday on this song and the soundtrack it is also instrumental in: **https://medium.com/songstories/tiny-hands-and-wrong-eyed-jesuss-**. It's so sad, such a haunting remembrance, and the Handsomes are all I want to play on my porch, as day turns to night and as I think back on those who made me. Songs of the personal apocalypse, as reading Harry Crews and Flannery O'Connor bring us to bear/bare.

10. **"Goin' Up the Country,"** Canned Heat, from 1969's *Living the Blues*. Back in '69, when I was barely musically alive, a guy I knew— let's call him STAN—disparaged this song as only thirteen year-old

guys can do. It was singer Al Wilson's voice that he most hated, and as you and I know, distinctive voices are key elements in any sound. The same guy later disparaged Queen's "Bohemian Rhapsody," so clearly, he didn't know then—and does he today?—what music is: GOOD MUSIC. So, I wrote a story using this title, and I hope I'm forgiven by poor old Al Wilson, who's been gone for decades now. It's the story I'm reading tonight from my collection, *Secrets I'm Dying to Tell You.* The story isn't about death, though dying comes into play. It's more about traveling, which, as I think about it, amounts to the same thing. It's the country I'm going to know.

You might think that the bleeding has stopped. Former and now disgraced Minneapolis police officer Derek Chauvin was found guilty this week in the killing (lynching?) of George Floyd. I'd breathe a sigh of relief, but I'd rather accent that I CAN breathe, and for most of my life, have been able to do so without worry that if I do something wrong (I never intentionally passed bad checks, though I didn't always check to count the total funds in the account on which I was drawing!) I'll be stopped, arrested, and forced to lie on a city street until the ones apprehending me decide that I'm no longer much of a threat.

The sentencing is still to come, but I'm thinking that for the next 30 or 40 years, Chauvin ought to be kept in some little room, his TV set to eternal "Play," while an endless loop of the last ten minutes of George Floyd's life courses past his eyes at maximum volume. With maybe a five-minute break every three hours to use the facilities, knowing what awaits him upon his return.

And then, there's the case of Blake Bailey, someone who should be held down until he confesses all he's done. Not that I want anyone to put his knee on Bailey's throat for nine minutes, but I wish he had to face all the women he's harmed, and atone to them. He's apparently worried about what the news will do to his wife and young daughter, and much the same way I thought about Brett Kavanaugh's daughter, I wonder and fear what it has and will be like to grow up under Bailey's parental auspices, especially knowing that at age thirteen, others in her image were being groomed for sick altercations to come.

I bought his damn biography maybe five days before the stories started emerging.

Now, I want to stick my largest, sharpest butcher's knife through it.

Not that, you know, I'm a violent sort.

Chauvin will still get a million-dollar pension, and Bailey still has whatever he got in advances from W.W. Norton.

And half the country still refuses to get the vaccine, while the former OP is moving his golf services up to his Bedford club in New Jersey soon, because Mar-a-Lago closes in the summer due to the excessive humidity. I can't make shit like this up because I haven't had enough coffee yet, and the dogs are screaming to be walked.

Howlin' is more like it.

And speaking of howlin' let's turn now to some tunes that won't evoke crisis, won't dismiss or make us forget all the pain out there, but that might put you into a mood for intervention and maybe even some good barbecue—because my grill is open today, I'm very privileged to be here, and I'm more than ready and inspired.

AMERICAN CRISIS PLAYLIST #43

1. "**You Gonna Wreck My Life**," Howlin' Wolf, from *More Real Folk Blues* (1967). I was trying to find an appropriate Wolf song to kick this off, and it took about three seconds to locate this one. When you consider blues, folk, and rock voices, why would you look anywhere else but here? The Blues have always been about what we do to each other, *how* we do each other wrong. Given the period/era in this country when this form took off—when segregation and lynchings still ruled—it's still sadly fitting for us now. The music, the voice, always will be, too. The conditions? We'll see.

2. "**Crawling Kingsnake**," The Black Keys, from an album coming out next month: *Delta Kream*. When I saw that they had a record coming out soon, I thought about shouting from my porch a thank you to all who hear and whom I hope will hear. And then I listened. I love how

they keep pushing deeper, into blues, a howling lead guitar, hoping to move us out of this place and into some other dank hole. The holes must be felt so that we understand what crawling out feels like, too. So I can't wait for the rest of this...and is a tour coming, Patrick?

3. "**Weightless Agai**n," The Handsome Family, from *Through the Trees* (1998). "This is why people OD on pills, and jump from the Golden Gate Bridge. Anything to feel weightless again." Are you haunted yet? I am, and even though my life is fairly sublime, Sunday night is approaching, my daughter will leave town again, and we'll sit outside tonight, listening to all the tree frogs and owls, and I'll wonder why it's gone this way—this time, this life. And I'll play more of The Handsome Family, because I can't get enough.

4. "**Sticks That Made Thunder**," The Steeldrivers from *The Steeldrivers* (2008). Recommended to me by one of my students as she listened last Sunday night to my virtual reading and the songs I chose to ground a theme and center my guided audio tour through that old "S-Town" back home. She wrote me that my Canned Heat selection reminded her of this, and she's right. The music is sweet, but the singing and the lyrics take us to some other place, to "the ones who'll never return." I appreciate sensitive listening and reading, so thank you Kiersten!

5. "**On the Road Again**," Canned Heat, from *The Very Best of Canned Heat* (among other places), in a 2005 re-release. Another fine selection including Al Wilson's voice, but with a relentless rhythm taking us farther and farther from what we know. and onto roads worth traveling. I hate that this band seems so forgotten, so unappreciated. So show them some love even though they'll likely not hear you—the ones left, that is. As for Al, he'll hear you every time from the vapors above.

6. "**Breathe (Taylor's version, feat. Colbie Caillat)**," from the re-released *Fearless* (2021). I woke up this morning, thinking about my playlist and how to find songs that spoke to George Floyd and the horrible way he died. And since my daughter and I were discussing Ms. Swift last night and how listening to this tune, this album, took her back to high school, I think the song and its theme got wedded to my subconscious, so then I saw it this morning, again, and almost didn't know that I had been searching for it for so long.

7. "**Place Names**," Nick Waterhouse from 2021's *Promenade Blue*. It's a cool, almost upbeat tune—"I never cry on cold days, am never set for the big change"—is it Nick's voice, his style, or is it those background voices, the strings? Where are we? What year? What era? My high school? Do we remember the places that caused us to veer, to swerve, to cry on cold and warm days when we couldn't get straight, couldn't understand why people fled when other people who looked unlike them appeared? And speaking of *Them!*...have you watched it yet (Amazon Prime)?

8. "**Another Place, Another Time**," Jerry Lee Lewis, from 1967's *Another Place, Another Time*. "Any place would be so much better than that lonely room of mine." I thought about including The Killer's hit, "**Breathless**," but I don't want to be accused of beating an old horse, so listen to it, too, if you want. But I love the country killer, and remember when he'd show up on *Hee Haw*, lantern adorning his piano, and I'd ask my daddy who that was. And Daddy would look at me like one of us was crazy.

9. "**Cry to Me**," Solomon Burke from 1964's *Rock 'N Soul*. "When your baby leaves you all alone, and no one calls you on the phone...." I wonder which radio station in my hometown played this song back in '64. WENN? WJLD? WVOK? How far did it cross over? How do we manage to forget such a voice, or did we ever hear it? Shit man, no one

in my house played such stuff, and in that way of complaining about the past that I know I'm guilty of, I have to ask why? Though I know I'll get no answer, or the same one as ever. Got it now, though, and it's definitely not too late.

10. "**Wonderful World, Beautiful People**," (1969) Jimmy Cliff from *Wonderful World, Beautiful People*. So let's end on a positive note, the first reggae song I ever heard, back when I was thirteen, riding home from school with my mom and my friend Robert. I didn't recognize the sound, the background, but I knew I loved it. My nature sang out, even though we were supposed to be entering that brooding stage, Robert and I. I guess we brooded, and then secretly sang along to this one whenever we could. And I'll do so now, too, despite everything in the outer zones.

The pill I took last night to induce sleep seems to work better after I awaken in the morning. Now, I want to fall asleep, whereas last night I kept hoping the magic substance would kick on in. Eventually it did, since I remember looking out past the treed-sky and then...nothing.

I hate being reliant on pills, but at some point, sleeplessness takes its toll, and so, here's to another few nights depending on a bottle left over from my mother's stash. Don't worry: my wife looked these over and pronounced them "safe." Still, I wonder about my inheritance, what we "copped" when looking through all the stored items in my mother's cabinets, drawers, and refrigerator.

We even kept back a few "special" pills prescribed by hospice toward the end. Don't tell, though, because I already went through enough with that agency.

What does all of this have to do with rock and roll? With the "music [that will] save our immortal soul?" Well, this:

My late night read over the past week is **David Mitchell**'s 2020 novel *Utopia Avenue,* about a rock band by the same name that rises from the dirty streets of London into something like fame, circa 1968. I should probably be reading the novel when I'm more alert, because Mitchell has a way of hiding patterns in his prose, and one of these comes in the way the four bandmates conceive their songs. Sometimes you see them composing the few lines that will anchor their latest hit. At other times, though, Mitchell will have a band member see or feel something, and you know that out of these images something new—and you get to play the game of which line will be the one—will eventually find its way to a studio and then to a vinyl pressing.

And though this is fiction and no band named Utopia Avenue exists (or does it?), the group runs into real rock stars like **Lennon and Bowie, Brian Jones and the cryptically aloof Syd Barrett.** What a scene, and as I said to Rob Janicke and Noah Levy over a fun Skype call, this is one of the periods of life that I wish I had been born into, for if I have to be awake for long stretches, seeing that London "Mod" scene as it was would make me enjoy my perpetually-opened eyelids.

When those eyelids of mine officially open for business these early mornings, I brew my Atlas, or Grounds for Hounds, or Red Rooster coffee and have an early read, which at this moment is **Laura Jane Grace's** *Tranny*. Laura Jane appeared on Trevor Noah's show a couple of years back, and I'm sorry it's taken me so long to enter her punk world. Or post-punk, or now post-post punk world. Her band is **Against Me!** and you'll hear a tune from them in just a bit. My only problem with my two daily reads is that they blur, and so I wonder sometimes who's real and who's not? Who has transformed and who hasn't? And...what would David Bowie think of either or both of these reads? At other times, I'm reminded of Joyce's last novel, *Finnegans Wake*, which, if you don't know, is a dream, or structured like one, because the last word on the last page is "the," and the first word on the first page is "riverrun," and if your bent is to connect all dots before you leave, then here you go: no beginning, no middle, and no ending.

Just the endless loop.

And for the obligatory political comment: after President Biden's address a few nights ago, my current state's (and by state, you know what I mean) junior senator, Tim Scott, got on the air to proclaim that "America is not a racist country," which might sound funny in a David Mitchell novel, but not so funny when you look around at your segregated neighborhoods and the ongoing wars about whose lives matter. But okay Tim—whatever it takes to keep you in dutch with those who watch over you as you sleep.

If I were going to start a punk band, I might call it "**Tim Scott's Mouth**," because whatever emerges from there makes me angry, makes me want to be an anarchist, and makes me want to rage against these stupid reality machines.

I guess I'm fully awake now, and so on to this week's music.

AMERICAN CRISIS PLAYLIST #44

1. "**All I Really Want**," Alanis Morissette, from 1995's *Jagged Little Pill*. "Do I stress you out?" Patience, deliverance—what do I really want? It's the pill talking, for sure. I remember when my friend Mickey told me he had been listening to this album because it helped him bond with his angry teenage daughter. I didn't know then what he meant, but a few years later, I would. Anger in teens isn't pretty, but when it's channeled, we all learn something about patience, deliverance, and maybe even creativity. For instance, my daughter delivered all the drawings for my books, and she's on the verge of buying her first house. "All I really want is some patience, peace, now...a wavelength... some justice." Check, check, check, check.

2. "**Fools**," Van Halen, from *Women and Children First* (1980). Now, I'm not certain who the fools VH are singing about on this one, but I would add some footnotes for them if they were ever to ask or listen to me. Poor Eddie, I didn't pay him enough mind, and I'm sorry for that. The harmonies here—not something you immediately think of in hard rock outfits—kill me.

3. "**Your Power**," Billie Eilish, from 2021's *Happier Than Ever*. A sharp break from the above two tracks, but whenever I see a new BE song, I have to listen. This might help me drift off but then I'd likely be listening too hard to drift. There's a park off Highland Avenue that I keep seeing—a night scene, with the avenue bending and twisting around that park. I see the Italian eatery nearby, and the little boys

playing beneath certain trees. I see this scene so often and I can't explain why it speaks to me so strongly. Just the images, I suppose, and the dreams I sometimes, or never, have.

4. "**Transgender Dysphoria Blues**," Against Me! from 2014's *Transgender Dysphoria Blues*. As Laura Jane sings, as the guitars transport me out of me and into another world, I want to participate in these rhythms and keep them pounding. You can still hear the punk sounds they emerged from, but so much else has entered their music, their world. Singing and playing about change, they wake me up. We look back, we should, because we all change in our many ways. Constantly and rhythmically. Listen to the other tunes on the record, and see if you can resist all that's inside you.

5. "**Lover Come Back (to me)**," Dead or Alive, from 1985's *Youthquake*. Somewhere in 1985, our musical train came to yet another crossroads, and we were wondering how we could take multiple tracks at the same time: rock, techno, glam, hip-hop, disco. Our mistake was thinking that only one or two ways led to departure. Have they ever? The transgenre-ed/gendered ways of the music world kept many of us running to catch up, to jump on, and so when Dead or Alive popped up on the poppy MTV playlists of early rock video, I kept wondering where they'd been all my dreamy life.

6. "**Rebel, Rebel**," David Bowie from *Diamond Dogs* (1974). An anthem of sorts, I can't believe I've waited this long—44 weeks—to attach it to a playlist. I first heard this song a few months after first seeing a live drag show in a bar called "Chances R." In Birmingham, Alabama, of all places. Androgyny was a word back then, but most of us didn't understand what it meant, and even more, when they saw Bowie, not only didn't understand, but wanted to fight whomever they could to

keep this from appearing before their very eyes. "You've torn your dress, your face is a mess." Beauty comes in many forms—"how could they know?" indeed. And, I wanted his hair to be mine.

7. "**Career Opportunities**," 1977, from The Clash's first record, *The Clash*. Just go with it: "Career Opportunities, the one that never knocks, every job they offer you's to keep you off the dock." In 1977, I was way too comfortable and so didn't notice or cotton to punk when I did notice—not then, anyway. God, who listened to The Clash in 1977 Alabama? Who played them on the radio? I thought I was "far out" by championing Bowie...and then, a revolution of sorts hit me. Hard core.

8. "**Under the Milky Way**," The Church from 1988's *The Very Best of The Church*. The night sky, as my old friend Guy keeps pointing out and writing about, keeps me staring at all I can't understand. Another old friend, Les, pointed this song out to me in a mixtape he made for our ongoing dialogue about friendship and musical taste. Soaring above me, the guitars and synths swirl and I think I'll just lie down on our lush fescue grass tonight and stare. Our stars, our universe. "Wish I knew what you were looking for. Might have known what you would find."

9. "**Friction**," Television, from 1977's *Marquee Moon*. I've had this tune on my personal playlist, playing it early, late, and in the middle of *Finnegans Wake* whenever I find room to allow the waking and dreaming selves to merge. I can't imagine what it would have been like to walk into an east village club back in those 70's and find Tom and the boys playing something like this. I was 21 in 1977, and so it could have happened, but my first trip to New York wouldn't happen for another four years, and what I remember most about that ride was driving at night through the Park, getting to an east side theater to see the Polish film, *Man of Iron*. Nothing makes much sense, until it does.

10. "**Break It Up**," Patti Smith, from *Horses* (1975). She was always a poet, and the only person I knew who bought *Horses* when it was first released was Jimbo, one of my three oldest friends. Do you still have this record, Jimbo? And if so, is it a first pressing, and do you know what it's worth, and do you know how I remember being with you at that old record store near Highland AV, and I wondered about your taking such a chance on Patti and punk, and how friendship requires us to stretch and ask each other to come along and remember these scenes, even if I've forgotten certain details? Exactly what the f**k was the name of that store? Oh yeah: **Charlemagne Records**.

Covid-19 has wreaked havoc on our lives in more damn ways than any of us can count. I won't go into the people we've lost, some of them close, some of them so far away. In my family, things are stable, and we've managed to get through this so far without serious illness, though some of us did have mild-to-moderate symptoms.

I have taught from home since April 2020, and I'm wondering what standing in a classroom again will feel like. This past year, I've taught from my writing study while my wife has seen clients from our basement studio or on the back porch, all climate permitting. We meet together for lunch every day at 12:30, and I'll miss that part of our lives come September.

What I've missed from this past year, though, is that personal interaction with college students, because discussion-based classes about literature and writing work best in-person. For all its benefits and graces, Zoom cannot reproduce that atmosphere, that vibe of discovering just who "**Joe Christmas**" is, and how/why his grandfather hates him, and how/why he becomes a victim of a truly sadistic lynching.

Of course, not everything is such a downer, but I do lean toward the darker truths.

And so, to make this all stranger, worse, I am not participating in our graduation ceremonies. I suppose I could and it would all be fine, but standing/sitting so close to anyone these days isn't a comfortable reality. I know I'll re-enter that world soon enough, but the sooner won't come before these students pass on into a newer world, not that so-called "real world," a phrase that seems so demeaning to me because college is real and there'll be no other experience quite like it. Please never doubt that when a group of people sits together discussing why a town like **Maycomb, Alabama**, would tolerate its

"Bob Ewell" while sentencing its "Tom Robinson" to die, and then watches a video about Emmett Till or examines closely the footage of a violent insurrection that is as much about Race as it is anything else, **REALITY happens**. And maybe it's all depressing, but it's right before us, too, and we should look closely and determine who we are as we embark on another phase in our real lives.

So, I'm dedicating this playlist to those students I've taught, mentored, and loved for the past few years—the ones I won't get to teach again, but who can always write or call just to chat about the world, and whatever book or film or new song they simply have to share with me.

And I'll be doing the same.

So here's to all of you: Matt, Ashley, Amber, Hyland, Alex, John, MK, Madison, Julia, and...Riley (man, I LOVE "Bessie!"). Find yourself, your song, below, because they've been curated with you in mind.

Have a good, good life.

🔲 AMERICAN CRISIS PLAYLIST #45 🔲

1. "**Questions**," Middle Kids from 2021's *Today We're the Greatest*. "And I got questions, and you got answers, and I'm not sure if they're fact or fiction... and I'm not sure if they're even worth asking." Think about it: a wise Jewish person once said that the answer to every question lies within the question itself. A new song to be with you on this road, and thanks to **Jimmy Kimmel** for featuring them last week. Keep asking, seeking, and discovering who you are and what you really want to do and be. It's all out there, and in there, too.

2. "**Stop!**" Against Me! from 2007's *New Wave*. The waves will never stop, and if Virginia Woolf wasn't the first to know this, at least she copyrighted the title. Newer waves pursue us, and every now and then, listen: a pause, a breath is all you might need. Though while

listening here, stopping is impossible. Play this at max volume and make sure whoever is with you understands what you need to do, or else, you'll be stopping for all the wrong reasons. Nothing is so urgent that you have to jump before you're ready. Just ask Lara Jane.

3. "**Freedom Train**," Lenny Kravitz, from 2009's *Let Love Rule*. Psychedelic rock guitar lovers unite. You have only your ears to lose, but not your freedom. I love how Lenny slides into various guises, allowing us to go on these riffed rides. So many styles to embrace, so much music to catch us when we fall. My wife said today that she read that someone else said, "The opposite of war is not peace...it's civilization." Just thought I'd toss that one in here.

4. "**This Is a Mean Old World to Live In**," Sister Rosetta Tharpe from 1962's *The Gospel Truth*. At the crossroads of gospel, soul, the blues, and a new rock vision, the good sister lays it all on the line. To know her is to love her, and you don't have to be particularly religious, or religious at all, to appreciate what's going on in her anguished, yet trusting voice. Listen to that steady rhythm, too, and see if you don't feel healed in some other way.

5. "**Slow Motion**," Blondie, from 1979's *Eat to the Beat*. I think I wrote once before about how this record scared a grad school friend of mine back in '79, when we were first figuring out how we fit into that new world of professors who were mainly more interested in our/their research. I played Blondie pretty regularly anyway, because there had to be an antidote to translating 500 years of Middle English and classifying it according to genre, and then writing papers on prosody. So I ask you, why on earth would Blondie be scary?

6. "**Motion Sickness**," Phoebe Bridgers on her first record, *Stranger in the Alps* (2017). "I hate you for what you did, and I miss you like a little kid." I'm just hoping that the stranger here is not one of those serial killers whose story I keep being advised to watch on Netflix. So, here's

another reason to slow down every once in a while, because not much can stay in constant motion—your career, your love, your place of being. I didn't know much about Phoebe until last year, and now....

7. "**Good Fortune**," PJ Harvey, from 2000's *Stories from the City, Stories from the Sea*. One of my two favorite Polly Jean songs. Fortune is such an interesting concept. Do we find it, make it, lose it, ever have it at all? How different is it from fate, or luck, or destiny, or even some concept of divine sojourning? You know, the love we take is equal to... Anyway, if I wish you good fortune, you know that I mean: make your decisions wisely, and try not to let life just happen to you while you're busy making other plans.

8. "**Debbie Denise**," Blue Oyster Cult from *Agents of Fortune* (1976). Someone in your life is bound to love a song like this, and as I keep reading rock memoirs like *Tranny*, I understand that for many, they're always seemingly waiting for the one they love to return. Don't wait on anyone else, please. Life roaming in a band is one thing. Love, another. "She'd wait by the window, so bitterly." Of course.

9. "**Hollywood Boulevard**," Big Audio Dynamite from *#10, Upping Street* (1986). Mick Jones had the beats and had a lot of help from his post-punk, reggae, and techno friends. Something happened to him, but he finds his way into other's records as if he was only ever meant to be a supporting character. For all of Hollywood, though, supporting players were backbones. For what would *Gone With the Wind* have been without **Hattie McDaniel**? And long live Chadwick Boseman (R.I.P).

10. "***We Go On***," The Avalanches (with Cola Boyy and Mick Jones), from 2020's *We Will Always Love You*. *See?* The main refrain is from a minor hit by The Carpenters, back in the 70's. I remember it well, and used to sing along when no one else was looking/listening, or so I thought. Anyway, we do. We will. I will.

226

So that didn't take long. Just let some group use its ransomware to disrupt the gas pipeline running through the southeast, and some motorist or tourist, or hell, maybe he's actually a resident of **Folly Beach, SC** (oh what a horror his life must be), decides that it's all the President's fault and, to paraphrase this nut, supposedly nothing like this happened under the previous administration. Nope, all was good and well then, nothing disruptive in our lives, our country, our world last year at this time, or the previous year, or the one before that.

Someone should write a song or two about this guy, an idea I can't take credit for, but which I'll gladly attribute to Keith R. Higgons who wrote this story yesterday:

Idiot Wind The modern Republican Party is a clown car of sycophants and racists.medium.com

So yeah, where are the protest songs we so badly need? The ones that will shame these assholes into understanding that "**We don't need no Mussolini, we don't need no orange plague. No diet coke buttons in our west wing. Republicans leave us the hell alone...**

HEY REPUBLICANS! LEAVE US THE HELL ALONE."

Seriously, what would Eisenhower or Goldwater, Rockefeller, or even Nixon say about this bunch?

Am I going to have to turn on the news again and double-up on my blood pressure meds? Or break down and have a couple of those imported gummy bears? Heading out to the CBD store soon. Any requests?

In better news, I used some recently found/distributed funds to buy a new turntable and speakers. Once we redo my study, I'm back to playing vinyl, which means I'm back to haunting my local record store here in Greenville, **Horizon Records,** and since my birthday arrives in two months to the day (if this is the 15th, that is), I'm ready for some treats. Any recommendations?

In the meantime, here's a list of ten songs I've been cranking out almost non-stop in the past few days. They aren't protesting too strongly, but they are a nice pause for reflection, and a good way to spend another weekend, hopefully, not stuck on some roadside pining for gas. Oh, and be on the lookout for **If Ever You're Listening**, who's going to send us all some love very soon.

▣ AMERICAN CRISIS PLAYLIST #46 ▣

1. "**Runaway Train,**" Soul Asylum from *Grave Dancers Union* (1992). "It seems no one can help me now, I'm in too deep, and there's no way out." Yeah, it does seem like we should be getting somewhere, and maybe we are. The CDC just announced that we can go mask-less (I can go where no one else can go) in closed places. I'm jumping on the Soul Asylum train because everyone at *The Riff* has been playing them, and back in '92, I was dancing with my baby daughter to older sounds. I'm seeing her this weekend if we make it all the way. Yep, seems like we should be getting to somewhere in Virginia (Bath County).

2. "**Changephobia,**" Rostam, from his upcoming release *Changephobia*. I know that I get fixated on certain artists, but don't we all? For the last five years, and maybe longer, I have listened to Rostam and all his iterations from his Vampire Weekend past. I have to admit, also, that change is hard for me, too. Maybe I do fear it, but I have to remind myself that we changed our guard, very legally and properly, last November, despite what Arizona Repubs might think. I get it: we really

don't know who is looming on the horizon, ready to drown us in words and lies. But we got through 2016–20 somehow, and I'm feeling fresh again. So is Rostam.

3. "**Fade Away**," Best Coast, from 2013's *Fade Away*. "People they change, and love, it fades." Sometimes I think Best Coast is simply my go-to band for when I'm blue and need something inspiring and soulful. Even when things end, we can draw something from the experience. Like, I was finishing a pretty great novel last night, **Lee Durkee**'s *The Last Taxi Driver*, and I felt that sadness when a good book ends, and for a minute I just sat in my chair—the one Max sits in when I'm gone because he recognizes all of me there—wondering why beautiful things keep passing my way, and if I can really appreciate the words that make the patterns we call art, before they fade away.

4. "**The Bottomless Hole**," The Handsome Family, from 2003's *Singing Bones*. When you fade away too far, you don't remember who you are. "I went out behind the barn and stared down in that hole. Late into the evening, my mind would not let go." This one, from another band I can't get enough of, reminds me of another novel I finished last week: **Lee Smith**'s *Saving Grace*. And speaking of endings, follow that one on out and decide if she's fading, or finding what she once had. Damn, these Lee people can write, and so can The Handsomes.

5. "**Summer Hill**," Middle Kids, from *Today We're the Greatest* (2021). Sometimes a single image can evoke all that we dream of. So imagine this summer hill. For me, it's the one out past Lakewood, heading toward McCalla near my old home in Bessemer. It's way back from the two-lane highway, and near it stands a lone tree—a tree that seems planted there by some accident we'll never understand. I never got to the hill, but I always imagined climbing it and sailing a frisbee from its peak, back in the days when summer frisbee tossing seemed not a past-time, but a destination.

6. "**The Sun Won't Shine on Me**," Teenage Fanclub, from 2021's *Endless Arcade*. Well, not if I'm standing under that tree. I just peeked at Max, who's sitting in the sun, while I write here on my shaded porch. He's looking at me, but now settles down again, warm and content. This song keeps shifting and while it's a bit melancholy, I don't feel so bad because writing these playlists certainly eases my troubled mind. I also just baked an apricot brandy pound cake again for my precious daughter. So, the sun does shine on us.

7. "**Style**," Taylor Swift from *1989* (2014). Trying to get back in the upbeat, though it won't be for long because endings are coming. I'm wondering whether this series will go on after we hit #52. How long can a crisis go on? Will it ever go out of style? You know I've been loving all this Swiftian sound, and feel the need to keep highlighting what is so good in the pop world. Soon I'll turn to **S.W. Lauden's** power pop books, and find even more upbeats. It's all about power, and speaking of which...

8. "**Your Power**," Billie Eilish from her upcoming record *Happier than Ever*. Saw her on **Colbert** this week, and she talked about how cocky she was about writing this one—how proud she was, saying that this is the greatest song she's ever written (she'll be twenty this coming December). I love how she kept calling Colbert, "Steve," and I also love that he and his producers bring out the strange and maybe the best in their guests. It was a cool video, too, and so my wife and I sat listening, and a little bit mesmerized. God only knows if this is autobiographical, or written about a friend, but in these Blake Bailey days, I take nothing for granted. Despite the exposure, the #MeToo stories aren't fading.

9. "**Where Would I Be**," Jim White from 2020's *Misfit's Jubilee.*" Where would I be if I was not myself? What would I be doing right now? Would I be an old man saying my prayers, or a nun dreaming of some football players?" Well Jim, who can really say? Jim likes to take

us into the old folds of his brain waves, wondering who we are, where we came from, and what we might be if we were alone and, "without you." It's all because he never found the Wrong-Eyed Jesus, or maybe it's that he did.

10. **#9 Dream**," John Lennon from *Walls and Bridges*. Speaking of dreams (weren't we?), my brother had this album way back in 1974 when it was first released, and the album folded out in parts, and we thought it was a true treasure, a real pleasure. He had a nice collection of all things Beatle, even a copy of *Let It Be* with the **Red Apple** label on the vinyl. I'll let him explain in the comment section what happened to his prized albums. It's a familiar story, a dream or nightmare with too many numbers attached. It might make him happy to know that I salvaged this one.

I knew the end of this series was coming. In some ways it was becoming fatiguing to write it every weekend; all routines, when they became "routine," should be examined and vacationed for a bit, I think. Also, I managed to hook up my new turntable and speakers—okay, in truth, my wife managed to hook these up, but at least I helped. Now, the music can flow as it once did, and so, look out record store (look out budget). I never want to be locked too tightly into anything, for as Shelley and Keane say,

"Everything is changing and I don't feel the same."

Is wearing a Covid mask really akin to wearing a yellow star? Do we have to negotiate and litigate this question, all because some yayhoo legislator has decided she's feeling persecuted for wanting to go around infecting others with her disease? How will history remember this epoch, or will we be remembered at all?

The good news: my wife and I celebrated our 37th wedding anniversary this year by actually going out to a restaurant, sitting outside of course, and noticing the free expressions of all kinds of love in downtown Greenville. On this same day, my daughter took me to a record store and bought me a Black Keys album for Father's Day. Count your blessings, I say.

Especially since in this period, Derek Chauvin, who deprived George Floyd's children of their father, received a 22-year sentence and then more or less expressed his condolences to Floyd's family. How you react to this news is your business, but come on. Condolences?

D-Day and Juneteenth passed again, and who noticed? Some also keep thinking that in August, the OP will rise again, like some creature from *The Walking Dead*. I think about August and how at the end of that month, I'll start teaching Holocaust literature again, and wondering how to make sense out of all of this. "This much madness is too much sorrow...impossible to make it today..."

The series ended with some repeat music from PJ Harvey, Angel Olson, and other sounds from Isaac Hayes, Paul Revere and the Raiders, Against Me!, The Doors, The Turtles, the Beatles, The Who, The Tragically Hip, Sampha, Sonic Youth, The Power Station, Sly and the Family Stone, Quincy Jones, Wilco, Neil Young, The Posies, and The Raspberries.

I know summer is here because when we're out walking, Max often turns to me and asks in his inimitable doggy way,

"What the hell are we doing?"

"Well," I tell him, "we're trying to work off those hamburgers we ate for supper last night, not to mention the cream cheese we slathered on our bagel this morning. And the ice cream."

"Oh yeah," he says, and then he stops, "Ice cream???"

"Ooops."

"But couldn't we have gone earlier in the morning?"

"Right. I'm adjusting, because last week we had some days that didn't make it out of the 50's, remember?"

"No, I don't. Do you remember that my memory goes back only about fifteen minutes?"

"Well, I forget things like that because you seem so...human sometimes. Like the way you tilt your head and smile when I ask if you want to go for a walk."

"Yeah. Hey, I have a question!"

"Sure buddy, what is it?"

"What the hell are we doing?"

And so it goes as we enter the last week of May here in upstate South Carolina, 90+ degree days, and nights in the upper 60's. But wearing masks has been modified to such a degree that as hot as it feels outside, I'm ready to venture out because we might have turned this major pandemic corner.

Sadly, I still see T***p signs in the usual suspicious locations, but eventually those colors will fade as our sun begins its scorching ways.

What I'm also seeing is my brand new turntable and my two new powered speakers. My wife and I (with special help from our friend Phillip) hooked it all up this morning, and I tried out some Hank Williams and Neil Young (*Greatest Hits* for Hank, *Tuscaloosa Live*, for Neil, a concert I saw live back in the Stray Gator days, and I was only 16).

So this week, I'm venturing out to my local record store, **Horizon**, to pick up something special on vinyl. I feel like a kid on a walk with his dad. What will I buy; what memories, what penumbra?

In the meantime, I have another playlist for you, as the Matt Gaetz affair becomes weirder and the Supreme Court begins considering, again, what to do with a woman's body or, as ELP once put it, "**The Endless Enigma**."

So walk early, walk late, and make sure you and your best pal are hydrated!

▣ AMERICAN CRISIS PLAYLIST #47 ▣

1. "**Get It On**," The Power Station, from *The Power Station* (1985). I think it's possible to feel lukewarm about Duran, Duran and about **Robert Palmer**. But add Chic drummer **Tony Thompson**, and then pull guitarist **Andy Taylor** and bassist **John Taylor** out of DD, and then add Palmer and it all sounds...better. I'm not saying they kill it here, because the song goes on too long. Tight songs like this one benefit from being shorter and leaving us wanting more. Still, Thompson's intro drum cadence demands attention, and for the next three minutes, I'm standing on chairs playing the air like nobody's business.

2. "**I Wanna Be With You**," The Raspberries, from 1972's *Fresh*. Did I ever tell you about the summer when my brother and another friend of ours went to see Eric Clapton play a stadium show—an all-day event—and the opening act was the Raspberries? I tell you, they cranked those Marshall amps and had some moments in the hot July Birmingham sun. This isn't a bad follow-up to "**Go All the Way**," and Eric Carmen's voice is a true pop tone. Power pop, right S.W. Lauden?

3. "**From a Motel 6**," Yo La Tengo, from *Painful* (1993). I mentioned this song last week in another story for The Riff. Guitars are singing to me today, especially the refrains where these Hoboken guys let go. The band's name is a reference to something baseball-related. I wonder if uber fan Kathryn Dillon. knows the answer? C'mon Kathryn. I have faith. You got it!

4. "**Ashes of American Flags**," Wilco, from 2002's *Yankee Hotel Foxtrot*. "We want a good life with a nose for things, the fresh wind and bright skies to endure my suffering...." Speaking of guitars, this one keeps echoing through the waves of despair that Tweedy feels and sends out to us. Yesterday, I passed a house in rural Virginia that had a Confederate battle flag and an American flag in adjoining windows. Why does the latter need the former? Whose ashes are we commemorating? Whose idea of a way of life? I also saw a T***p/Pence 2024 sign down that same road. I started to get out of my car and ask the guy whether he truly imagined ol Mikey was going to be asked to stem another insurrection, but my time was already up. "Speaking of tomorrow, or will it ever come?" Oh my god, this song makes me want to write about every road trip I've ever taken.

5. "**My Wife**," The Who, from *Who's Next* (1971). Sometimes I forget about the British Invasion, or in this case, its wake. John Entwistle didn't get to sing much, but here he goes, and Keith Moon follows. I used to crank this entire record on my first belt drive turntable ("I may

end up spending all my money, but I'll still be alive"). Man, 1971 feels like yesterday, but I still get excited thinking of my old copy of this one with my name in red ink written on the cover. "She's comin'."

6. "**Don't Wake Daddy**," The Tragically Hip, from 1996's *Trouble at the Henhouse*. "You teach your children some fashion sense, and then they fashion some of their own." I really love these lines, and thought about this band again after reading Jessica Lee McMillan's story on The Riff this week. And then there's the line, "Kurt Cobain reincarnated sighs and licks his face." Do with that one what you will, but as I've been reading in *Girl in a Band*, **Kim Gordon** has some tragic and hip things to remember about Kurt.

7. "**Madonna, Sean, and Me,**" (aka "**Expressway to Yr Soul**"), Sonic Youth, from *Evol* (1986). So I get it, the band here doesn't allow easy listening, and I, for one, have had my troubles with them. But that's what listening and not giving up are about. And I'll also confess that once I've read deeply into a band or performer's life, I do understand better who they are and what they're trying to do. This fairly long song has built itself into my head-fabric and while I don't know how much I understand, what I'm thinking is that if I named my band Sonic Youth, I'd want to live up to it, too. My soul's all right, after all.

8. "**Runnin' Away**," Sly and the Family Stone, from 1971's *There's a Riot Goin' On*. It's a difficult album, too, because by this point Sly wasn't feeling the everyday people vibe so much, and I don't know what we're feeling out there now. And yet, this song and "**Family Affair**" from the same album were Top 40 AM hits, and so bands that try to please us die hard in the end. I love the song's intentional tiredness, its way of saying, keep going even though there might not be anything left in your proverbial tank. I wondered back then if I was missing something, or if, unlike most of my friends, I knew something since this song has always spoken loudly to me.

9. "**Rise**," Public Image Ltd, from 1986's *Album*. I don't know, either, if "the written word is a lie," but I do know that often we're just trying to work out what we think as we write, sort of like I'm doing now. Something had to emerge from **The Sex Pistols**, anyway, and so why not this? Is this evolution, progression, or an aim for anger still seething in an 80's culture that couldn't distinguish hard rock from heavy metal, new wave from no wave, and whatever else music was attempting to be? "I could be wrong...I could be right...I could be black, I could be white." Or, I could be too tired to care, too hot to walk, and too hungry to know the difference. Anyway, we are on the rise, aren't we?

10. "**The Community of Hope**," PJ Harvey, from 2016's *The Demolition Project*. PJ likes to put us in her sweet spot, the sharp-eyed rifle sight and crosshairs of rock and hope and protest. I once wore a PJ t-shirt to an AP English grading exercise, and was besieged by other PJ fans, grading their lives away on essays regarding strange vicars in Thomas Hardy stories. Makes you wonder, and some of the writers thought vicars were aliens and then got off somehow on Channing Tatum. So, anyone thinking PJ is off should tackle AP English exams and then get back to me. And for fun, when I was ten, some guys stole both my bicycle and basketball goal, and miraculously, I got them back. The alley in back of our house deserves a story, so....

I know. It's rude to tell other people to "shut up." My mother taught me that lesson over sixty years ago, and while I faltered in my early years, I'd like to believe I haven't used those words against anyone directly at least since I've been married, and my 37th anniversary comes up in a mere three weeks.

I can't lie and say that when I watch TV, especially news segments, that I don't scream

SHUT UP

at the top of my lungs, especially if the speaker is our former fascist president, or people in government with the last name of McConnell, McCarthy, Hawley, Cruz, and especially, Greene.

So, Mrs. Greene has likened people being forced to wear masks to Holocaust Jews being mandated to wearing yellow stars. I have no words for such blatant ignorance. **Jimmy Kimmel** showed a clip of her from a time before she was elected when she appeared before her county council, pleading that they keep statues of fallen Confederate losers from coming down.

"It's history," she said in so many words, and in other words, she said that she would like to show these statues to her kids and explain the history behind them—which, if that doesn't make you shudder and want to scream **SHUT UP** then try this on for size. She claims that if statues of Adolph Hitler and Satan (at least she understands about like minds) were erected, though she wouldn't like it (sure) she'd advocate that they stay up so she could also explain these to her kids.

I don't want to rain on her damn parade, but there are a few books on these subjects, and if she wants her kids to get educated, she might try moving out of the way and let someone who understands complexity, or even simplicity, have a go at them. Kimmel had a great line about placing statues of Satan and Hitler in Mrs. Greene's front yard so she can explain away any old time of night or day.

This is, of course, assuming that they aren't already there at her gate posts, the guards holding on to swastikas, Q flags, Confederate battle flags, and those lovely "An Appeal to Heaven" banners—all flags used in the Jan. 6 insurrection which McConnell and his mates have filibustered out of existence, or [so far] prevented a congressional commission from studying by their loose and sinister talk.

It's funny about the past. Some things we want to talk about and remember, some things we want to forget. That McConnell is the arbiter of "which is which" makes me want to vomit. So while he did call Mrs. Greene's words "reprehensible," he guards his own noxious, post-history words with nonsense and the smug assuring grin of a man who believes that whatever harm was done to the Capitol, to other human beings, and in a way, to him, too, should be consigned to some dust bin along with our loose memory of people like Timothy McVeigh, another so-called "patriot."

There. Do I feel better now? Well, not yet, so it must be time to listen to some tunes, ten ideas about words that, I hope, matter to you and help you remember some of the truer parts of our land, our culture, and ourselves.

AMERICAN CRISIS PLAYLIST #48

1. **"Everything That Happens,"** David Byrne and Brian Eno, from 2008's *Everything That Happens Will Happen Today*. A beautiful sonic gift from Byrne and Eno, but the sound is more than matched by these lyrics: "O my brother, I still wonder if you're alright...From the milk of

human kindness/from the breast we all partake/Hungry for a social contract, she welcomes you with dark embrace." They didn't know how relevant these words would become, or maybe they did realize that such worry and concern are timeless, even here, even now.

2. "**Blood on Me**," Sampha, from *Process* (2017). Thanks to **If Ever You're Listening** for bringing this record to my attention. I feel the desperation here, and though "they" aren't likely to come "for me," our household has experienced some terror.

3. "**Suddenly Mary**," The Posies from *Dear 23* (1990). "Loving," she told me "is a question of bravery." I've been having fun listening to and reading about that thing called Power Pop, aka, love. I admit to not having listened much to The Posies, but back in the '80s, a guy named Brian told me to check them out. It took only thirty-five years, but at least I haven't been filibustering. **S.W. Lauden** has some good books like *Go All the Way (with Paul Myers)* on the genre if you want to check them out as I have. So, just to be clear, politics, apparently, has nothing to do with love.

4. "**Words (Between the Lines of Age)**," Neil Young from 1972's *Harvest*. "Someone and someone were down by the pond/looking for something to plant in the lawn. Out in the fields, they were turning the soil. I'm sitting here hoping this water will boil...when I look through the window and out on the road, they're bringing me presents and saying hello...singing Words...." A guy named Jason Taylor, in **David Mitchell's** dreamy evocation of an English novel boyhood, *Black Swan Green*, comes across this song. It's almost too much for him, as it was for me when I was his age. In some ways, it still is: "Thinking your mind was my own in a dream." I got nothing to add.

5. "**My Rights Versus Yours**," The New Pornographers, from *Challengers* (2007). I keep seeing people in fancy neighborhood SUV's

bearing stickers that say, "We Love Jesus" and "My 2nd Amendment Right is my Glock." Has it boiled down to this: our rights being measured by who can and who can't own a Glock? My wife and I love to watch the BBC series "**Father Brown**." Why? Because, though we don't believe what he believes—at least the religious version— we understand that FB has everyone's rights in mind, and none of these is predicated by a Glock. And what a great band, by the way. Pornography is a right, too, right?

6. "**White People for Peace**," Against Me! from 2007's *New Wave*. "And bureaucrats engaged in debate to try to reach a resolution." I wonder where the protest songs stemming from Jan 6 are? Are the white rockers and folkies going to sit back and leave it to the rappers? And then this begs the question as to whether white people are for peace, if they can be for peace. Can we? Not that white people don't create, we do. And of course, war comes to everyone, no matter the color of our skin. Yet, yet, yet, who has waged the greater, the MOST wars? Who writes history and where is all of this heading? I saw a white person yesterday at Costco with another flag proclaiming that "T***p is still our president." Uh, No, white man.

7. "**John Wayne**," Lady Gaga, from *Joanne* (2016). Oh god, check out the lyrics, "I'm sick of their city games/I crave a real wild man/I'm strung out on John Wayne/Baby let's get high, John Wayne." The junkies, the druggies, Joan Didion, John Wayne. White culture for sure. Ol' John sold us a myth about ourselves for sure. White White White, and nothing can stop us now, or at least on the set of Monument Valley, so if you haven't, or haven't lately, do watch *The Searchers* and see another part of the myth. Or just listen to Gaga.

8. "**Love is Here to Stay**," Lou Reed from 1980's *Growing Up in Public*. "It gets proven every day/love is here to stay." Comic books, Mean Joe Green, hot dogs and gestalt therapy. Now there's a list for you.

My brother got a dog this week, a two-year old Husky/Shepherd mix named Blue. So, love is here, and they'll (he and his two sons and Blue) be joining us this week, to stay for ten days. We're excited, Max especially. Love, brotherhood, dogs. Family. And love again.

9. "**Superstar**," Sonic Youth, from the compilation *If I Were a Carpenter*, from 1994. So I've fallen back in love with this song. "Loneliness is such a sad affair," and so I want to stay engaged, but it's hard when you insist that I have to believe that the worst leader in our country's history is somehow legitimate, relevant, and a caring individual. Anyway, not to tarnish this fine song, because I want to embrace Sonic Youth over and over for making me live it all again—my own sonic youth.

10. "**It All Feels Right**," Washed Out from 2013's *Paracosm*. So I'll go ahead and shamelessly plug this other story I wrote last night about this song:

https://medium.com/songstories/it-all-feels-right-.

It might feel right, it might be right, but every day I wake up, still worrying about the cost of freedom, and how much I have, or might want to give. I think it's a good place to stop; I like to think that I know when to cash out, so have a great week. Now, "Close your eyes and think about the old times."

August.

Actually, in August we'll take our annual family beach trip to Edisto, so I don't mind August even though here in South Carolina, you might be hearing a lot of...

"It's not the heat, it's the humidity."

And really, it's BOTH.

I also won't mind that my college's opening will come very soon after that trip because I'm excited to be back in a live classroom, teaching Holocaust Lit (well, let's find a better word than "excited" for this course) and Modern Novel, which always revs me up.

No, what I do mind is hearing/reading about the expected, so-called resurrection of the OP back onto what he perceives to be his throne (you and I might call it his commode). Now, I don't for one second think that he is coming back—and man, I'm getting the whole Second Coming thing—but until August passes by smoothly, it will almost be like the slight trepidation I had when 1999 turned into 2000, and many wondered about whatever our computers might do. I wasn't really scared then either, but apocalyptic thinking can be infectious.

So, it's only the beginning of June, and while tomorrow—June 6—is D-Day, and I honor that day because it truly was a day of bravery and courage —I have to wonder where courage lies anymore, or how it lies, or how we define it and really, if we can even come close to agreeing about what it is. What was WWII all about anyway, and how does it feel to see Nazis marching in our streets today?

Will we make it through this summer together, watching, listening?

Remember, it's only music. Or rather:

It's Always Music that brings us together.

Now that I have my new turntable and speakers set up, I've been diving back into vinyl and restoring (resurrecting?) my older faves, as well as sneaking off to the record store and adding, but shh. Don't want certain people to get anxious about what's exploding on the shelves of my study!

▱ AMERICAN CRISIS PLAYLIST #49 ▱

1. "**No One Knows Me (Like the Piano)**," Sampha, from 2017's *Process*... "in my mother's home." Such a soft lament for Sampha's relationship with home, with an instrument that he's been wedded to for so many years. I remember trying to play the piano a few times, but even if I had succeeded, where were we gonna put a piano in my mother and father's home? So, I had to find another creative outlet, but I always appreciated my friends who took piano lessons across the street at Mrs. Terry's—another mother, another form of love and knowing for the kids in our neighborhood.

2. "**I've Got a Thing About Trains**," Johnny Cash, from 1970's *Hello, I'm Johnny Cash*. "Maybe I'm just a little sentimental, cause I know that things have to change." And, "I get a sad kind of feeling when I see a passenger train." It was always freight trains for me, especially hearing them go by from my bedroom window, late on a Sunday night. So lonely, so country, and yet, the only trains I've been on were connecting me from DC to New York, from Dublin to Sligo riding across Ireland, and from Dover to Paris on/in the Chunnel. What's so sad about that? Hard to say, except the loneliness is palpable and John surely knows.

3. "**Glenn Tipton**," Sun Kil Moon, from 2003's *Ghosts of the Great Highway*. More traveling, more reflecting from a haunting/haunted

record. "Cassius Clay was hated more than Sonny Liston/Some like KK Downing more than Glenn Tipton/Some like Jim Nabors, some Bobby Vinton/I like 'em all." I can't do this song justice: a lamentation about what's lost, what we loved, and what we might have done, and so those first lines speak so vividly. Mark's voice creeps up on a person, and that's fairly appropriate for this sung persona.

4. "**I Love How You Love Me**," Bobby Vinton, from 1968's *I Love How You Love Me*. Somehow I think I have to prove to you that I do like Bobby. I don't listen to him much, or at all really, but the previous song reminded me of this one, and how much my mother loved it, and truly, how much I did, too, back when I was twelve. I have it on a 45, and when I think of all that 1968 was in our world, it kind of kills me that this song was such a hit. Maybe we needed it along with "**Born to be Wild**."

5. "**My Heart Skips a Beat**," Buck Owens and His Buckaroos, from the 2016 compilation, *The Complete Capitol Singles 1957–1966*. Let's go honky-tonkin'! We had a neighbor who kept asking/threatening to take my grandmother, my "Nanny," honky-tonkin' up to The Bluebird Cafe on Highway 11. That sounded funny then, back in 1968-9; now it sounds like all I want to do: go hear a nice rock-a-billy combo pleading with us to dance, to have fun, and/or to waltz in time to slower moods. Buck was nobody's fool, either, and I'm looking for his cover of "**Twist and Shout**," now.

6. "**It Was a Very Good Year**," Herb Alpert and the Tijuana Brass, from *What Now My Love* (1966). I've written before about my parents not only buying Herb Alpert records, but also seeing Herb and the Brass live. That's maybe the coolest thing they ever did. In second place is introducing me to this sound. This was the song I'd play over and over when I was ten years old, and you can try to figure out what that says about me, then and now, because I still feel its seductive power,

its beauty, and something I never quite understood about how music transcends generations. I'm just so glad for it, though.

7. "**Honky Tonk Blues**," Hank Williams, found in many places, but try it on *Live at The Grand Ole Opry*, a compilation from 1999. So, Ma and Pa will "lay down the law" when you get home from cattin' around those honky tonks. Man, did Bessemer have a few. Anyway, I pulled out my old Hank vinyl, a two-record set called, aptly, *I'm So Lonesome I Could Cry*. Of course whenever I hear Hank I think of **The Last Picture Show**. You should, too. But even if you don't, give it a listen and think about all we lost when we lost him so early.

8. "**Oh Lonesome Me**," Neil Young from 1970's *After the Gold Rush*. My birthday isn't till next month, but my brother is in town, and when we journeyed to the record store yesterday, he decided to get me what I wanted now, because, well, because he can and he knows that pleasing me isn't so hard, but it's best done live. I plan to write more about this record soon, but now I have the 50th anniversary reissue, and I'm not feeling so lonesome, but proud. This was the first Neil record I ever owned, and I remember wondering what was going on, because I just wasn't used to this kind of lament, this voice, back when I was fourteen, though judging from what I've written above, you might not buy that.

9. "**When You Dance (I Can Really Love)**," same artist, same record, though I love it most from *Live Rust*. Because it's Neil (with help from Steve Stills, Nils Lofgren, and **Crazy Horse**), and because I love him, and because my life was changing in so many ways back then, and this record sent me veering off into stranger mental places, knowing as I did that not many people in my midst would ever like Neil, and many of them would never like me because I didn't love playing soldier or

football hero. And, I learned to dance, because, you know, when you dance....Feel the beat, the rhythm, the love!

10. "**What Goes On**," The Beatles from *Rubber Soul* (1965). How fun! How **Buck Owens**! How country! And, how **Ringo**!!! It just feels right to end with this ditty that certainly showed how playful the band could still be, and how well they knew the roots of the music they/we love. I'll admit that I didn't get why they'd do such a song, or cover Buck's "**Act Naturally**," but that was because I thought so foolishly back when I was a child that you had to keep music genres segregated, but give me a break: I lived in Alabama, after all.

So here we are at **Juneteenth**, thinking about how the previous administration wiretapped members of Congress, and me thinking that the FBI could have taught them some other tricks like wiretapping Black leaders back in the '60s to show that men were men, regardless of skin color, political persuasion, or reverence for a higher authority.

I don't know about you, but my heroes haven't always been cowboys, lawmen, soldiers, or certain state and national politicians. It's funny how we pick and choose whom to adore.

My mother loved JFK, my father believed mightily in Harry Truman, my maternal grandmother lived and died with FDR, and my paternal grandmother—on the Jewish end of things—**used to apologize for Joe McCarthy**, and then she and Dad did a hard right turn toward Nixon and later R. Limbaugh.

None of my elders knew anything about Juneteenth, or Ralph Ellison who wrote a novel with that title about a dying US Senator who attempts to understand his own life, and really American life. I remember reading Ellison's *Invisible Man* in my sophomore year of college, and thinking,

"Now here's something that's been kept from me."

Of course, others had gotten the message, had lived the message, and I was coming late, but not too late, to this particular cotillion. But then, it took HBO's *The Watchmen* to help me see that a **race massacre occurred in Tulsa, Oklahoma, back in 1921,** and I try not to be ignorant about American reality, but our history books just don't do our life justice, or at least not all of the time, or at least not if you happen to be in a minority.

Yesterday, I was reflecting on a time after some friends and I had watched Daniel Day-Lewis in 2012's *Lincoln*; one of these friends turned to me as we were exiting the theater and asked:

"Why is there no White History Month?"

"Well, you can read about history and celebrate it anytime you want," I responded.

And as a character in defrocked Woody Allen's *Crimes and Misdemeanors* proclaims,

"History is written by the winners. If the Nazis had won the war, we'd know the war and its history in a very different way," or something to that effect.

But what if we don't know certain stories? What if they're kept from us? What if we don't have enough curiosity to seek them out? What if we refuse to investigate the investigators, watch the watchmen? How will any of us be remembered?

Back to Juneteenth, and music. Let's have some soul, some funk, some deep grooves to remember that even in the midst of segregation, we could listen to sounds from places we couldn't enter, people we couldn't dine with, or for god's sakes, worship with.

The time is now, and it's so right.

AMERICAN CRISIS PLAYLIST #50

1. "**Gotta Hold On to This Feeling**," Jr. Walker and the All Stars, from *The Definitive Collection* (2008, though the single came out in 1970). I could have selected any of several of Junior's hits, including "**Shotgun**," but somehow this one was a favorite of mine back in the year I turned fourteen. I loved the sax, and thought the lyrics spoke to that elusive love I wanted to find and keep. A great song to keep you moving in the summertime swoon.

2. "**Soul Bossa Nova**," Quincy Jones, from 1962's *Big Band Bossa Nova*. Last summer, Jessica Lee McMillan did a summer challenge of Bossa Nova and other Latin-influenced music, and so I held this one over because it was so much fun to listen to and reflect that no one I knew in '62 would have owned this or cared. And I still don't understand why. So sophisticated, so smooth and tight. We forget, right, that in the advent of rock and roll, other sounds were still hitting the waves and showing us that there truly is something for all tastes.

3. "**Just for a Thrill**," Ray Charles, from *The Genius of Ray Charles* (1959). I would gladly choose this song as my last dance at any club with my wife, and when I listen to it, I wonder how the hell we have tolerated the bullshit of a land where we think someone is better than someone else just because of accidents of birth. Listen to this man sing and play, and focus on that border between love and lament. Isn't that what art is: "You made my heart stand still...well, it was just for a thrill."

4. "**Black is the Color**," Rhiannon Giddens, from 2015's *Tomorrow Is My Turn*. Rhiannon has a brand new album out this week, so if you haven't run out to celebrate National Record Store day, join me and pick up her latest. My wife and I saw her live a few years back in glorious Greer, South Carolina, so don't say that nothin' good ever happens in your home environment. The show was mesmerizing, and we were as close to her as I am to you right now. Love this tune, as it speaks to love and celebrates what is often not written about for White History Month.

5. "**Family Affair**," Sly and the Family Stone, from 1971's *There's a Riot Goin' On*. "Blood's thicker than the mud," for sure. "You can't cry cause you'll look broke down/But you're cryin' anyway because you're all broke down." In 1971, we hadn't figured out the crisis in families who lived near and below the poverty line, and guess what? We are still figuring. Who would have figured that this song would make it to the Top 40, and yet it did. I heard it often and even at fifteen, I knew we had moved far beyond "**Hot Fun in the Summertime**."

6. **"If You Need Me,"** Solomon Burke, from *Rock 'N Soul* (1964). **Peter Guralnick**, in *Looking to Get Lost*, made me a Solomon Burke fan, which is great and sad, given how old this song is, how old I am now that I've really started listening to the man, and given how some white people actually get it, write about it, and honor it. Soul, Rhythm and Blues, Funk—wherever and whenever they find it. Anyway, segregation certainly kept me on this side of the fence for a long time. No fences, no borders.

7. **"Respect,"** Otis Redding from 1965's *Otis Blue*. I understand that another artist made this song into her own, but I don't want to forget, before we get to her, that Otis did it first, and if it wasn't an anthem for him about being truly oppressed, it still spoke to an issue that had difficulty being put into practice by too many people across race and gender lines. Anyway, THAT VOICE, and those horns. Hard to ignore, though some tried, and keep listening to more from this record, including the song right after: **"Change Gonna Come."**

8. **"Good to Me As I Am to You,"** Aretha Franklin, from *Lady Soul* (1968). With a guitar solo from **Eric Clapton**, this song captures soul for me. We can hear the blues it all sprung from, the heart of loss, and an expectation of how to treat your love. Who sings like this, please tell me? I have to thank my old friend Randy Manzella for making me notice how good Aretha really sounds, and he told me back in this year, while we suffered through seventh-grade science (or at least I suffered). But who could suffer while we had this kind of soul music?

9. **"Come See About Me,"** The Supremes from 1964's *Where Did Our Love Go?* Gotta be my second favorite Supremes' song of all, since my heart will always belong to **"Someday We'll be Together,"** since for whatever reason, endings are hard to take or forget. But I love how this song builds right from the very beginning and never lets up for its two+ minutes. What a hit and it's not even the biggest song on the

record, as the title tells you. And "**Baby Love**" is there, too. This was just 1964, and the trio seemed invincible. For many of us, they were, even those of us who had to listen under the covers.

10. "**Nowhere to Run**," Martha Reeves and the Vandellas, from *Dance Party* (1965). So, if you haven't read **Andrew Grant Jackson**'s *1965: The Most Revolutionary Year in Music,* what are you waiting for? This song wasn't the biggest hit of that year, or perhaps even the group's biggest hit, but when you start thinking about the Watts riots, the Viet Nam War, and the assassination of **Malcolm X**, the title alone makes, or should make, you quiver a bit. But despite all that, the song gets inside and helps you move, even if you don't think you can dance. What's the harm in trying? And, by all means, dance with anyone you can, because life is too short to be so selective or so "discriminating."

My younger daughter in Charlotte just closed on her first house, and we've been with her as she continues to negotiate making her place over in the image she's likely envisioned for years, or maybe for her entire life. It's a first home, we continue to remind her, so it won't be perfect. Yet, knowing her, I'm reasonably certain it will be close to that.

For Father's Day, she took me to **Repo Records**, a pretty cool store in a part of Charlotte I might not be able to find again without some strict guidance. Not a huge den of records, though what they had was pretty sublime. I went into the store with three bands in mind: **The Handsome Family, Against Me!, and The Black Keys**. The day before, I had lectured my daughter— because that's what I do professionally—on the importance of having a vision of what you want before entering a record store, or else you'll flail around and end up purchasing something you likely won't listen to but once, or maybe never.

I'm thinking here of that *Grand Funk Live* record I bought back in 1970.

She had been talking about the tile for her kitchen backsplash, and after my mini-lecture, she glanced over at me, with that smile, and said,

"Yep. I already know what I want."

I'm sure she'll get it, too, though I wish I could be with her to see. The tile stores were all closed on Saturday afternoon, and good for them, though I was selfishly thinking about our own needs.

So, walking into Repo Records, I was ready. Did you know that **Against Me!** records are awfully hard to find, as are Handsome Family discs? I suppose that's not surprising, but I had harbored vague hopes. Fortunately, **The Black Keys** bin had a few choices, so I opted for

Let's Rock, which has a song I'll say more about later. And if you're wondering why I picked the Black Keys, for one thing, they're terrific and are always seeking sound changes, and for another thing, I took my daughter to see them live (opening act, **St. Vincent**) for Christmas a few years back. So, Greenville, SC, does get a few cool shows. I wrote a story about this experience not long after it happened and will reprise it for *The Riff* soon (ok Rob Janicke?).

So I thought as long as we shared that evening, I'd honor her honoring of me with this remembrance. I really wanted their latest, *Delta Kream*, but it was sold out.

And if you haven't had this experience, I will say that there's nothing like hitting the record store with your child—adult though she may be—and having her whip out her card to pay for your music. She's growing her vinyl collection, too, but buying a house will put you off other kinds of purchases for a while.

Today we're celebrating my wife's and my 37th wedding anniversary. We ate out last night at our favorite place in Greenville—Jianna—where the black-ink squid pasta can't be beat (Jianna is closed on Monday, in case your OCD is wondering). So, many ups this week—a few downs that I am too struck by to mention—and since we just passed the longest day of the year, I'm making this story/playlist just a bit longer.

Before I get to the music, I want to recommend a book I started last week: **Curtis Wilkie**'s *When Evil Lived in Laurel* (WW Norton Co.). The Laurel is that town in Mississippi where my favorite HGTV show, *Hometown*, is produced. Such a welcoming show about bringing people of all sorts into Laurel to settle and build a hopeful and diverse community. People of all colors, gender identity, and economic class have been helped in the series, and it's about as wonderful as a show can get.

But Laurel, like so many southern towns, also has a dark and violent past, one, sadly, featuring the Klan, and in this case, one of the worst, most virulent Klan chapters of them all. So, not an easy, but rather a harrowing read, but so important to know because if you want to understand the present...

And I do, and so, when I came across this passage, referring to my home in Greenville, SC (as opposed to Greenville, MS, where racist Klansman—what a redundancy—Byron De La Beckwith gunned down Medgar Evers in 1963 and still strolled the streets for decades after, un-indicted much less imprisoned), I stopped and now have to share. The focus of the book is FBI spy **Tom Landrum** who infiltrated the Laurel KKK in the early '60s to gather info. He was driven to his swearing-in ceremony by a part-time preacher who believed that God had ordained segregation, because, after all, look at the segregated bird species. Can you make this stuff up? Really? Apparently, this man learned all he needed to know about segregation and race hatred from Bob Jones, Sr...

"...whose ministry had been supported over the years by contributions from the Ku Klux Klan before he settled down at a university he named for himself in Greenville, South Carolina [don't you love white men who go around naming institutions, or towers, for themselves, while claiming to love Jesus or the American flag?]. Jones found justification for racial separation in the scriptures. In a famous easter Sunday radio address in 1960—weeks after the first sit-ins by Black students in North Carolina—Jones spoke of a 'satanic agitation striking back at God's established order.' And in that 'order,' God had established racial separation. 'Racially, we have separation in the Bible,' Jones assured his listeners" (27).

While BJU has been integrated for a few decades—like many

other southern colleges and universities—its modern-day founder (the college started in 1927) was not only intolerant of integration, he used God as his source.

This is the point where the **Phantom Zone** enters. If you remember your *Superman* comics, this zone was a place where Superman could zap you for a few eons until you changed your ways. And please give me a ray gun so I can also put it to the head and zap old Mr. Jones Sr. (yeah, I know he's dead), and whoever it is putting up those billboards along I-85 proclaiming that the Orange Plague's vote totals outdistance President Biden's.

I'm afraid someone is going to have to rewrite that biography of **Kafka**, the one entitled *The Nightmare of History*.

So now, get out your ray guns and join me in the following tunes as I try to restart again enjoying this new year of my marriage, and both of my daughters' sweet ol' world.

▢▬▢ ▮ AMERICAN CRISIS PLAYLIST #51 ▮ ▢▬▢

1. "**Cross to Bear**," Tricky, from 2008's *Knowle West Boy*. This one seemed most appropriate for the words I wrote and quoted above. Just how white does anyone believe Jesus's skin was, or how much he cared about such accidental trivialities? Someone in our last Riff album discussion of Sampha brought up Tricky, so I thought I'd give my favorite Tricky record another listen. Worth it. Hope you think so, too, so please give the lyrics a turn. I know you'll appreciate them in the spirit in which they were intended.

2. "**I Walk the Line**," J. Cash from 1964's *I Walk the Line*. Picture me as an eight year-old, sitting in Cliff's Drive-In BBQ in Bessemer, and even in this year, Cliff's still had a pickup window around back for, you know, "**Them**." My grandmother wouldn't set foot in Cliff's, but mainly because she thought it was unclean and Cliff himself had once had

tuberculosis. Anyway, I don't remember the bbq, but I do remember that John resided in many spots on the table jukeboxes, and I thought he was something old and though white, definitely not cool, definitely not The Beatles. It's that history thing again.

3. "**Back in My Day**," The Handsome Family, from *Unseen* (2016). Did you ever live at a time when there were no locks on the door, when you could count the stars but never make it past four? How many times have you told your child something from "back in your day?" My daughter asked me yesterday how much a new album should cost, and I said, between $24–$30, and she couldn't believe it, because she knew that I used to spend from $3.99 to $7.99 even when she was little. What's happened? I told her about finding a good used copy of Elvis's Sun years recordings for $20, but to get used discs only from a reputable record store, and not that antique mall dealer who sold me a scratched copy of an old Merle Haggard record. Back in my day...

4. "**Have a great day**," life's a beach, from *life's a beach* (2021). Since we're in the business of quoting cliched phrases, here's another, though the sound is pretty calming and funny. This reminds me a bit of what The Beach Boys would sound like had Tricky produced them, or maybe even what they sound like anyway when you move past the hits. It all sounds so easy, these pointed phrases telling you what to do: **Just Say No. Whites Only. No Jews Allowed. Tomorrow is the First Day of the Rest of Your Life**. And today?

5. "**Today**," The Smashing Pumpkins from *Siamese Dream* (1993). It's impossible, isn't it, that this record is almost thirty years old. I remember hearing it on **The Planet**, Greenville's New Rock station, which may or may not still exist. Today is the greatest day, for sure, even in its darker moments, and if you don't know why, then let's have my dog Max explain: "Because I get to take a walk; because I'll

get my burger later; and because whenever my dad or mom look at me, I know how loved I am. And I'm not a cat, though I have only love in my heart for most of them as long as they don't want to pop my nose again."

6. "**Dreams**," Solange from 2019's *When I Get Home*. Yeah, like my daughter, every child grows up with dreams. Some of us want to own our own home. Others want to buy whatever they want at a record store; still others want to be able to live, or dine, or use a restroom in an equal setting, fashion, without feeling the incriminating gaze, the transplanted cross, the redlining, or continued restriction, or reimposition of restrictions to voting. And speaking of record stores, do we really need to separate the music by genre? Can't we just use alphabetical order, as appears in my computer's music library? What are we accomplishing anyway, and, anyway, isn't it difficult to place into categories artists like Solange and the Handsomes?

7. "**Boyfriend**," Against Me! from *Shape Shift With Me* (2016). "I don't want to hang around the graveyard waiting for something dead to come back." Do you wonder what our generation's fascination with zombies is all about? So as I continue to look for their vinyl records, I try the Punk, the Alternative, and the Rock bins in my store, and they just don't exist anywhere. I'll keep trying, though, and I'm sorry that I was ever a lousy zombie boyfriend to anyone. I hope 37 years of happy marriage prove that I can be steady, faithful, and a better living husband.

8. "**Shut Up and Kiss Me**," Angel Olson, from 2016's *My Woman*. Now, that's no damn cliche. "Stop pretending I'm not there." We got to sit on the balcony at Jianna last night, and looking down onto Main Street, we saw happy people walking their dogs—and even dogs happily relieving their bowels—as well as in love couples, and pairs of men holding hands, and women walking together being true

to themselves, and my wife asked, "*What if Greenville becomes the new Provincetown?*" and I thought for a second and considered that at least there were no Bob Jones students preaching that heathen tongue. You never know. And then she said, "Shut up and..."

9. "**Ready to Start**," Arcade Fire, from 2010's *The Suburbs*. "My mind is open wide, and now I'm ready to start. You're not sure, you open the door, and step out into the dark." You know they're one of my top five favorite bands, right? Whenever I'm in a shaky mood, they definitely open me up, and I'm feeling that it's all worth starting, continuing to start, and the dark is only a place.

10. "**Walk Across the Water**," the Black Keys from *Let's Rock* (2019). Not on, but across. Finishing up a semi-theme. If someone can and will walk across the water, would you really think he or she is doing so in order to keep you or me apart? How far have we come? How much farther do we have to go? Not sure, but this series has one more week. Let's rock and make it a good one. Thank you Layla. Love, Dad.

I don't care for endings or goodbyes, so this isn't really either of those, but 52 weeks does seem like a milestone, and maybe time to move on, forward, or somewhere, in hopes that if I quit calling what we have and are a "crisis," maybe I will actually believe that what we've experienced over the past year and a few months, or in the case of the person I've deemed the OP, the past five years, is finally over. Done.

I'm not naive, however, and so I have to look closely at myself and decide what I think about what America is, and how we are responding to continued threats to our moral sanity.

So Derek Chauvin received a 22-and-a-half-year sentence for murdering George Floyd. I'm sure the sentence was within the guidelines of the charge, though the prosecution had asked for thirty years, but it is a strange number and as we all know, were the colors reversed, even if Floyd had been a cop, that sentence would have been different, and likely, significantly so.

Chauvin expressed his "condolences" to the Floyd family, and if that statement isn't the definition of "surreal,' I don't know what is. Chauvin will be eligible for parole when he's sixty. What else can I add?

It's been a year—just over, actually—since that brutal murder. So what's changed in the Republic of America? I suppose that every person will answer in their own fashion; if they answer, that is.

I had no real plan when I started this series, other than to write about my confusion, my fear, our collective trauma, and to hope that some music would at least help us get through these troubled times and maybe even do some healing, that is if we weren't already too far gone.

I'm hoping, with moral and intellectual support from Riff founder Noah Levy, to compile this year of playlists into a book. Working hard toward that end now, so thank you to all who have responded, clapped, read, and made me feel in such good company: Rob Janicke, Steven Hale, Kevin Alexander, Chris Zappa, and Jessica Lee McMillan, who have been my most avid, loyal, and supportive readers and advocates here.

So, while I must acknowledge this ending, my final playlist for this series is more about beginnings, which while daunting, are my favorite part of any endeavor, because the end is so far away in the beginning, and who knows where the many different roads will lead, and what will happen, unpredictably or even with great foreknowledge, along that way.

Or as **James Joyce** wrote in *Ulysses*,

"Each life is a series of days, day after day."

Amen to that.

AMERICAN CRISIS PLAYLIST #52
The end of the beginning...

1. "**From the Beginning**," Emerson, Lake, and Palmer from *Trilogy* (1973). Not to start so obviously, but I do love this song, a ballad about all of us being here/there and trying to see what we can do if we want to carve a path that isn't so full of chaos and tumult. In my high school years, my head spun with all the different types of music that my friends and I could and did listen to. Guess what? It's still like that, as reading *The Riff* daily shows.

2. "**Beginnings**," The Chicago Transit Authority, as they were known on their first, *self-titled*, record in 1969. My favorite song on this record is and always will be "**Questions 67 & 68**," their first hit. But

"Beginnings" is a strong song, too, with "a color of chills all over my body," and everything, "When I'm with you," that is, for it is all that matters. Ahhhh, the trombone and trumpet! They held such promise, I thought, and while Chicago II was also strong, it all waned for me after, even though there were still a few good tunes on those mammoth albums.

3. "**Five Years**," David Bowie from 1972's *The Rise and Fall of Ziggy Stardust and the Spiders from Mars*. The first Bowie song I ever heard: "And it was cold, and it rained, so I felt like an actor, and I thought of Ma and wanted to get back there...." What an intro to a sound, and even if I didn't understand all the words, I knew that I was beginning a new sort of journey with an artist who dared it all, bared it all, too. So life-changing. "Five years, what a surprise...my brain hurts a lot." And his band: cheers **Mick Ronson**.

4. "**Walk on By**," Isaac Hayes from 1969's *Hot Buttered Soul*. I didn't understand what anyone meant by "soul music" until I heard this record. Remember: I was only thirteen, and when the AM disc jockeys put this on late at night, I didn't know what to do with that lonely guitar, that haunting voice, or about Hayes himself. Not that I had to do anything but listen. I knew about Motown; I knew about Aretha; I even knew that **Dionne Warwick** had made this a hit back in 1964—a Bacharach/David composition. A man "breaking down and crying" for a woman whom he loves. "I just can't get over losing you, so if I seem broken in two..." Another song that intones the phrase "foolish pride." Still appropriate.

5. "**Happy Together**," The Turtles, from *Happy Together* (1967). The first single I ever bought and kept (more about that later) on the **White Whale** label. This song was everywhere, and I saw the Turtles perform it on every variety show in existence. My parents loved the

song, too, and isn't that every eleven-year-old kid's dream? As pop songs go, it's hard to beat this one, and I still have that little 45 deep in my downstairs bin. So happy to preserve it.

6. **"Rain/Paperback Writer,"** The Beatles, from a double-sided hit single released in 1966. Now, this was the first record my parents ever bought me. We put it on our turntable, but since it was the first 45 anyone in our house ever bought, period, no one recognized that we needed to shift the phonograph's speed from 33 to 45. So Lennon sounds like he's taken some acid—which he likely had—and when we figured out our problem and made the switch to 45 and then played "Rain," my parents seemed to hate it even more. So, they asked me ever so politely to get rid of it. I then traded the record for my friend Steve's copy of **"Love Is Blue,"** by Paul Mauriat and his orchestra. Please don't hate me.

7. **"Broken Arrow,"** The Buffalo Springfield from *Buffalo Springfield Again* (1967). Their second record, but my "first induction" into their music, and particularly to Neil Young's contribution. It's a song that when I first heard it, I thought I had already heard it somewhere, somehow, many times before. Like many Neil songs, the images carry more meaning than the words seem to. "Eighteen years of American dreams. He saw that his brother had sworn on the wall. He hung up his eyelids and ran down the hall. His mother had told him the trip was a fall, and don't mention babies at all. Did you see him?" I've got nothing to add here, because I'm still standing on that shore of teendom, holding on to what I've got.

8. **"Free,"** Paul Revere and the Raiders, from *Something Happening* (1968). The hit from this record is **"Too Much Talk,"** a song I also love. You might know that this band was my favorite from childhood, and I still find much of their sound as happy and shining as I ever did. But this song—a kind of psychedelic love song—was the one that twelve-

year-old me—in that morass/nightmare of seventh grade—listened to the most, thinking about a poor girl I hardly knew—a girl ridiculed from afar for being poor and in the wrong crowd. It's a wonder any of us ever escapes adolescence, and clearly, too many don't. My first rock and roll love; my first understanding that what we think and say hurts.

9. "**Riders on the Storm**," The Doors from *L.A. Woman* (1971). The song I once proclaimed would be the first song I'd play were I ever to become a disc jockey. Did you know that the Doors played a show in **Birmingham, Alabama**, once with **Paul Revere and the Raiders** on the same bill? Think about it. I was too young to attend, and wasn't sure I should say that I liked The Doors out loud. Even I understood that "**Light My Fire**" was sexual, even if I didn't completely understand sex. But "Riders" has always appealed to that part of me who loves rain and storms and riding off into distant clouds. Oh, and Ray Manzarek's piano.

10. "**Jungleland**," Bruce Springsteen from 1975's *Born to Run*. The most epic of all Springsteen songs, from the first record I ever heard/owned by a man who's come to define rock and roll for so many of us, right Paul Combs? Cinematic in every way, the lyrics run perfectly with the music and Bruce's crying voice in the night, in all nights to come. I don't write about him enough, but it's not because I don't care. Could have listed "**Backstreets**" here, too, but maybe I did once, long ago.

So many others I could/should have named: "I Got You, Babe;" "Rapper's Delight;" "I Wish It Would Rain;" "Atomic Dog;" "Catch the Wind;" "Crimson and Clover;" "Wild Horses;" "Got to be Real;" "Harvest;' "Dim All the Lights;" "Madonna, Sean, and Me;" "Us and Them." But, I'll have other days, more time. You will, too.

It's now mid-August in the second summer of Covid. The Delta variant is running amok and it seems I hear, on a daily basis, about someone I know contracting the virus. Someone I know who has already been vaccinated. I live in one of those states whose governor refuses to allow mask mandates. My college is requiring everyone to wear a mask indoors, but the student vaccination rate hovers around 56%.

I despair sometimes of the disinformation campaign waged by minions of the OP, and of his refusal to publicly declare that people should get the vaccine. For those I know who have gotten Covid are getting it from the unvaccinated who claim it is their freedom, their right to not follow scientific guidelines.

So I can't say that we've emerged from the crisis exactly.

What I can say is that my brand new turntable and powered speakers have kept me sane and relatively happy. In my privileged world, vinyl albums have made a hearty and steadfast mark on my soul again. Of the new and old albums I've purchased, here are ten more names and songs for you to play while our world and our citizenry do whatever they're going to do:

1. **Jackson Browne's** "For Everyman" (*For Everyman*)

2. **Neil Young's** "The Old Laughing Lady" (*Neil Young*)

3. **Pink Floyd's** "Us and Them" (*Dark Side of the Moon*)

4. **Emmylou Harris's** "May This Be Love" (*Wrecking Ball*)

5. **Pink Floyd's** "If" (*Atom Heart Mother*)

6. **Middle Kids'** "Summer Hill" (*Today We're the Greatest*)

7. **The Jimi Hendrix Experience's** "Long Hot Summer Night" (*Electric Ladyland*)

8. **The Kinks**' " A Rock n Roll Fantasy" (*Misfits*)

9. **Neil Young's** "Razor Love" (*Silver and Gold*)

10. **Sly and the Family Stone's** "Everyday People" (*Greatest Hits*)

Without music, where would we be?

And, my friends, I have to ask:

Where are we now?

Edisto Beach; Greenville, SC

August 2021

Bonus Tracks II

The Jan. 6 House Select committee is meeting to investigate the conspiracy to undermine our Constitution. Reps Bennie Thompson and Liz Cheney are heroes for now. Fleetwood Mac knew decades ago that *Heroes Are Hard to Find*. But for my money the song defining our times is and will always be King Crimson's "21st Century Schizoid Man."

—June 16, 2022. Bloomsday.

Bonus Tracks III

Cassidy Hutchinson is a hero. Liz Cheney, despite her politics, is now my hero. For them it's that David Bowie song I love so much. Michael Flynn, who took the 5th Amendment when asked if he believes in a "peaceful transition of power in the United States," is a coward and a traitor. For him, I have Donny Osmond's tune, "Sweet and Innocent," one of the worst things I could wish on anyone, musically speaking. Speaking of cowards, oh Josh Hawley, you poor sad thing (and aren't we the poorer and sadder for having to witness you?). For you, after we all witnessed your coup complicity and then your moon-walk down the stairs and through the hallways, I play "I Ran" by Flock of Seagulls. If only you had the sweeping hair to match. And for the Orange Plague, no piece of music is good enough or bad enough. I hope his jail cell has a constant loop of an infant's startled cry for its 2:00 AM feeding. And visually, I hope he sees the image of Liz Cheney forever, taking back the bottle just before the nipple hits the toad.

▣ Bonus Tracks IV ▣

August 8: FBI seizes Top Secret documents from Mar-A-Lago. Violation of Espionage Act possible. America now must transplant new name for domestic traitor to replace Benedict Arnold and Edward Snowden. That name: The Orange Plague.

Some time in the future: In a maximum security prison in some rough place, officials ask the ghosts of Johnny Cash and Merle Haggard to perform. When they examine the "guest list," they refuse. "The Fightin' Side of Me" has never sounded sweeter.

—TB, Greenville, SC 2022

▣ Terry Barr's *The American Crisis Playlist (2020-2021)* is the fourth essay collection he has published with Redhawk Publications, along with *Don't Date Baptists and Other Warnings From My Alabama Mother* (2016); *We Might As Well Eat: How To Survive Tornadoes, Alabama Football, and Your Southern Family* (2018); and *Secrets I'm Dying To Tell You* (2020). He is a three-time Pushcart nominee, and his essays have been widely published in national literary journals. His most recent work, "Greyhound Seats," won first place in Tell Your Story's Spring 2022 Nonfiction contest. He writes regularly about music and culture at medium.com/@terrybarr, and teaches Creative Nonfiction at Presbyterian College. Barr lives in Greenville, SC, with his family. ▣

www.ingramcontent.com/pod-product-compliance
Lightning Source LLC
Chambersburg PA
CBHW031150270326
41931CB00006B/209